2/14

Roots of the Arab Spring

Roots
of the
Arab Spring

Contested Authority
and Political Change
in the Middle East

Dafna Hochman Rand

PENN

UNIVERSITY OF PENNSYLVANIA PRESS

PHILADELPHIA

Copyright © 2013 University of Pennsylvania Press

Published by
University of Pennsylvania Press
Philadelphia, Pennsylvania 19104-4112
www.upenn.edu/pennpress

Printed in the United States of America
on acid-free paper
10 9 8 7 6 5 4 3 2 1

Library of Congress Cataloging-in-Publication Data

ISBN 978-0-8122-4530-1

Contents

Preface

In the mid-2000s, I lived in Morocco, Tunisia, and Bahrain, conducting research on the political strategies enabling authoritarian governments to persist in the Middle East and North Africa.[1] Middle East comparative politics specialists considered the endurance of authoritarianism in this region a puzzling anomaly. Most of the developing world had at least experimented with some type of democratization from the 1970s through the 1990s—even if many of these states later regressed back to "hybrid" regime types, neither fully democratic nor fully authoritarian.[2] Yet the states of the Middle East and North Africa remained undemocratic, lagging on all of the global rankings that measure political freedom and civil liberties.[3]

After conducting over a hundred interviews in these three countries, sitting in on parliamentary sessions, and participating in civil society and political activities, my search for a generalizable explanation for the democracy deficit in the region seemed beside the point. Though there were constitutional, bureaucratic, and socioeconomic explanations for authoritarian endurance, this endurance did not appear to be the most apparent trend in the region. On the ground, from the Casbah of Rabat, Morocco, to the ports of Bahrain, the most remarkable characteristic of the region's politics during the first decade of the twenty-first century was its widespread dynamism, including a pervasive uncertainty about the future of both regional and local politics.

Of course, the authoritarian state appeared just as strong as I had expected. Internal security services, including, in some places, despised secret police, exercised powerful oversight roles, often interfering in daily life. Political opposition activists traded stories—some real, some imagined—of arbitrary detentions and deplorable prison conditions. The rulers commanded a pervasive physical presence, with pictures of leaders adorning everything from public buses to hotel lobbies, reminding the citizens of the established political order. Yet in Morocco I also found journalists and women's rights activists trying to push the monarchy's limits. These groups and individuals were seizing upon the relatively permissive atmosphere under a new king to publish daring and critical newspaper articles, to mobilize protests in front of parliament, and to advocate for minority and human rights. In Bahrain, I saw a political opposition deeply divided, and a public growing increasingly disillusioned with a new king whom most had expected would be a reformer. In Tunisia, the public was increasingly fed up with the methodical efforts by the president and his cronies to transform a once moderate, pluralistic state into one of the most closed political systems in the world.

Thus, my field research suggested that the autocrats in the region were not at all uniformly "robust," as described at the time by Middle East and North Africa experts. While it was true that many of these leaders had ruled for decades, and had successfully overcome intense public opposition and intermittent crises, by the twenty-first century, most were nervously trying to manage the varied political changes occurring around them.[4] Some were doing so more successfully than others. Often, economic, social, or political reforms could appeal to popular and elite allies, minimally allay opposition or civil society demands, and solidify the autocrat's rule by building credibility or by co-opting opposition groups. In the short term, these strategic efforts seemed to be working: The autocrats appeared in some cases to be cleverly staying one step ahead of the changing political pressures surrounding them—whether by revising press codes to rein in the expanding media space or by revising constitutions to carefully limit the electoral participation of political challengers. But their ability to stay a step ahead of the game was precarious at best. It seemed apparent that top-down efforts to manage the changing dynamics could easily go awry, and could generate unknown and unintended consequences.

My field research found a degree of flux at odds with the widespread conclusions reached by academics studying the Middle East and North Africa at the time, as well as the consensus among policy makers working on the region.[5] Both groups considered the regimes and rulers of the Middle East and North Africa robust, persistent, and strong. At the time, scholars and policy makers were focused not on the dynamism in the region, but rather on analyzing the explanations for what appeared to be a nearly monolithic freedom deficit. Given this overarching lens, few academics or policy makers were searching for political cracks—sources of instability. So focused on the vast power imbalance between the state and societies, neither community dedicated sufficient analysis to the potential sources of political change.[6]

Many scholars subscribed to what was loosely dubbed "the authoritarian resilience research agenda"—offering a set of hypotheses to explain how the region's autocrats used economic, institutional, and electoral strategies to wield power, typically by outwitting and outmaneuvering other actors, including the international community and political opposition.[7] As the author of one seminal article argued, these autocrats' "robust and politically tenacious coercive apparatus" could overcome "any opposition with strength, coherence, and effectiveness."[8] While regional experts had previously explained Middle East and North African authoritarianism by studying external rents and foreign patronage, the natural resource curse, or the Islamic world's religious and cultural traditions, over the past ten years they were focused increasingly on the micro foundations of authoritarian rule. In particular, they homed in on the institutional logics governing constitutions, party systems, and electoral rules.[9] This literature also explored how selective economic growth, cronyism, and economic crises sustained authoritarian systems.[10] Regional scholars found that many leaders were choosing proactive strategies to deliberately divide and co-opt opposition factions, particularly Islamist parties and movements from secular opponents.[11]

By emphasizing how and why the region's regimes were so extraordinarily successful at staying in power, however, this research agenda often painted, with broad brush strokes, a picture of a stagnant region.[12] The Middle East regionalist scholars pursued a very useful set of research questions by focusing on the nuts and bolts of authoritarianism, but they sometimes marginalized, whether intentionally or not, the political orientations, attitudes, and changing views of the region's citizens.[13] Hypothesizing why authoritarianism survived not only reflected a bias toward studying elites, but also diminished the attention paid to social movements in the region, whether youth, workers, or the new communities that were developing online.[14] The prevailing scholarly approach, in short, inadequately addressed the potential of individuals and non-traditional actors to mobilize.[15]

In Washington during this time period, U.S. policy makers began advocating for a "Freedom Agenda" in the Middle East and North Africa. They turned their attention—at least temporarily—to the promotion of democracy and human rights in a region where both were flagging, in addition to new trade and investment programs. New U.S. government funds focused on the capacity of independent civil society organizations and media, as well as small business and entrepreneurship promotion programs, most notably under the new Middle East Partnership Initiative (MEPI) and the multilateral Broader Middle East and North Africa (BMENA) program. President George W. Bush and Secretary of State Condoleezza Rice offered unprecedented public support for democracy and universal rights in the region—in the former's second inaugural address and in the latter's address at the American University of Cairo in 2005.[16]

The logic of the U.S. Freedom Agenda began with the assumption that the states in the region were durable and strong, with the leadership firmly entrenched. The policy makers who championed this agenda often overlooked the local movements and organizations that were advocating for change, many of which had existed for decades.[17] They discounted, like many academics, the potential for collective action by the region's citizens. Policy makers interested in promoting democratization in the region were also particularly interested in national-level elections, and to some extent they failed to imagine how political change might come about any other way. This failure of imagination meant that policy makers paid less attention to the non-electoral spheres of political society. Focused on promoting freer and fairer elections, many policy makers did not adequately consider other sources of political change, including the potential for cross-cutting revolutionary movements.

Although many policy makers were committed to the principles behind the Freedom Agenda, particularly during its first few years, in practice U.S. efforts had mixed results. Many people in the region rejected the U.S. foreign policy approach to the region post–September 11, 2001, particularly the 2003 Iraq War, and these policies tainted the Freedom Agenda. U.S. democracy-promotion strategies also failed to differentiate between those tactics appropriate for the stable authoritarian regimes of the region and those more suited for the unstable, ethnically divided, and conflict-ridden states, such as Iraq and Lebanon. Finally, when elections in Egypt, Palestine, and Lebanon in 2005–2006 yielded victors considered inimical to U.S. interests, policy makers' enthusiasm for democratization in the region withered.

U.S. public rhetoric about democracy moderated after 2006 for a number of reasons. Policy makers' emphasis shifted—from public messaging and large-scale new initiatives to a greater emphasis on private diplomacy and programmatic assistance focused on building the capacity of civil society organizations, independent media, and institutions. Nevertheless, even the new, more subtle approach rested on the assumption that the political status quo in the Middle East and North Africa—a set of strong, autocratic regimes—would endure for the foreseeable future.

This book presents a new argument about three drivers of political change that were occurring in the region from the 1990s through the 2000s: (a) an increasing demand for free expression, which over time created an enlarged public sphere, a space for public debate beyond state control; (b) top-down de-democratization efforts, as authorities initiated new rule-of-law reforms in order to restrict political rights; and (c) a pattern of liberalizing reforms that, over time, stalled, as new leaders who had come to power at the turn of the twenty-first century lost interest in reforming.

A decade after these drivers emerged, they had begun to change the relationship between states and societies, between authorities and citizens. These three drivers of change were catalysts of the Arab Spring protests, though they neither explain the origin of any particular individual uprising nor are together exhaustive explanations for the broader systemic change that was occurring during this period. Rather, the combination of these three drivers of change generated public frustration, anger, and alienation, contributing to the intensity of the unprecedented public protest movements. These drivers were widespread in particular during the fifteen years before the Arab Spring, due to the rise of new innovations, new leaders, and new norms during this period. They did not all occur to the same extent in every Arab state, but in some states the convergence of two or more of these drivers proved to be particularly combustible.

Temporally, the argument in this book extends until January 2011 and does not explain why the protest movements took on different degrees of intensity and scope in different countries. Each of the uprisings has taken a divergent path, leading some states toward tentative democratic openings, others toward civil conflict, and still others toward violent crackdowns. Scholars have begun and will continue to study these divergent outcomes for years to come.[18] In fact, the three cases discussed in this book, Morocco, Tunisia, and Bahrain, have each emerged from the protests of 2011 on increasingly divergent political trajectories. Instead, this book looks backward from the start of the Arab Spring, analyzing how three drivers of change generated greater regime insecurity, as the public grew bolder in its willingness to mobilize and to participate in antiregime activism.

Introduction

Authority in Flux: Three Drivers of Change
in the Middle East and North Africa

The self-immolation of a fruit and vegetable vendor in a central Tunisian town in December 2010 seemed an unlikely spark for revolutions across three continents. Tunisia's populist uprising initially began as local affairs—workers and youth congregating in the town square to express years of pent-up frustration against petty bureaucrats considered corrupt and abusive. The demonstrations began in towns far removed from Tunisia's coastal elite—in Sidi Bouzid, Menzel Bouzaiene, al-Ragab, and Miknassi—with protestors demanding economic opportunity as well as greater dignity, justice, and political freedom. The protestors were united in opposing the cronyism and repression that had characterized President Zine El Abidine Ben Ali's twenty-seven-year rule.[1] By January 2011, the streets of Tunis were filled with lawyers, engineers, young women, and old housewives, a broad cross section of the Tunisian middle class. These were average citizens who, it had appeared to most outside observers, had accepted the authoritarian political order. Within eighteen days, the protestors unseated one of the most entrenched authoritarian regimes in the world. With Ben Ali's hasty departure, his ruling Constitutional Democratic Rally (RCD) party quickly dissolved, and the infrastructure of a regime that had seemed so omnipotent began to crumble.

Inspired by the Tunisians' peaceful ouster of their dictator, activists, youth, workers, and other average citizens took to the streets, from Cairo to Benghazi to even sleepy Muscat. By the end of 2011, none of the Arab states of the Middle East remained untouched by the wave of uprisings dubbed the "Arab Spring."[2] Antigovernment protests emerged everywhere, albeit in different forms. The protests quickly grew, fusing cries for economic justice with demands for greater political rights. By mid-2012, the upheaval had toppled four entrenched dictatorships, generated irreversible political crises elsewhere, and dramatically reshaped the politics of the region.

That the dissolution of long-standing authoritarian regimes happened so quickly came as a surprise to many, within the region and beyond. The conventional view, shared by both policy makers and academics, considered the region's authoritarian systems resilient, and presumed their invulnerability to populist upheaval.[3] Prior to 2011, in light of the autocrats' strong security forces and other mechanisms designed to control political mobilization, bottom-up upheaval sufficient to challenge the regimes in the region seemed unlikely. By early 2011, however, the supposedly clever and adaptive rulers were now backed into a corner, cowed into surrender. As the spark spread from the Tunisian Casbah and Cairo's Tahrir Square across the region, it became clear that the political structures that had seemed so robust were actually vulnerable. The unrest revealed how ruling parties and even in some cases internal security services, such as ministries of interior, were more insecure than previously understood.

It is too soon to gauge how each individual Arab state will emerge from the uprisings that began in 2011. Each revolt has thus far yielded varied political trajectories. As Tunisia, Egypt, Yemen, and Libya embark on precarious, and by no means certain, paths toward democratic transition, elsewhere authoritarian retrenchment and consolidation are likely. In some cases, such as in Morocco and Jordan, the governments are making careful constitutional and electoral reforms to expand some political rights, even as they try to stay ahead of any potentially combustible mass mobilization. In Syria, civil and ethnic strife will likely endure. This book does not explain the varied outcomes of the uprisings of 2011, nor why protest movements varied in intensity from country to country. Instead, it offers a macro explanation for the Arab Spring's origins.

Explaining the Arab Spring: Drivers of Political Change

Three systemic drivers of change, which emerged over the course of two decades, contributed to the uprisings of 2011 by changing the relationship between the region's ruling authorities and their publics. The three drivers are (1) an increased popular demand for free expression, which expanded the public sphere, opening a substantive debate among the public that was beyond the state's full control; (2) a set of top-down reforms restricting political rights and civil liberties; and (3) a stalemate in the liberalizing reform programs of the late 1990s and early 2000s, many of which had been introduced by a new generational cohort of leaders, sons or other relatives who had succeeded their fathers.

Even as the coercive apparatuses of the states remained intact, particularly the strong security services capable and willing to suppress dissent, these three drivers played a central role in changing the nature of political life in the Middle East and North Africa. This book explains where and why these drivers arose, how authorities tried to proactively employ or manage them, and how they ultimately contributed to the political frustration and discontent that culminated in the Arab Spring.[4]

Defining Political Change

Most social science research treats political change as a one-way pathway, which transforms exclusive, repressive governing structures into more inclusive, accountable, and fair ones—even if there are periodic setbacks. Political change has often involved dramatic events, such as the storming of the Bastille or the fall of the Berlin Wall two hundred years later, though it can also come about through more gradual processes such as the consolidation of democratic institutions in Latin America and Eastern Europe. While most scholarly work on political change assumes a teleological orientation, here political change has no predetermined direction. I use the term "political change" to describe macro processes that, over a medium term of decades, augment or contract political rights and civil liberties, in directions typically considered liberal, illiberal, democratic, or undemocratic, even if the official regime type does not change. For instance, constitutional changes can expand the contestation afforded political parties (e.g., the 1988 Algerian constitutional revision) or limit political parties' participation (e.g., the 2002 Tunisian constitutional revision). Press reforms often increase or decrease the media's ability to publish freely without censorship, either limiting civil liberties or broadening them, even as authoritarian systems remain intact. Moreover, political change as conceived in this book is not linear. The process is characterized by advances and reversals, starts and stops, with no standard pace or outcome.

Political change as discussed here involves two key substantive areas: first, democratic rights, such as the right to be represented in parliament or to run and vote in elections; and second, civil liberties, such as the freedoms of expression, speech, press, and association as well as group rights. Democratic rights and civil liberties are the two broad analytical areas identified and measured annually by Freedom House rankings, commonly used by policy makers, and two key aspects of political life measured by the Polity Project data used by social scientists.[5]

These two areas of focus roughly hew to the two processes commonly called "democratization" and "liberalization." There are myriad definitions of these two terms in the academic literature, but here "democratization" refers to the expansion of political rights and freedoms, particularly the right to contest and participate in a representative government. "Liberalization" refers to the expansion of civil liberties, both individual rights such as freedoms of press, speech, and assembly/association and group rights, such as those protecting women and minority groups. Democratization might be preceded by liberalization, but democracy is never the assured outcome of any liberalization experiment. While liberalization opens up "space" for individual or group action, democratization changes the structure of "authority."[6]

By making both political rights and civil liberties central to this book, I weigh in on the central debate in the democratization literature on the definition of "democracy." Some comparative scholars of democratization, following the example of Joseph Schumpeter, argue that democracy is defined solely through the presence of contested elections, and therefore political change occurs when governments move closer to the ideal of free and fair elections.[7] Instead, I consider political change as a broader process, which includes the exercise of civil liberties as well as procedural democratic rights, reflecting the ways in which both elements affect political life and the relationship between the states and their publics in the Middle East and North Africa.[8]

The field research for this book, conducted in the region from 2005 through 2008, took place before these revolutions occurred. While I did not predict the tumultuous and dramatic events that would soon sweep through the region, my research found an unexpected prevalence of political flux, and found that the authorities presiding over the states in the region seemed remarkably vulnerable to the dynamic changes afoot.[9] Though this seems in retrospect to be an obvious finding, at the time it contradicted the prevailing academic consensus and the widespread assumption held by policy makers regarding the robustness of the ruling regimes in the region, which were considered to be invulnerable, particularly given their strong coercive apparatuses.[10] In contrast to the prevalent assumptions, I found autocrats struggling to manage change, and in many cases enacting strategic reforms to preempt or counter opposition challengers. Rather than safe and secure, these regimes seemed highly vulnerable to miscalculation. It seemed likely that the survival strategies employed by the region's autocrats, despite their best efforts, were not foolproof, and indeed sooner or later these strategies would themselves trigger unanticipated outcomes.

Furthermore, the political change that I observed occurring in Bahrain, Tunisia, and Morocco in the mid-2000s did not hew to the linear paradigms offered by the academic literature on liberalization and democratization processes. This literature built its theoretical foundation on the multiple cases of top-down transitions from closed, repressive regimes into liberalized democracies that had occurred with great frequency in Southern Europe, Latin America, and, to a lesser extent, Africa over the past fifty years. From Portugal to Botswana to Brazil, the approximately thirty countries that transitioned from 1974 through 1991, in what was later dubbed "the third wave" of democratization, established a generalizable template for political change: most of these transformations began with a period marked by the expansion of individual and group rights such as freedoms of press, expression, and association and changes that opened a previously closed economy, reforms often initiated by the incumbent leaders. Then, the opposition and the regime agreed upon a process to expand political participation and the contestation of executive power, often by calling for new elections.

The third wave cases gave way to a transition model, which delineated a pathway out of authoritarian rule. Before 2011, given the endurance of Middle Eastern autocrats, it seemed improbable to imagine any of the fifteen stable authoritarian Arab states embarking on this pathway any time soon, however.[11] Therefore, while political change was underway in the region, it did not conform to the most researched model of how political transitions occur, a model derived largely from the experiences of other regions of the world. This is one of the reasons why the changes I observed on the ground were undertheorized and overlooked by academics and policy makers alike. What was happening in the Middle East and North Africa simply did not fit the existing academic template; it did not conform to the model of political change that had been occurring with great frequency throughout the late twentieth century in other regions of the world.

Rather than focusing on the potential sources of democratization and liberalization in the region, by the mid-2000s the prevailing scholarly framework took the opposite approach, exploring the foundations of the robust authoritarianism. Middle East regional experts did not try to explain or predict sources of change but rather sought to offer explanations for its absence. These scholars offered a series of hypotheses for the political stagnation of the region, focusing in particular on how the leaders of the Middle East and North Africa used economic, electoral, and patronage networks to wield power.[12] The robustness of Arab authoritarianism literature emphasized in particular the strength of coercive institutions, including militaries and security services, as a major factor underlying regime stability.[13]

The pervasive assumption that Middle Eastern regimes were extraordinarily successful at staying in power—and forestalling political change—seemed at odds with the dynamics that I had witnessed as part of my field research in the region from 2005 to 2008. Activists were organizing demonstrations, political movements, and new types of civil society. Many leaders were nervously scrambling to contain demands from below by offering carefully calibrated reforms, which they hoped would sufficiently address these demands while avoiding opening a Pandora's box. On the whole, though the coercive institutions were as strong as ever, the behavior of the regimes suggested vulnerability. In the words of one author describing Hosni Mubarak's efforts to deal with labor unrest in the late 2000s, the leaders in the region seemed "embattled on many fronts."[14] The political change occurring conformed to neither the models offered by the transitions literature nor the status quo predictions assumed by the authoritarian robustness hypothesis. Given the dynamic changes occurring in the region, it seemed impossible that even the most strategic, deliberate leader would be able to stay a step ahead of the public's increasing mobilization. The risk of miscalculation seemed high, especially as leaders tried to respond to the unpredictabilities inherent to twenty-first-century governance.

The Three Drivers of Change

The three drivers of political change discussed in this book broke barriers between authorities and the public and in some cases discredited many of the ruling parties, political institutions, and the rulers themselves. In many instances, these three drivers generated widespread anger, frustration, and alienation, leading, over two decades, to the sense of stalemate and political desperation that contributed to the mass mobilizations of 2011.[15]

First, in many countries in the region, particularly in Morocco, Algeria, Egypt, Jordan, Kuwait, Yemen, and Bahrain, over the past two decades, independent journalists and bloggers began pushing the boundaries of acceptable free press and speech. In many cases the regimes themselves tacitly unleashed this driver of change—by relaxing some of the extreme censorship rules that had prevailed during the 1970s and 1980s and by promoting widespread Internet use. Enabled by new technologies, whether satellite television such as Al Jazeera or new social media such as blogs, individuals, journalists, and activists began testing the limits of government tolerance for free debate. As the boundaries for acceptable free expression expanded, the public's demand for more open media and free discourse became insatiable. A public sphere emerged, creating an environment where previously taboo subject matters could now be discussed and debated, often online. While many regimes tried to respond, promulgating new press laws and launching arbitrary crackdowns against popular independent journalists, their efforts proved to be futile—and counterproductive. In some isolated cases, by the late 2000s, government measures successfully silenced individual journalists or media organizations. For the most part, however, the repressive countermeasures intended to rein in the newly expanded public sphere served only to mobilize greater political activism. As the region's citizens grew habituated to greater free expression and the experience of unrestrained public discourse, it became increasingly contentious each time the authorities tried to suppress public debate, or to monitor the blurry line between free speech and political activism.

In the 2000s, academics studying the Middle East recognized how new media technologies were changing the nature of political discussion. At first, the thrust of the research in this area focused on the pan-Arab discussion and identity that was emerging across the Arab world, as a result of new pan-Arab media such as Al Jazeera.[16] A few authors probed how local bloggers and journalists were shaping local debates, increasing the demand for free expression and the opportunity to engage in discussions largely outside state control.[17] Observing the clever ways in which the regimes in the region responded to Al Jazeera, blogs, and the Internet, however, many authors concluded that Arab authoritarian systems would survive the challenge of open media and new technologies through adaptive measures, including by propagating new types of state-run media to counter satellite television or by conducting online censorship. In short, most regional experts concluded that that Middle Eastern government could weather the storm of Al Jazeera and the emergence of the Internet, offering further proof to support those already convinced of these leaders' adaptability and resilience, rather than their potential vulnerabilities.[18]

Second, during the 1990s and 2000s, many autocrats in the region began reforming rules of law—affecting the electoral code, the judiciaries, and even the constitution itself—in order to limit the political rights and civil liberties afforded their citizens. This formal de-democratization and deliberalization, institutionalized through rule-of-law reforms, deliberately limited certain civil liberties and political rights in states such as Jordan, Tunisia, Egypt, and Yemen.[19] By the end of the 2000s, in many countries elections were less free, constitutions less protective of citizens' rights, and freedoms of press and association more curtailed compared to a decade earlier.

This driver of change, which I call here a "de-democratizing" trend, was anathema to many Western academics and policy makers, who considered rules of law and legal institutions as the potential vehicle for the expansion of individual rights, rather than a vehicle that could be used to constrict these rights. Earlier autocrats had simply solidified their power through brute force. Now, the autocrats of the region were not abandoning any tools of repression but rather adding de-democratizing rules of law to their tool kit. These de-democratizing reforms were, more often than not, announced through grand proclamations about human rights. No one was fooled, however, either at home or abroad.

At first, in the 2000s, it appeared that by passing new de-democratizing rule-of-law reforms, many regimes could strengthen their standing, with little cost or risk. In many cases, rules of law were strategically deployed to weaken and divide political oppositions.[20] Repressive rules of law also elicited far less of an international outcry than traditional repressive tactics, such as suppressing demonstrations or incarcerating activists.

At the same time, however, de-democratization through rule-of-law reforms had unintended medium-term consequences: the regimes' cynical exploitation of key institutions such as electoral laws, constitutions, and the courts convinced key political elites and opposition leaders that genuine government-led top-down reform was impossible. The promise of an incremental political reform process, achieved through negotiation and compromise with regime moderates, proved illusory. Instead, the process of "reform" became a cynical farce, and many political opponents, even less radical ones, came to the conclusion that only fundamental change—indeed the end of the regime itself—could protect their political rights.

Third, a wave of hereditary successions from ruling fathers to their sons or near relatives in the late 1990s and early 2000s contributed to a third driver of change. In the beginning of the 2000s, most of these sons and relatives began enacting liberalizing reforms to appeal to elite and public constituencies. While these "sons" preferred social and economic liberalizing reforms, in some cases they initiated limited political reforms as well, particularly to extend political participation. In Syria, Qatar, Jordan, Morocco, Saudi Arabia, and Bahrain, the new rulers all experimented with different types of reforms upon assuming power, although the scope, substance, and the longevity of these experiments varied.

In the early 2000s, scholars studying the region noted the wave of regime-initiated reforms, enacted primarily by the sons but also in some cases by long-serving rulers, as well as the ways in which the reforms fell far short of the liberalization and democratization processes that had opened up regimes in other regions.[21] As the decade progressed, the failure of these reform programs to produce meaningful political, social, and economic changes generated disappointment among the public, and served as a rallying call for many domestic opposition movements. The limited reform programs enacted by the sons often triggered inequitable economic growth. In the political realm, the very limited reforms, whether changes to party laws or electoral laws or, in some cases, constitutional revisions, had failed to broaden political representation in government institutions or to allow for legitimate electoral contestation.

In the 2000s, Middle East experts confidently called the type of liberalization measure initiated by the sons a "trap"—machinations to maintain and strengthen a regime's rule.[22] To authoritarian robustness scholars, the regimes were initiating reforms to increase the scope of patronage, to neutralize putative democratizers, and to create a positive, though ultimately false, image of the autocrat as a liberalizer.[23] However, these same limited liberalizing reforms that Western scholars might have dismissed as inconsequential window dressing did in fact, over time, influence events on the ground: in some cases these reform agendas—started and then stalled—were paradoxically raising public and opposition animosity toward the regime rather than neutralizing or allaying the political opposition and the public's demands. In other words, the liberalizing reforms introduced by the sons, and in some cases other leaders, while intending to strategically co-opt and mitigate opposition and public demands, had the opposite effect—raising expectations and then failing to meet them. Disappointment with the willingness of the new leaders to follow through on their promises generated widespread frustration, motivating public participation in the 2011 protests.[24]

Alternative Arguments

In the weeks and months following the overthrow of the dictatorships in Egypt and Tunisia, analysts debated the causes of the unanticipated revolutions in the Arab world, attributing the upheaval, most frequently, to the rise of pan-Arab media such as Al Jazeera television and new social media such as Facebook and Twitter, demographic factors such as the youth bulge, and the global economic downturn of 2008–2009, which had dramatically squeezed the coffers of many states, raising food, gas, and oil prices and deepening already high unemployment. Some of this analysis partially answers the question of why the protests emerged in 2011, rather than earlier or later.[25] In the immediate wake of the Arab Spring, social scientists and Middle East scholars were particularly seized by the role new media had played. Those scholars who had studied the effects of new media in the region for the past decade sounded a note of caution about offering monocausal arguments, however.[26]

During this same time period, the participants and leaders of each revolution pointed to the importance of the contagion effects inspiring protests across borders: the Tunisian "Jasmine revolution" of December and January 2011 inspired the subsequent Egyptian and Libyan revolutions, and all three inspired the Moroccan, Syrian, and Bahraini protest movements.[27] In some cases, cross-regional Facebook pages and Twitter feeds helped to create a pan-Arab revolutionary cohort. In other cases, activists offered their neighbors practical and technical advice, such as how to avoid tear gas injuries and police roundups.[28]

The early analysis of 2011 and 2012 identified what can be termed micro causes. This book focuses instead on macro causes, that is, permissive, catalytic explanations for the outbreak of the Arab Spring. The three macro drivers of change discussed here are not exhaustive. There are other compelling alternative arguments outside the scope of this book, particularly involving macro- and microeconomic variables, which contributed to the widespread dislocation, anger, and unemployment that contributed to the scope of support for the protests.[29] As the demands articulated at the demonstrations of 2011 revealed, often personal desperation drove individuals to overcome their fear of the repressive security forces and to demand jobs and dignity.[30] At a more macro level, rising educational opportunities afforded to youth in the region occurred without a commensurate increase in employment opportunities. Educated young people who could not find jobs were particularly important participants and organizers of the Arab Spring demonstrations.[31] In addition, the benefits of economic growth were unequally distributed in the 1990s and 2000s. In some countries, a nouveau riche elite class benefited from the liberal economic reforms. The number of college-educated middle class young people grew, without the commensurate development of the private sector to employ newly eligible workers. Finally, in addition to these systemic socio-economic shifts, the economic downturn of 2008–2009 triggered an immediate food and gas price increase and increased unemployment. The immediate shock of food insecurity in 2010 offers an explanation for the timing of the Arab Spring in early 2011, rather than during some other time over the course of the previous ten-year period.[32]

Though beyond the purview of this book, these macroeconomic and socioeconomic drivers were critical. In many cases, they reinforced the political drivers of change discussed here. In Tunisia, for instance, popular support for the RCD party was, in part, predicated on the relative prosperity its economic policies had generated. For over a decade, Ben Ali had offered an implicit bargain to his people: in exchange for economic security and middle-class amenities such as home ownership, some Tunisians reluctantly accepted their limited political rights.[33] The downturn of the Tunisian economy after 2008 directly upset this bargain. In addition, though the corruption and nepotism inherent to the ruling regimes had long infuriated the public, after the 2008 economic downturn, with the price of basic food items soaring, the excesses of Ben Ali's inner circle became increasingly offensive.[34]

Methodological Approach

Roots of the Arab Spring offers a broad, macro-level argument applied to a diverse set of states in the region, including presidential republics and hereditary monarchies.[35] Rather than formally testing hypotheses, this book argues that three drivers of change over time reshaped the relationship between the authorities and their publics in many Middle Eastern and North African states. It is my hope that this book will contribute to the empirical research that has begun on the sources of the Arab Spring, by allowing others to derive testable hypotheses from these drivers of change.

The argument presented here does not engage in process tracing to pinpoint the local triggers of any particular revolutionary movement.[36] A set of very particular socioeconomic, cultural, and ethnic tensions converged in each country—and, in some cases, in each city—proving combustible. Even the locations of each revolution's origin—whether Benghazi, Libya; Daraa, Syria; or Sidi Bouzid, Tunisia—reflect important and particular domestic geographic and demographic factors. Moreover, the scope and salience of each the three drivers discussed in this book varied across different states and sub-regions within the Middle East and North Africa.[37]

Finally, the book does not explain the wide variation in the outcomes of the different protest movements—that is, why uprisings that began amid similar circumstances led to democratic transitions in some cases and sectarian violence or authoritarian retrenchment in other cases. The trajectories of the Arab Spring uprisings are still evolving. The loyalty of the military, the role of international pressure and intervention, and the degree of violence involved in the government's response have and will continue to shape their direction. The drivers of change discussed here are still salient in the region. They will, in certain cases, continue to play an important factor in shaping the political trajectories for those states that survived the initial upheaval of the Arab Spring with the ruling regime impact. Nevertheless, this is a book about the sources of the Arab Spring instability, rather than the outcome of the protests.

The Role of International Factors

This book focuses on domestic sources of political change. Over the course of the field research conducted for this project in the mid-2000s, activists and citizens in the region continuously emphasized how political change was (and should be) an indigenous process.[38] Nonetheless, during this time period, at the end of the twentieth and the beginning of the twenty-first century, three major global and regional trends were exerting an influence on the domestic politics of the region as well as clearly influencing local leaders' decision-making processes. All three augmented and heightened the three drivers of change described in this book.

First, international norms regarding democracy, human rights, and good governance began to consolidate at the end of the twentieth century, in part because the preponderance of states worldwide had transitioned to democracy by the 1990s. Some regional leaders were likely influenced by these normative pressures, wanting to "appear more democratic" or at least to satisfy international norms regarding governance and human rights superficially.[39] The fall of the Soviet Union, the transition to democracy in many developing countries in Africa, Asia, and Latin America, the triumph of free market economics, and the expanded reach of globalization made it harder for authoritarian regimes to justify their existence. This was as true for monarchies as it was for presidential dictatorships.[40] Global normative pressures translated practically into diplomatic pressure exerted behind closed doors or public critiques issued by foreign governments or international organizations, whether the UN or nongovernmental organizations. In the twenty-first century, media and transnational organizations such as Human Rights Watch, Amnesty International, and Reporters without Borders could quickly disseminate accurate information about local human rights abuses. Though some academics have tried to measure the effects of normative pressure on autocratic behavior, such effects are often difficult to gauge.[41]

At the very least, even if Arab autocrats were not persuaded by these normative global pressures, in response to these pressures, they quickly learned the importance of adopting the "democracy language." According to some analysts, "Arab incumbents quickly learned the language of what was expected internationally; talking the 'donor talk' became a prerequisite for political rent-seeking."[42] Building institutions such as legislatures or courts, even if they only rubber-stamped regime policies, appealed to regional rulers; this is perhaps one reason why de-democratizing through rule-of-law reforms became so pervasive.

Second, in the 2000s, international actors (Western governments and nongovernmental organizations) became increasingly interested in the region's domestic politics, with unquantifiable but observable effects. The most dramatic type of intervention occurred in 2003 with the U.S. invasion of Iraq. Many have argued that this invasion had a negative effect on the region's democratization and liberalization prospects; because people in the region so universally reviled this war, when the United States later defended the invasion in the name of democracy promotion, the legitimacy of many democratic activists elsewhere in the region suffered.[43] In the 2000s, however, greater Western interest in democracy promotion also took other forms, including a greater focus on public and private messaging regarding political freedoms and human rights and programmatic support to build the capacity of civil and political society in the region. While it is hard to measure how Western support affected the political change occurring on the ground, in some self-reported cases, the increased international spotlight on the nondemocratic nature of their states inspired and helped to amplify the message of local opposition groups interested in democracy and human rights.[44] In many cases across the region, international resources and programmatic support directly bolstered the work of regional independent journalists, activists, and civil society organizations.

A third type of international pressure involved the emergence of strong demonstration effects across the region in the 1990s and 2000s. Both the regimes and their oppositions often copied the behavior and response from neighboring states. Indeed, regimes as well as oppositions likely studied their neighbors' domestic politics—watching and learning from each other's trials and errors.[45] For example, Egyptian President Mubarak might have gauged public reaction abroad and at home to Tunisian President Ben Ali's 2002 constitutional reforms before he initiated similar ones in 2005 and 2007. It is probably not a coincidence that the sons who succeeded their fathers as a generational cohort in the late 1990s and early 2000s followed a particular pattern en masse—initiating reforms during the first few years of their rule in the similar substantive areas of economic privatization, economic development, and human rights. The presidents of Algeria, Tunisia, and Egypt may have watched how the Moroccan public responded to King Mohammed VI's response to independent journalists, as they gauged where to draw their own lines regarding freedom of expression in their states. The Gulf states watched each other's domestic politics carefully—activists coordinated and shared strategies, while the ruling families eyed each other's experiments with parliamentary process and permitting political societies (legal organizations short of political parties). While regional mimicry was most pronounced within sub-regions such as North Africa and the Gulf, by 2010 some of the most important Arabic bloggers in particular but other political opposition actors as well began to pay attention and draw parallels to events unfolding across the Arab World.

Future research is necessary to measure and estimate the precise effects of these three factors in shaping regional leaders' decision making in the 1990s and 2000s. While it is unclear whether and to what extent these international forces contributed to the Arab Spring, as the following chapters describe, these international drivers interacted with and in some cases amplified the three drivers of change.

Presenting the Argument

Chapter 1 argues that as the popular demand for greater free expression increased over the 1990s and 2000s, a public sphere emerged particular to each state that began to erode the barriers between the public and the authorities. The growth of a public sphere beyond state control allowed debate on subjects once considered taboo, from religious practice to dating and marriage norms to corruption allegations involving government officials. Authorities tried to respond, passing new press laws and in some cases convicting emboldened journalists and editors. Because of the new technologies at play and the public's heightened demand for the free flow of information, however, it was nearly impossible to contain and limit the expansion of free expression. Chapter 1 focuses on the case of Morocco to exemplify the contentious expansion of the public sphere over the course of the 1990s and 2000s—and the protracted battle between authorities and independent journalists and bloggers over the limits of free expression. The Moroccan case reveals how state efforts to rein in free debate in some cases backfired, as governmental crackdowns often prompted an even greater public outcry, blurring the lines between free expression and political mobilization.

Chapter 2 describes a second driver of change: the systematic deliberalization and de-democratization efforts introduced by many regimes in the region, often in the form of new rule-of-law measures. In the fifteen years before the Arab Spring, regional autocrats increasingly employed de-democratizing rule-of-law reforms in an effort to limit competition and protect their rule. The prevalence of this strategy led many citizens to conclude that a sitting autocrat would never genuinely oversee an authentic process to expand political rights and civil liberties, even incrementally.

Chapter 2 highlights the case of Tunisia in the last two decades of Ben Ali's rule, when a series of constitutional, electoral, and other legal revisions, which all narrowed the space for political and civic competition, began to erode public trust in state institutions as well as the fairness of the electoral system, the police, the judiciary, and other authorities.[46] As Ben Ali exploited the rule of law in order to consolidate his authority and impose "legal" justifications for his repression, many opposition leaders and members of the public concluded that only radical change—the end of the regime itself—could secure their rights.

Chapter 3 argues that the partial liberalizing reforms initiated by a set of new leaders in the early 2000s in the social, economic, and even political realms raised—but then disappointed—public and opposition expectations. Most of these limited reform programs were introduced by the "sons," a new cohort that came to power at the turn of the century (including mostly sons and other close relatives of the deceased leaders). Some of their reforms, whether in the area of economic development or education or women's rights, derived from genuine motives. By the end of the decade, however, the promise of a new era had not materialized—the reform programs did not augment political rights or civil liberties. A political stalemate and sense of frustration prevailed. Chapter 3 focuses on the case of Bahrain, where King Hamad immediately oversaw a political reform process upon coming to power, from 1999 through 2001. Ten years later, however, with expectations dashed and the king's reform process languishing, public disappointment and a sense of stalemate prevailed, setting the stage for deeper political instability.

The choice of these three case studies reflects a critical case research design.[47] Simply put, Morocco, Tunisia, and Bahrain clearly exemplify each of the three drivers of change in the fifteen-year period before the Arab Spring, even though these drivers were emerging elsewhere as well. In choosing Morocco, Tunisia, and Bahrain as my three primary cases, I am selecting cases where the Arab Spring upheaval led to different outcomes to date: Morocco thus far has weathered the Arab Spring without a regime crisis, with the king introducing a new constitution and calling for new parliamentary elections. In Tunisia, a tentative democratic transition is ongoing, even as the freely elected leaders are finding it challenging to fulfill the protestors' demands for economic opportunity along with political freedom. In Bahrain, instability prevails. The reoccurring and intensifying protests, have, in some cases, turned violent.

Chapter 4 analyzes the implications of the three drivers of change for U.S. policy makers, recognizing that its assessments are relevant to other international actors—whether foreign governments or international institutions—intent on promoting political change in the region. The popular demand for greater free expression raises the question of how Western governments might offer support for the independent and the often uncoordinated movement of journalists, bloggers, and other private individuals expressing free viewpoints. Rule-of-law de-democratization that diminishes the credibility of institutions such as elections and constitutions often prompts an insufficient response from the international community. Meanwhile, the new autocratic leaders tend to be most interested in reforms during their first few years, in order to buttress credibility. Over time, they often cease to introduce or implement reforms. This pattern offers a cautionary tale to Western policy makers, who tend to embrace new autocratic successors by placing high hopes in their promised commitments, without leveraging demands for follow-through.

Policy efforts initiated during the first decade of the twenty-first century to promote political change in the Middle East and North Africa faltered in part because they were rarely based on a careful analysis of the nuanced political changes already occurring in each state in the region. Had policy makers understood the political change tentatively afoot, they might have calibrated their strategies to ensure greater complementarity and support for local opposition actors, including civil society, journalists, and political parties.

Academics shared the flawed assumptions held by policy makers, primarily the fallacy that the region's authoritarian systems were robust and therefore would likely continue in their current form into the foreseeable future, no matter how strong the political opposition or civil society became. However, academics and Western policy makers were not the only ones to suffer from a failure of imagination regarding sources of potential bottom-up political mobilization. The region's autocrats themselves failed to imagine how their own regimes—which had in some cases lasted three decades—could become vulnerable to drivers of political change.

At Century's Dawn

The three drivers of change described in this book derived in part from particular factors that converged in the 1990s and 2000s, including new technologies, new patterns of international pressures, and new types of political opposition organization. Nonetheless, many of the states in the Middle East and North Africa had experienced earlier periods of gradual political change, including movements to increase popular sovereignty and political participation. For example, in some parts of the Arab world, in the mid-nineteenth century an elite constitutional movement, inspired in part by European liberalism, took hold. In 1866, Khedive Ismail Pasha, the Ottoman viceroy of Egypt, approved a set of basic laws creating Egypt's first representative Advisory Council. Ismail proudly wrote to a fellow Egyptian, living in Paris at the time, "You will be interested to know that the election turn-out was tremendous . . . people seem to fully comprehend the benefits and advantages which will occur to them from the Council. The commoners say that from now on higher and lower officials alike will have to give up their arrogance and to observe a straight proper path in all their conduct. The elections . . . were conducted in full freedom."[48] During this same period, when Midhat Pasha became the governor of Baghdad, he implemented a series of Tanzimat reforms, including the establishment of provincial representative assemblies and elected municipal councils. Khair al-Din also experimented with political, administrative, and legal reforms as the chief minister of the Tunisian government in the 1870s, representing the Ottoman Empire.

Periods of political change again swept through the region episodically throughout the twentieth century.[49] Many of the modern states of the Middle East and North Africa were born in the 1940s and 1950s amid nationalist independence movements that often included a cross-section of the public and brought citizens to the streets in Egypt, Algeria, Tunisia, Syria, Iraq, and elsewhere. Therefore, the three drivers of change discussed here do not constitute a radical break from the history of the region, including the modern history of the region over the past two hundred years.

By the 1960s and 1970s, however, a long respite from the populist pressures of the Arab independence movements allowed many leaders, their loyalist political parties, and their elite bases to solidify. Over the second half of the twentieth century, Middle Eastern leaders successfully neutralized nationalist and anticolonial fervor, in part by co-opting and weakening the strong political parties that had formed as part of the independence movements. Strongmen began to dominate most aspects of political and civic life. By the twenty-first century's dawn, however, regime persistence became an increasingly complicated venture. As the region's autocrats were forced to manage political change, it became more difficult—and unclear—about how to best calculate and ensure regime survival.[50] Staying ahead of political change required a good deal of high-risk guesswork. Efforts to do so were fraught with the potential for miscalculation. In many cases, what seemed at the time to be clever regime management strategies produced unintended consequences, creating the conditions ripe for revolution.

Chapter 1

The Demand for Free Expression
and the Contested Public Sphere

Over the course of the 1990s, in some countries in the Middle East and North Africa, authorities began to relax the previously strict media censorship laws, often informally, allowing the emergence and broader dissemination of independent print media. The slightly more permissive environment inspired individuals and journalists to test the limits, probing the regimes' tolerance for dissent. By the mid-2000s, the limited opening in some countries began to expand public debate among a cross section of elites and middle-class citizens, including independent journalists, activists, and nongovernmental organizations. Journalists published daring articles about nepotism in ministerial appointments or the siphoning off of foreign aid for private use.[1] Bloggers with transregional and transnational networks began debating local and international politics, including issues once considered taboo—such as the role of women in politics.[2]

The demand for freedom of expression created a new arena for debate among entrepreneurial journalists, bloggers, and citizens. New technologies and the fourfold growth of Internet usage certainly enabled the growth of the public sphere, facilitating the expansion of networks for discussion, regionally and globally.[3] This chapter focuses on the systemic expansion of the public sphere that created substantive changes to the discourse, rather than the technological innovations used by citizens to communicate with each other. Both in the decade before and immediately after the Arab Spring, other regional scholars studied the political effects of new media such as Twitter and Facebook, or new pan-Arab satellite television such as Al Jazeera.[4]

Initially, this public sphere existed largely in elite, literate circles. Nonetheless, over time, as it expanded, the psychological barrier limiting criticism of the state began to erode as well. Citizens grew accustomed to discussing sensitive topics "publicly," even if the public sphere that they encountered was comprised solely of Internet sites. New technologies such as blogs allowed the region's citizens to express themselves beyond the control of state censorship, and these citizens grew habituated to airing their opinions freely and discussing issues such as workers' rights, elections, corruption, and citizenship. Because they had become used to expressing their views in public, many citizens grew emboldened. Over time, the risks of political mobilization seemed less threatening.

By the end of the 2000s, some governments in the region tried to reign in the burgeoning public sphere, recognizing that the expanded marketplace of ideas might potentially pose a political threat. A new wave of censorship led to arbitrary legal crackdowns against high-profile journalists and independent media companies, in an effort to limit free speech and to deter those who had overstepped the perceived boundaries of acceptable expression. The crackdown came too late, however. Though authorities tried to assert control over the newly expanded public sphere, to a large extent it was impossible for the state to reclaim its writ. In some cases, the intimidation measures silenced important investigative journalists. In other cases, however, these measures backfired by transforming journalists and bloggers into glorified public figures. By the end of the 2000s, the public sphere of debate in many Middle Eastern states could not be constricted, as the public would not accept a reduced space for free expression.

Freedom House's annual freedom of the press rankings of Middle Eastern states reflect the trend discussed in this chapter, first a tentative opening and increase in free expression, followed by a region-wide reversal. Beginning in the late 1990s, journalists, bloggers, and activists, particularly in Morocco, Kuwait, Bahrain, Yemen, Egypt, and Jordan, grew increasingly daring. At a point in the 2000s, Freedom House responded by elevating the annual press freedom ranking of each of these countries from the "not free" to the "partly free" category, in light of the limited openings authorities in each state were affording journalists, the media, and the public to express their opinions. Yet in each of these cases the partial openings for free expression stalled or reversed course. By 2010, Freedom House had downgraded each of these Middle Eastern states' free expression ranking back to "not free."[5]

This chapter focuses on the Moroccan case to exemplify the broader regional trend. Morocco offers the clearest case of this driver of change, as the issue of free expression emerged there saliently, becoming a controversial source of political debate over the course of the first decade of the twentieth century. In the 1990s, King Hassan II had begun to tacitly relax the draconian state control over all media that he had imposed for decades. When his son succeeded him in 1999, activists and journalists expected the new young king to advance free expression even further. They therefore became increasingly bold, probing the extent of King Mohammed VI's permissiveness and tolerance for free expression. Over the course of the 2000s, daring Moroccan journalists, bloggers, and activists faced off against authorities trying to limit the reach of these actors with a series of high-profile arrests and exorbitant fines levied against those considered to have crossed red lines. By the mid- to late 2000s, King Mohammed VI decided to exert more control over the burgeoning public sphere, enacting a series of legalistic changes intended to monitor and regulate free expression. According to Freedom House, Morocco's press was "partly free" from 2001 to 2003, but then regressed to "not free" for the rest of the decade.[6]

In Morocco, the regime's efforts to crack down yielded mixed results. On one hand, the authorities' efforts to contain individual journalists, editors, and bloggers reimposed in some cases the practice of self-censorship around certain substantive red lines. A series of convictions against high-profile journalists, for example, seemed to limit the scope of investigative journalism in print, although with restrictions and penalties primarily focused on the formal press, many frustrated journalists turned to the blogosphere. There, government authorities could not prevent journalists and citizens from engaging with one another and with colleagues from across the region. After relaxing the limits imposed on free expression for at least a decade, the authorities in many states in the region found it difficult to reimpose these constraints.

We will see as this chapter progresses that there were three key pathways through which the growth of the public sphere likely led to greater citizen political mobilization in a way that contributed to the Arab Spring protests. To develop the argument that the expansion of a public sphere helped to catalyze the Arab Spring, I draw on examples from the Egyptian case as well. In Egypt, the gradual opening of the free press in the 2000s, followed by a crackdown in the late 2000s, followed a pattern similar to that of the Moroccan public sphere.[7]

The New Arab Public Sphere

Social and political theorists, from John Milton to John Stuart Mill, considered the unfettered and independent flow of information and freedoms of expression, press, and association as essential foundations for the expansion of political freedom.[8] For instance, Jürgen Habermas famously posited a link between the rise of free expression and political discourse and systemic political change: In *The Structural Transformation of the Public Sphere*, Habermas argued that the growth of newspapers, journals, reading clubs, Masonic lodges, and coffeehouses in eighteenth-century Europe gradually replaced the "representational" culture, where the state sought to ensure that all cultural representation focused on reflections of itself. Over time, the new public sphere that arose existed outside of state control, allowing a place for individuals to exchange views, ideas, and knowledge. In this sphere, critique and dialogue were acceptable and embraced. According to Habermas, the French Revolution resulted in part from the collapse, over decades, of the French representational culture and its replacement by a public sphere where individuals either met in conversation or exchanged views via the print media.[9] Whereas Habermas and his contemporaries considered the public sphere a bourgeois phenomenon only, by the late twentieth century scholars studying the third wave of democratization recognized how a marketplace of free ideas, once liberated in a democratic transition, could shape the views and political predilections of a more diverse cross section of the public, contributing to the shared experience of democratic citizenship.[10]

The Liberalization of State-Controlled Media and the Demand for Free Expression

In the Middle East and North Africa, for most of the second half of the twentieth century, pervasive censorship and government regulations limited free speech and free media, enforced by strong, coercive institutions such as ministries of communication and information. By the late 1990s, even as these institutions remained intact, a series of factors eased the strict control on new types of media and accessible information, increasing the public's demand for greater free expression.

First, in some cases regimes began informally relaxing censorship norms by tacitly allowing the rise of independent newspapers. Some analysts have argued that these independent papers filled the space left open by the weakening political parties—and their ossified, moribund press outlets.[11] In the multiparty republics of Egypt, Morocco, and Tunisia, where newspapers affiliated with parties had once offered independent views, the legal independent political parties grew increasingly weak (and co-opted in some cases by the government), reflected by their newspapers' increasing tendencies to toe the government's editorial line. As a result, the public sought new sources of independent information and analysis. In the late 1990s, an independent press emerged, with private owners unwilling to adhere to any particular party line.[12]

Second, the democratization of the print media and rising literacy rates within many of the region's countries meant a more extensive circulation of all types of media, particularly newspapers. Third, the dramatic increase in Internet use in the early 2000s changed the landscape for media and journalism and offered a means of access to a wider audience. Internet usage grew four times faster from 2000 to 2010 in the Middle East and North Africa than in any other region around the world, and the percentage of the population in the Middle East and North Africa using the Internet (30 percent) in 2010 even surpassed the international average of 28.7 percent.[13] Blogs and independent online media created central, easily accessible and safe venues for popular expression, particularly among the region's youth. The blogosphere in particular offered an increasingly attractive alternative to the print media for many journalists eager to express themselves; by 2009 there were approximately thirty-five thousand regularly updated Arabic-language blogs.[14]

These technological innovations were a double-edged sword. While habituating many citizens to free expression, the technologies also allowed savvy security services to generate new types of censorship mechanisms, such as Internet filtering and surveillance systems.[15] Still, despite the willingness of many regimes to counter Internet freedom, on net, the systemic technological changes helped to protect a space for debate beyond the authorities' complete control.

A dialogue particular to each state in the region began to arise. Citizens deliberated and discussed politics and social issues, holding online and in some of the independent press debates that would have been unthinkable in classrooms, boardrooms, or local civic meetings.[16] Citizens debated corruption, social mores, and religious freedoms and began to demand accountability, transparency, and the rights of citizenship long denied by the authoritarian state. As citizens began to find venues to express their views beyond government restrictions, the expanded public sphere allowed people to confront controversial issues as well their fellow citizens' points of view. While the focus in this chapter is on the local public sphere, particular to each country, a regional network also emerged, and it connected activists, journalists, and citizens across the Arabic-speaking world.

The Sclerotic Response

Even if many of the region's leaders had tacitly allowed the growth of free expression in the first place, by the early 2000s—recognizing the potency of the independent media and the new voices it had unleashed—many began scrambling to manage the consequences. Each state tried to protect certain "red lines" in terms of acceptable content for free speech and press, prescribing the boundaries of the public sphere. When individuals or journalists began testing these lines—often by expressing antiregime, anti-Islam, or other controversial sentiments—they incurred fines and jail sentences. The red lines were often fluid—and subject to interpretation by loyalists in the courts and within the ministries of communication. At times, authorities arbitrarily and erratically enforced the red lines, unsure themselves of the limits they wanted to impose on the newly expanded public spheres. By the end of the 2000s, many governments had launched episodic, often capricious, legal campaigns against bloggers and journalists. Many of these campaigns were symbolic in nature and failed to delineate a consistent position on the acceptable boundaries of free speech and expression.[17]

In addition to imposing fines and jail sentences, and exerting financial pressures on individuals or media, many governments in the region began promulgating legal reforms in order to manage this driver of change, favoring new press codes or laws to regulate the media industry in order to navigate the acceptable boundaries of speech and press.[18] From 1995 to 2006, the governments of Bahrain, Morocco, Tunisia, Egypt, and Jordan all revised their countries' press codes or press laws in order to manage and control free expression.[19] The new and "reformed" Kuwaiti press law, issued in 2006, criminalized the publication of material criticizing the constitution, the emir, or Islam and inciting acts that offended public morality or religious sensibilities. The vagueness of these laws encouraged self-censorship, with editors and publishers preferring to err on the side of caution rather than risk the often steep penalties.

Nonetheless, efforts by many regional governments to stanch the increased demand for free expression could not entirely reverse the trend. Authorities in Bahrain, for example, cautiously allowed the operation of the independent opposition newspaper *Al-Wasat* for most of the 2000s, despite the publication's often critical coverage of government policies.[20] During the same time period, the Moroccan authorities allowed the publication of the independent weekly *TelQuel* (and its Arabic companion, *Nichane*), even as they launched a campaign to undermine the independence of the publication, culminating in an open attack against its editors and publishers.[21] Moreover, state efforts to limit the public sphere often backfired, inspiring independent journalists to test the authorities' limits. Those journalists who were targeted used the Internet to mobilize sympathetic support among local and international media watchdog groups.[22] While in some cases local independent newspapers retreated, bloggers—perhaps emboldened by their sometimes anonymous identities—were often unwilling to succumb to self-censorship pressures. The government exerted control over independent media by applying financial pressures on the media companies that owned the publications, but low-cost blogs were beyond the reach of these pressures. In most cases, regime efforts to control the Internet through surveillance and filtering also could not limit the power of the blogosphere, as new technologies continued to arise to circumvent censorship efforts.[23] By the end of the 2000s, in some, though not all, Middle Eastern and North African states, authorities were engaged in protracted negotiations with journalists, opposition groups, and media owners and consumers regarding the acceptable limits of the public sphere.

The Drive for Free Expression
in King Mohammed VI's Morocco

The End of King Hassan II's Rule

For the first two decades of King Hassan II's rule, the Moroccan monarch oversaw the brutal repression of his political opponents.[24] Security officials arrested thousands and executed or disappeared hundreds, while violently suppressing major urban and rural insurrections. Prisoners were detained indefinitely and tortured.[25] The Ministry of Interior tightly controlled freedom of speech and restricted print journalism to a half-dozen government-produced dailies.[26] By the late 1980s, local and international organizations began vocally criticizing Morocco's human rights conditions. A few foreign governments echoed these concerns.[27] King Hassan initiated a series of limited reforms from 1988 through 1992 in an effort to appeal to his domestic opponents, primarily a bloc of parties interested in political reform, and to try to allay growing international criticism. In 1988, the king legalized the Organisation Marocaine des Droits de l'Homme (OMDH), the first civil society organization in Morocco dedicated to human rights. In 1990, the king established the Conseil Consultatif des Droits de l'Homme (CCDH) as a consultative body to recommend human rights reforms to the palace.[28]

By the mid-1990s, when the king reached out to the coalition of prodemocracy opposition parties, the Kutla bloc, to try to reach a political accommodation with them, the issue of press freedoms emerged as a key demand. Since the 1960s, the Union Socialiste des Forces Populaires party (USFP) and the other opposition parties within the Kutla bloc had protested the highly repressive Moroccan Press Code, which had been promulgated in 1958 by the first post-independence Moroccan king, Mohammed V.[29] In 1973, King Hassan II strengthened the already punitive code, augmenting executive power to ban or to seize publications, and mandating extensive jail sentences and fines for offenders.[30] By 1993, however, as part of his efforts to reach an agreement with the USFP and the other parties in the Kutla bloc, the king indicated his willingness to amend the press code in order to enhance freedom of expression.[31]

While the discussed amendments were never promulgated, in the wake of the dialogue and the subsequent reconciliation between the palace and the Kutla bloc in 1996, Moroccan journalists began taking more liberties.[32] In 1997, for the first time, the Moroccan government picked a prime minister from an opposition party. This move signaled to many Moroccan journalists the launch of a new era, and they began to expand their coverage of the government's policies and practices, though still cautiously. By the late 1990s, independent weeklies with a collective circulation of a hundred thousand (which was large by Moroccan standards) were regularly breaking substantive taboos by investigating issues such as human rights abuses committed by the security apparatus, the corruption of government officials, and the king's wealth.[33] Publishing articles on such topics would have been unthinkable a decade earlier.

Technological Innovations

The political liberalization of the 1990s helped foster a new marketplace, where the increase in independent press and media supply generated increased public demand. By 2001, there were a total of 644 dailies and weekly papers (430 in Arabic, 199 in French, 8 in Berber, 6 in English, and 1 in Spanish) and over 700 periodicals with an aggregate circulation of 3,671,000 Moroccans. Morocco's press emerged as one of the most robust in the Middle East and North Africa.[34] (By 2002, only Kuwait and Jordan also had earned a "partly free" ranking status according to Freedom House's freedom of the press rankings, compared to the "not free" rankings earned by the other states in the region.)[35] The demand for print media was particularly impressive given the high illiteracy rate—between 50 and 60 percent at the turn of the twenty-first century. Though many of these publications were affiliated with the government or political parties, by the late 1990s an independent Arabic and French press also emerged.[36] One of the first independent weeklies, Le Journal, established in 1997, began covering previously taboo topics. Stories appeared for instance focusing on the infamous Interior Minister Driss Basri, who had overseen the repressive practices of the regime for twenty years through a web of informants and ruthless security forces.

Meanwhile, in addition to the growth of the Arabic and French print media, the emergence of the Internet quickly transformed the marketplace of information. While the first Moroccan Internet connection was established in 1995, ten years later Morocco had over one million users among a population of about thirty-two million, one of the highest per capita rates in the Arab world. The spread of cheap cybercafés (numbering over fifteen hundred by 2005) offered Internet usage to Moroccans living beyond the elite, urban enclaves.[37]

The Internet also began changing the nature of Moroccan politics and political discourse, on all sides of the ideological spectrum. By the late 1990s, government ministries, political parties, and parliament had built their own websites. Civil society and opposition groups used the web to advocate for their positions and local campaigns and to criticize the monarchy. In 2000, the illegal Justice and Charity Organization (JCO), the popular Islamist political movement, launched a website. The JCO used its website to publish, among other things, its organization's letter to the king, which urged King Mohammed VI to redistribute his father's wealth. The letter had been banned by the regime from publication in any of the independent Moroccan print newspapers. The JCO website also featured information resources, news, and audio and video clips about the movement's positions, thus bypassing the government censorship that had previously prevented JCO from mobilizing supporters in the formal Moroccan press.[38]

The Transfer of Power from Father to Son

In 1999, when the thirty-six-year-old King Mohammed VI acceded to the throne upon the death of his father, many assumed that he would not only continue his father's increased tolerance for civil liberties, but also relax constraints even further.[39] This expectation was not unfounded, given that the new king immediately initiated a series of human rights and social reforms, as Chapter 3 discusses. He ousted the notoriously repressive Interior Minister Driss Basri.[40] He revised the family status laws (the moudawana) to increase women's rights. He also established the first reparations council in the Arab world to compensate political victims who had been incarcerated and tortured during his father's reign. These reforms won him instant acclaim abroad. In 2005, the reparations council, called the Equity and Reconciliation Commission (IER), began to hear the claims of political prisoners held without trial in prolonged detention between 1959 and 1999 and those of the family members of victims who had never returned. By the end of 2007, the state had compensated over twenty thousand individual victims or their family members, paying out $85 million to individuals and proposing communal reparation programs for disadvantaged minorities and regions.[41] This truth, reconciliation, and compensation process was unprecedented in the Arab world.

The IER and other reforms, including women's rights reforms, led many journalists, activists, and the public to believe that the new king would also relax constraints on free expression. During the first years of Mohammed VI's reign, the press began testing the waters of what they believed to be a newly permissive environment.[42] As they covered the IER process, for instance, journalists published exposés on the human rights abuses committed by King Hassan's security services.[43] For the first time in Moroccan history, the press reported on the makhzen—the clique surrounding the king that often operates as a shadow government—as well as corruption linked to palace officials. *TelQuel* published a daring story discussing the salary of the king.[44] During the first months after King Mohammed VI's succession, *Le Journal* published a story reporting that the new king's advisors were launching a "hostile takeover" of the private sector.[45] The public could now see pictures of the royal family, including the king's wife, in the media and learn about their private lives.[46]

In addition, the independent press began to serve as a peaceful forum for public discussion of controversial social issues—a space that had never existed before in Morocco.[47] In June 2002, for example, *Le Journal* (whose name was changed to *Le Journal Hebdomadaire*) sponsored a debate about the proposed reforms to the personal status code (moudawana) regarding women's rights, between Nadia Yassine, the daughter of the JCO's founder, and a former minister who had first proposed the reforms. At the time, the topic was still highly sensitive and politically charged and the JCO had expressed only unflinching opposition to the reform. In the *Le Journal Hebdomadaire* debate, however, Yassine signaled some flexibility regarding the proposed reforms to some of the family laws affecting women's rights.[48]

The new atmosphere derived in part from a basic expectation: many assumed that the new young king, educated abroad, would support a progressive approach to civil liberties, particularly freedom of expression. Many journalists also felt emboldened by the liberalizing reforms that the king was initiating in the social and economic realms. Taking their cues from the palace's pursuit of these reforms, they assumed that the new king would be equally enlightened when it came to coverage of once-taboo subjects in the press.[49] According to one human rights lawyer, Abdelaziz Nouyadi, a new generation of journalists began publishing stories on issues such as corruption, palace budgets, and drug trafficking because they did not practice the political calculations of earlier journalists who had tried to avoid government control—they "believe[d] we are in a democratic society [where] the only calculation [was] with their readers."[50]

The 2002 Press Code

Even as the new king embraced economic, social, and human rights reforms during the first two years of his reign, he seemed uneasy with the press. He was reluctant to grant a personal interview to Moroccan newspapers upon his succession. And only a year after the king assumed power, the government began punishing the preeminent independent news weeklies—in an opening salvo of a battle that would last the entire decade. In December 2000, authorities banned editions of *Le Journal* and its Arabic counterpart when these weeklies published stories questioning Morocco's military activities in a disputed part of the Western Sahara.[51] In April 2000, the editors of *Al Ousbou* and *Al Shamal* were sentenced to jail, fined, and banned from journalism for three years after publishing an article in late 1999 titled "The House That's There: Company with Capital of 500 Dirhams Sells Morocco a House Worth Five Million." The article alleged that the Moroccan Foreign Minister Mohamed Benaissa had misappropriated public funds while serving as ambassador to the United States.[52] In 2001, the managing editor of the *Le Journal Hebdomadaire*, received a three-month suspended sentence and was ordered to pay a fine of $240,000 for publishing an article making the same allegation.[53]

Soon the king began to argue publicly in favor of imposing regulations on the press. In July 2001, he had told the widely circulated pan-Arab daily *Asharq Alawsat*, "Of course I am for press freedom, but I would like that freedom to be responsible." He called Morocco's freedom of press a "responsible freedom that respects the institutions and does not slander them with laws that regulate them."[54] In a July 30, 2003, address, the king guaranteed the right "to information through the consolidation of the freedom of the press and independent audiovisual networks" but "within a framework of respect for our religious principles, national components and the kingdom's laws."[55]

In February 2002, the palace issued a royal decree promulgating a new national press code.[56] The 2002 text was somewhat more lenient than the 1973 text. It contained fewer criminal penalties for libel and decreased the length of sentences for defaming the king or the royal family, from twenty to five years; made it easier for journalists and editors to start a new publication; and required the government to state a reason for banning newspapers.[57] Nevertheless, the new code included legal loopholes and vague libel and defamation clauses, which could be used in order to limit independent publications.[58] The code defined libel broadly, making it easy for regime loyalists in the Moroccan courts to fine journalists who were found guilty of publishing false information. Moreover, the new press code allowed the government to sentence journalists to prison for three to five years, fine them up to $120,000, and ban a publication when it was perceived to be damaging to "Islam, the monarchy, or territorial integrity."[59] By maintaining these three red lines, the government retained its right to shut down what it deemed to be offensive substantive coverage. Territorial integrity was a thinly veiled reference to a discussion of the Western Sahara, and though this journalistic taboo was well understood, many journalists never-theless tried to bypass it, even reporting from the Western Sahara.[60] The press law failed to define, however, the acceptable boundaries for covering Islam or the monarchy.

Although the new code reduced the maximum sentence from twenty to five years for those found guilty of defamation, and transferred responsibil-ity from the executive to the courts to try journalists, the revised code also institutionalized restrictions on free expression.[61] To those who expected the new, young king to be more progressive in his approach to civil liberties than his father had been, the new code was disappointing. While in some cases the new code improved registration opportunities for new publica-tions, it also allowed for greater government discretion to censor those articles that it deemed most sensitive, particularly when combined with the provisions of the 2003 antiterrorism law.[62] Immediately after the announce-ment of the new press code, the government began confiscating copies of publications that authorities considered in violation of the code. The Minis-try of Interior provided informal regulations or "guidance" to journalists, encouraging self-censorship. The Moroccan Press Union reacted to the new press code critically, lamenting its failure to eliminate penal sanctions en-tirely as well as the government's retained power to revoke publication licenses and to confiscate and suspend publications deemed threatening to the public order.[63]

TESTING THE RED LINES: THE CONTENTIOUS DEBATE
ABOUT THE MOROCCAN PUBLIC SPHERE

The 2002 press code and the subsequent 2003 antiterrorism law offered Moroccan authorities new legal means to monitor the substance of the debate begun by the emboldened independent press, an independent dia-logue that now ascended into the realm of blogs and civil society organiza-tions.[64] As the 2000s progressed, Moroccan authorities used these laws on occasion to impose limits on the journalists, activists, and bloggers focused on issues once considered taboo.[65] When authorities tried to exert control over the independent print media in order to influence editorial substance, editors and the owners of the independent media publications often acqui-esced, in part because battling continuous lawsuits often had significant financial costs.

Yet, even as Moroccan authorities began implementing the new code and in some cases filed suits against independent journalists and others, the Moroccan public's demand for independent information continued to increase—exponentially. Whereas in 2001 less than 1 percent of the population had Internet access, by 2009 over 33 percent did. Interest in online news sources increased.[66] Sales of Moroccan weeklies reached nine million cumulatively by late 2008.[67] New mandatory universal primary and secondary education and a more literate youth heightened the demand for diverse media and Internet sites.[68]

By the mid-2000s, government efforts to crack down against independent journalists often became a battle of wills, as the defendants would often capitalize on the attention, transforming into media and blogosphere celebrities. For instance, when Ali Lmrabet published an article on the status of Western Saharan refugees in his satirical newspapers *Demain* (French) and *Doumain* (Arabic) in 2004, he promptly received a $6,000 fine and a sentence banning him from the practice of journalism for ten years. The imprisoned Lmrabet went on a hunger strike in prison, instigating an international outcry. Authorities quickly released him.[69] At the time, although a number of journalists were testing the taboo against covering the Western Sahara, the government chose to fine and punish Lmrabet, in part to settle accounts.[70] In another incident, Moroccan authorities tried to block access to YouTube after the site hosted videos of pro-independence Saharan demonstrations in 2007, but these videos quickly reappeared on other sites.[71]

Over time, the limits imposed by the government on the public sphere began to seem arbitrary. The courts and the Ministry of Communication often capriciously interpreted the red lines identified in the new press code. In 2008, this ministry banned the distribution of the international edition of the French weekly *L'Express* after the feature story depicted portraits of Jesus and Muhammad considered to be disrespectful of Islam.[72] In January 2007, a judge banned the Arabic newsweekly *Nichane* for three months and fined editor Driss Ksikes and journalist Sanaa Elaji $9,000 for an article titled "Jokes: How Moroccans Laugh at Religion, Sex and Politics," calling the article offensive to Islam and traditional morality.[73] Yet none of the jokes were particularly new or sordid and the fine surprised many. In general, the interpretation of the code was inconsistent, with authorities trying to make a point by issuing highly punitive indictments against isolated scapegoats.

As the decade progressed, Moroccan authorities responded inconsistently when the independent media began to push the limits of its coverage of the royal family. During the first few years after his succession, in an attempt to introduce himself and appear more accessible to the Moroccan public, the king and his family made themselves available to the press, at least informally. Pictures of the king's wife appeared in most Moroccan dailies and weeklies—the first time a picture of a royal wife had ever appeared in print.[74] By the mid-2000s, however, the king began to react with deep sensitivity to any press stories about himself or his family. In 2007, the Ministry of Interior seized and destroyed a hundred thousand copies of the independent weeklies *Nichane* and *TelQuel* because they contained an editorial considered disrespectful of the king. (That year, the Committee to Protect Journalists labeled Morocco among the ten worst global "press backsliders" largely due to the efforts by the Moroccan authorities to restrict the content in these two publications.)[75]

In September 2008, one day after he published an article critical of the special favors the king sometimes accorded his citizens, Moroccan blogger Mohammed Erraji was arrested and sentenced to two years in prison. The first Moroccan blogger to be jailed for his writings, Erraji was released on bail less than a week later by an appellate court.[76] Even individuals making jokes or light-hearted remarks about the king received penalties. A student in southern Morocco was sentenced to eighteen months in prison for replacing "King" with "Barcelona" in the country's national motto "God, Country, King" (in reference to the popular soccer team).[77] In November 2009, the editor of *Al Mishaal* received a one-year prison sentence and a fine of $12,000 for publishing "false information" about the health of the king.[78]

By the end of the decade, journalists could no longer write stories about the king's close family members and advisers, reflecting an increasing level of insecurity on the part of the palace. In August 2009, the Moroccan authorities questioned a dozen journalists and seized two independent newspapers that had published an opinion poll about King Mohammed VI's reign—even though the poll they had published indicated favorable public attitudes toward the king. (Of the Moroccans surveyed, 91 percent judged the king's performance positively, while 49 percent said Morocco had become more democratic under his leadership.)[79] Defending the censorship, the Minister of Communications and Government Spokesman Khalid Naciri argued that—no matter the polling results—treating the king as the subject of an opinion poll violated the constitution and showed disrespect to the royal family.[80] In September 2009, authorities detained—and later fined—journalists and editors for *Al-Jarida al-Oula, Al Michaal,* and *Al Ayam* for reporting on the King's health.[81] In October 2009, the editor and cartoonist of *Akhbar el-Yom* were interrogated for forty-eight hours by police after publishing a cartoon that satirized the wedding of King Mohammed VI's cousin Moulay Ismail.[82]

A FAILED GAMBIT

During the mid to late 2000s, some Moroccans argued that the arbitrary way in which the regime upheld its press red lines reflected the king's ambivalent beliefs regarding the acceptable boundaries for free expression.[83] Initially, King Mohammed VI had continued the process of expanding civil liberties begun by his father in the 1990s, allowing the evolution of a carefully prescribed avenue for free expression. King Hassan likely decided to gradually relax limits on free expression in part to help enable a smooth succession for his son: better to allow nongovernmental organizations, activists, and journalists to collectively "vent" in the press or at public demonstrations than repress all expression and drive activism underground—perhaps triggering more dramatic, revolutionary activism. Allowing the limited liberalization of civil liberties was a calculated gamble that seemed to have been successful in the 1990s and early 2000s, when the relatively more free and tolerant environment helped to create high public regard and trust in the new king and paint him in a positive light internationally.

Yet King Mohammed VI's decision to reverse course by the late 2000s was shortsighted. In the short term, the king had been able to prevent popular demands for greater political rights, in part by initiating liberalizing reforms upon taking power, as discussed in Chapter 3, and in part by opening up a limited space for free expression for a few years. Yet, over time the gambit proved less effective. By the second half of the 2000s, the regime's efforts to control free expression—through the crackdowns discussed earlier—were both ineffective and counterproductive.

The regime's decision to begin select campaigns against journalists and bloggers had the effect of transforming these individuals into national and international heroes. Subjecting journalists and publishers to isolated and seemingly unfair lawsuits glorified them and encouraged even bolder and more defiant activism across a wide political spectrum. The once sleepy and ineffectual national press union, the Syndicat National de la Presse Marocaine (SNPM), for example, became increasingly active, demanding

that all fines levied against the press be proportionate to the alleged dam-
ages. The SNPM leadership, now empowered by its ties to international
press watchdog groups, such as the Committee to Protect Journalists, monitored each government case against Moroccan journalists. Criticism of
Morocco's press laws intensified in the second half of the 2000s.[84] In 2009, a
SNPM report claimed that Moroccan journalists were subject to "arbitrary
harassment, aggression and unjust prosecution" and complained that the
judiciary was not making "any move to protect journalists," despite the
courts' inclination to "take legal action."[85] In late 2009, Noureddine Mef-
tah, the publisher of *Al Ayam*, tried to resign in protest as secretary general
of the Moroccan Federation of Newspaper Publishers (FMEJ)—a government-sponsored federation—after police interrogated him and raided *Al
Ayam*'s office.[86]

Crackdowns against newspapers became a rallying cry across a broad
array of nongovernmental opposition groups. In a rally organized by
twenty-three civil, trade union, and human rights groups in November
2008, two thousand Moroccans denounced the defamation case against *Almassae* that had resulted in a fine of $790,000 the year before. The protest-
ors at the rally accused the judiciary of complicity in "a battle to silence
the free press," while speakers "enumerated the abuses of the freedom of
expression in the so-called new era."[87] In late July 2009, a court imposed
heavy fines on three independent dailies for defaming Libyan leader Muammar Qaddafi. A day after the ruling, many of the country's newspapers
defiantly published blank editorials.[88]

Political activism in defense of free press also garnered international
attention. In 2008, for example, authorities charged Fouad Mourtada with
a three-year sentence after he created a fake Facebook page in the name of
Prince Moulay Rachid, King Mohammed VI's brother.[89] The Moroccan
blogging community took up the Mourtada case and planned a number of
protests within Morocco. The bloggers also attracted international attention
to the sentence. Within weeks, in the spring of 2008, Mourtada received a
royal pardon.[90]

In short, by the end of the decade, the government's effort to limit
media coverage of the so-called sensitive issues, particularly the king and
the royal family, became increasingly unpredictable. In some cases regime
efforts to censor journalists and bloggers, and in particular to use legal
proceedings to punish publishers, resulted in the desired effect of reimpos-
ing self-censorship. For example, the state was successful in forcing the

independent *TelQuel* and *Nichane* weeklies to change their editorial tones. Yet, the crackdown against the media in the late 2000s also precipitated greater activism and generated protest movements directed directly against Moroccan authorities. And even as the government tried to control the mainstream media, preventing the publication of topics considered taboo in newspapers and magazines, newer forms of media, whether blogs or other Internet sites, could freely cover the same issues. It was nearly impossible to limit what had become a market-based response to the public's demand for greater free expression. The authorities' often inconsistent and rash efforts to impose censorship did not stanch the public debate, which was no longer confined to individual media outlets and had instead expanded, generating an independent public sphere beyond state control.

Pathways to Political Change

As Marc Lynch and others have argued, multiple mechanisms or pathways may have linked the growth of free press and the emergence of a more independent public sphere in the Middle East and North Africa to the political actions of early 2011.[91] Yet it is empirically difficult to prove that any one of these potential pathways below was determinant. This chapter has argued that in many countries in the region, over the 1990s and 2000s, a realm for free expression, increasingly free from state control, began expanding. It could not be reined in, despite the authorities' best efforts. There are a number of ways in which the growth of a public sphere could have influenced the unprecedented political mobilization that occurred in 2011.

Functional Innovations

The first pathway, as the Moroccan case suggests and as other scholars have documented, involves the particular technological innovations and new media—from independent newspapers to Twitter to satellite television to local blogs—that enabled the driver of change. In this regard, most scholars have focused on the new types of social media and pan-Arab television as the key technological innovations, but the growth of independent print newspapers in the 2000s can also be considered a similarly "functional" innovation.

New means of communication allowed citizens and activists to organize the protests of 2011 in a manner that was free from governmental control. By 2011, Facebook had over twenty-one million Arab users, more than the estimated total number of newspaper readers in the region; both Egypt and Tunisia had particularly high levels of membership.[92] The fact that the Tunisian and Egyptian revolts inspired the emergence of protest movements in other countries can be attributed to the celerity of social media and traditional media outlets in disseminating information and images.[93]

While scholars will continue to measure the specific ways in which social media mobilized the participants in the 2011 revolts, the net effects of new technologies should not be overestimated. Technological innovations *also* enabled governmental regulation, censorship, and control throughout the 2000s. For example, new technologies offered new types of censorship methods, allowing authorities to respond to the growth of the public sphere by imposing Internet filters and new forms of online censorship. Technology was therefore both an enabler and a way to impose limits on the burgeoning protest movements.

Perhaps the most interesting aspect of the functional technological pathway is that in both Morocco and other regional states, the governments themselves had either actively or tacitly encouraged many of the technological developments that allowed for the expansion of the public sphere in the first place. King Hassan had affirmatively allowed the rise of independent weeklies in the late 1990s, and then he had encouraged greater print media dissemination. Similarly, Hosni Mubarak also gradually relaxed Egypt's censorship policies in the late 1990s and allowed the "explosion" of Egyptian independent media.[94] As in Morocco, by the turn of the twenty-first century, the Egyptian government allowed journalists unprecedented freedoms.[95] During this period, the authorities began granting newspaper publication licenses to opposition parties and private investors. A new crop of Egyptian independent newspapers and political talk shows broached topics that would have been unthinkable only a decade earlier, including by covering the positions of political opposition groups.

By 2010, there were six hundred newspapers, magazines, journals, and other periodicals published in Egypt.[96] Though many of the traditional media outlets were government owned or managed, these media outlets covered a much wider range of viewpoints than previously was the case. The government allowed foreign satellite channels and permitted the establishment of locally-based private satellite television stations. Finally, in

Egypt, as in Morocco, thanks to aggressive government efforts to promote Internet use, the number of citizens with Internet access quadrupled over the first decade of the twenty-first century. This growth of Internet usage allowed the public unlimited online debate, as the Egyptian government did not typically engage in online censorship.[97]

Indeed, there is no question that new forms of communication made possible by the Internet enabled the Egyptian revolution, particularly online organization and activism.[98] In order to catch the government by surprise, the organizers of the general labor strikes of April 6 and May 4, 2008, the most important set of political protests leading up to the revolution, relied almost entirely on the Internet, including blogs, YouTube, and Facebook. Government authorities responded to these labor strikes with heavy-handed repression, believing they had eviscerated the movement. Ultimately, the authorities failed to see how their violent reaction could backfire, leading to the establishment of the organized April 6 political movement, which was named in honor of those who had stood up in the face of police repression in 2008. Indeed, the strike of April 6, 2008, and the police's heavy-handed response proved to be catalysts, mobilizing the political action that culminated in the January 2011 protests in Tahrir Square.

The fact that new means of communication could sustain more robust political mobilization was not lost on the regimes clinging to power in early 2011. Given the obvious technological innovations enabling the political protests of early 2011, it is not surprising that as both Mubarak and Ben Ali saw the demonstrators engulfing their capitals, they both immediately moved to block Internet servers. In Bahrain, progovernment mobs went further—attacking the offices of the main opposition newspaper *Al-Wasat*, shortly after the antigovernment protests began. The Bahraini government, recognizing the power of one mainstream independent newspaper to encourage the opposition, began filing a series of lawsuits against it, shutting down the newspaper for a few weeks and filing a series of charges against *Al-Wasat*'s independent-minded editor. Eventually, in August 2011, the Board of Directors reinstated the editor of *Al-Wasat*.[99]

Collective Action and the Public Sphere

In a second potential pathway, greater free expression in the public sphere spills over into the political sphere, encouraging greater activism. Citizens were simply unable to keep up a barrier between the free views they were expressing online and reading in new newspapers and the limits to their political rights they were experiencing practically. Soon, the barriers to collective action began to erode. In addition, as observers of other revolutions have argued, the rise of the public sphere could have acclimatized more citizens to collective action by creating greater and more accessible information about their fellow citizens' viewpoints. Typically, people avoid political protest because they fear social or official sanctions. Even individuals who detest a regime may refrain from making their views public, worried about the response from their neighbors, friends, and families. However, as the region's citizens more frequently saw and heard instances of journalists and bloggers airing contentious political views, reflecting the pervasive nature of these views, such barriers began to dissipate.[100] The costs of dissent gradually appeared to decrease, as individuals saw the plethora of other voices seemingly sharing the dissenting perspective. They recognized that they would not be alone in expressing antiregime sentiments.

There is ample evidence that Moroccans and other citizens of the region were growing increasingly daring in their political expression over the course of the 2000s. As the public grew accustomed to greater free expression, political protest and activism grew more common. From the late 1990s until 2011, it was a common sight to stumble upon Moroccan protestors congregated in public squares, demanding workers' rights or jobs. In the mid-2000s, on the main street of the capital city of Rabat, across from parliament, unemployed graduates began gathering almost daily to protest the dearth of jobs. Noisy mass demonstrations regularly filled the streets. In 2000, citizens participated in simultaneous marches in Rabat and Casablanca to advocate for and against, respectively, a March 2000 proposal by a government minister to augment women's rights, which would eventually become the revision to the personal status code discussed above. The protests for and against a pending legislative measure were unprecedented in Moroccan history. Other notable large-scale protests occurred in Morocco in the 2000s, first in sympathy for the plight of the Palestinians (2000, 2002) and then to protest terrorism after a deadly attack struck at home (2003).

By the end of the 2000s, Moroccans were growing increasingly bold in their political behavior as well. During the September 2007 parliamentary elections, almost a fifth of Morocco's voters went to the polls and defiantly defaced the ballots or deliberately left them blank to protest the limited political rights these ballots afforded them. This unprecedented act of political protest may have revealed an electorate increasingly accustomed to free expression and willing to make bold political statements. Political activism and expression came to a head in the winter of 2011, when online activists began organizing the February 20th movement with a protest planned for that day to express grievances against the government. The lines were increasingly blurred between exercising free expression and political activism and mobilization. Much of the organizing was done online via a Facebook group, which had more than twenty thousand members.[101] A popular YouTube video featured a diverse array of Moroccans explaining why they would be joining the protest on February 20. These reasons included the desire to get a job "without paying a bribe" and accessible education "for everyone, not only the rich."[102]

In Egypt, over the 2000s, there was a similarly blurred line between new opportunities to exercise free expression and the growth of political opposition activism. Bloggers and other Internet users began playing key roles in Egyptian politics. First, they voiced direct criticism of Mubarak's regime, particularly but not limited to Article 76 of the 2007 constitution, which, as the next chapter will discuss, dramatically restricted the candidate eligibility for presidential elections. Second, the bloggers often defended the reformist judges who were subject to systematic attacks by circles close to the regime. Third, bloggers played a crucial role in uncovering abuses by institutions loyal to the regime. The spread of mobile phone video technology enabled bloggers to reveal incidents of torture in a number of detention centers, incidents that later became legal cases before the courts. Such efforts began to build bridges between Egyptian bloggers and domestic human rights groups. Some blogs went so far as to systematically map the detention facilities in which officers had physically abused detainees.[103]

In short, there was clearly a deep correlation between the growth of a new public sphere for free debate in each state in the region and new types of bolder, more defiant political activism. The direct and explicit causal relationships between the two phenomena will be the subject of empirical social science research for decades.[104]

The Unintended Consequences of Crackdowns

The case of Morocco discussed in this chapter makes the argument for a third potential pathway linking the rise of the public sphere to the political mobilization of early 2011: the paradoxical effects of greater governmental crackdown. Having experienced freer expression, many citizens of the Middle East reacted with indignation when authorities began to reimpose limits in the late 2000s. The states' overly punitive response to the growth of the Arab sphere may have in fact catalyzed greater political activism—the exact outcome the regimes were trying to avoid.

As this chapter has argued, despite their best efforts, Moroccan authorities could never fully regain control once the public began exercising greater free expression and the public sphere had expanded. By the end of the decade, citizens grew accustomed to participating in a domain of free expression beyond state control. Watching the authorities try—and fail—to rein in independent journalists and bloggers proved to be inspiring. The inability of the government to control and reimpose limits on the public sphere was one of the first instances in citizens' memory of potential regime vulnerability.

By the end of the 2000s, Egyptian authorities also seemed increasingly nervous about free expression, particularly the newly emboldened journalists and bloggers. As in Morocco, the Egyptian government first tried to introduce new limits by revising the Egyptian press law in 2006, criminalizing any publication considered to have published "false news." In addition, the new law banned writing stories about certain types of individuals, such as foreign heads of state, with a penalty of $900 to $3,600 and up to five years of imprisonment. With few professional protections, journalists remained vulnerable to prosecution under these laws.[105]

The authorities began imprisoning journalists and bloggers in a few high-profile cases by relying on provisions of the Egyptian emergency law and the Egyptian press law. A series of symbolic prosecutions also suggested regime efforts to target those journalists and members of the media who posed the greatest political challenge to the aging Mubarak and his inner circle, including his National Democratic Party. For instance, officials detained and eventually sentenced Al Jazeera journalist Huwaida Taha Mitwalli for making a documentary about torture in Egypt, charging her with "possessing and giving false pictures about the internal situation in Egypt that could undermine the dignity of the country." In addition, the state security prosecutor brought charges against Ibrahim Eissa, editor of the independent daily *Al-Dustur* for publishing reports about President Hosni Mubarak's health "that were likely to harm the public interest." The Alexandrian blogger Abd al-Karim Nabil Sulaiman, better known by his pen name, Karim Amer, was sentenced to a four-year prison term for "insulting the president."[106]

An expansion of free expression followed by government-led efforts to limit the public sphere created a similar pattern in Egypt as it did in Morocco: the state's efforts to curtail online and independent bloggers and journalists transformed these previously unknown individuals into glorified champions of individual freedom. Almost all of the bloggers arrested in 2008 after the labor strikes became important leaders of the new April 6 movement. These individuals included Abdel Moneim Mahmoud, editor of the Ana Ikhwan ("I am a Brother") blog; Esraa Abdel Fattah, who started a Facebook group calling for Egyptians to join the April 6 strike (over 74,000 joined the group); and the blogger Wael Abbas, editor of the *al-Wa'i al-Misri* ("Egyptian Awareness") blog, who had been vilified in the government media due to his success in documenting Egyptian police brutality inside detention centers in video clips he posted on YouTube.[107] In short, the government's traditional methods of suppressing free expression—whether through arresting, fining, or imprisoning the perceived offenders—were counterproductive. They typically gave the accused greater prominence, prompted online solidarity groups, and increased the impetus for political mobilization.

The Regionwide Drive for Free Expression

From Algeria to Yemen, citizens across many Middle Eastern and North African states increasingly demanded free expression over the course of the 1990s and 2000s. They were led first by bold independent media outlets and, later, by bloggers willing to test the limits of the tentative openings, probing the regimes' boundaries. In Morocco, Egypt, and elsewhere, the regimes themselves were ultimately responsible for this driver of change because they had—often just tacitly—relaxed the draconian censorship policies of the 1980s.

Given the similar conditions confronting journalists and bloggers across the region, by the late 2000s many began joining forces, creating regional coalitions to coordinate across borders. In March 2009, Moroccan bloggers formed a new association, the Rassemblement des Blogueurs Marocains (RBM), in part in order to work with international bloggers and blogging

associations to defend the rights of bloggers and Internet users and to promote the principles of public freedoms and human rights.[108] Journalists
across the Middle East established the Arab Observatory for the Freedom of
the Press and Media as a watchdog organization to report on press freedom
violations in the Arab world. Mahmoud Maarouf, the head of the Union of
the Arab Journalists in the Maghreb, called the Observatory necessary because "a democratic and independent press" needs "a democratic and independent organization."[109] Bloggers and journalists in one country aided and
assisted their compatriots elsewhere, particularly calling attention to the
plight of individuals arrested or exorbitantly fined by their local authorities.[110] The transregional coalition to protect free expression in the region
was one among many cross-regional linkages that established a foundation
for the regional mobilization during the Arab uprisings of 2011.

By the end of the 2000s, across the Middle East and North Africa, some
leaders were beginning to rue the permissive environment that they had
fostered.[111] Though they tried to crack down through fines, sentences, and
arrests, these repressive efforts were too late. In some cases, independent
publishers were driven out of business or forced to change their editorial
line. Overall, however, it was impossible for the authorities to reverse what
had become a two-decade trend. The drive for free expression had swept
across the region, and the public had begun to expect that independent
news sources would act as a forum to deliberate and discuss political, social,
and economic issues, many of which questioned the absolute rule of the
regime.

Try as they might to control the burgeoning public sphere, the region's
leaders found themselves in a bind: jailing a bold journalist would simply
call attention to his or her plight, and sometimes foster new waves of political activism, including by Western watchdog groups. It was therefore too
late to retreat to total repression and censorship. The state could levy fines.
It could not, however, reverse the fact that its citizens had grown accustomed to airing their grievances and thoughts through new types of journalism and online media. To autocrats who had prided themselves on
strategic means of control, they had miscalculated, misunderstanding the
ways in which free ideas, once liberated, could not again be suppressed.[112]

Chapter 2

De-democratizing through the Rule of Law

Tunis's main thoroughfare, Avenue Bourguiba, is a broad avenue lined with ficus trees, where men and women in business suits walk briskly across the grassy divide, navigating the lively open-air cafes and stately embassies. Until January 2011, twin billboards flanked each end of the avenue, each with a picture of the country's president, Zine el Abidine Ben Ali, smiling imperiously into the distance. These looming pictures of the president had been a fixture of the landscape for so long that most of the city's denizens had ceased to notice them. To a visitor, however, the portraits stood out as a memorable facet of the downtown Tunis landscape, and the imposing pictures of Ben Ali seemed to be scrutinizing everyone who passed by.

The fact that the Arab revolts of 2011 began when a mass protest movement engulfed Tunisia surprised some in the region. For years, analysts, academics, and local activists considered President Ben Ali's political rule to epitomize the type of ossified authoritarian rule that was stable and enduring. Although Ben Ali had come to power in 1987 promising to oversee a series of reforms, including abolishing lifelong presidencies, twenty-four years later he comfortably presided over a one-party state controlled by his Democratic Constitutional Rally (RCD) party.[1] For over two decades, Ben Ali and his regime had executed a thoughtful, deliberate campaign to weaken every element of political and civil opposition—from lawyers' and journalists' unions to opposition political parties to the once vibrant network of independent women's rights organizations. By the 2000s, all of the president's opponents, including the main Islamist movement, en-Nahda, were in exile, forced underground, or in jail. Political dissent was nearly impossible, with the Ministry of Interior, conveniently located on Avenue Bourguiba, wielding absolute control through its intimidating network of plainclothes police.[2] Reporters without Borders listed President Ben Ali

among the world's thirty-four "worst press freedom predators" by the mid-
2000s.[3] In 2008, Freedom House ranked Tunisia 177th out of 196 countries
in terms of freedom. Tunisians demanded free expression but did so cautiously, with the public sphere limited by tight governmental control. Given
these constraints, free expression had not expanded to the extent described
in Chapter 2, suggesting how some but not all of these drivers were present
in regional countries before the revolutions of 2011.

Ben Ali's strategy of "de-democratization" by way of specific rule-of-
law reforms in the short term eviscerated his opposition and prevented
independent civil society activity. Over the longer term, however, this strategy undermined the legitimacy of Tunisian institutions and the substantive
meaning of the rule of law.[4] In Ben Ali's case, by exploiting the rules of the
game to serve his own personal and party ends, he forced a reckoning
among many members of the political elite: by 2011, most had concluded
that only dramatic change, including the dissolution of the ruling RCD
party, could advance political freedoms and civil liberties, rather than piece-
meal rule-of-law reforms undertaken with an autocratic regime still intact.[5]
Some analysts observed in the late 2000s that Ben Ali had been able to
eliminate the independent spirit and will of the Tunisian people, creating a
passive society acquiescent to authoritarian rule.[6] Yet, the opposite was the
case: his de-democratization created a fundamental rejection of the political
system in its entirety.

President Ben Ali's deliberate and methodical process of de-
democratization over a twenty-year period included two particular rules of
law, which are the subject of this chapter. First, he passed a civil society
organization law in 1992 intended to cripple a key nongovernmental organization that had successfully challenged the policies of the Tunisian government for decades—the Tunisian Human Rights League. The law did not
ban the League outright but cleverly allowed regime loyalists to infiltrate
and to exert control over its membership and activities. Second, in 2002,
Ben Ali irrevocably revised Tunisia's constitution, rolling back previous
constitutional constraints on executive power, including presidential term
limits. This "legalistic coup d'état," as it was dubbed at the time, assured
Ben Ali's presidency through 2014 and narrowed the field of possible presidential candidates. Though the regime cast each of these reforms in the
language of democratization, in actuality these two laws—combined with a
series of additional legal changes initiated in the 1990s and 2000s—
strengthened the exclusive authority of the president and the ruling RCD

party, limiting the rights afforded other institutions, political parties, and nongovernmental organizations.

By the end of the 2000s, other autocrats in the region seemed to be taking a page out of Ben Ali's playbook. In 2007, Hosni Mubarak initiated similar de-democratizing constitutional reforms in Egypt and in late 2010, Ali Abdullah Saleh proposed revisions to the Yemeni constitution to cancel term limits, effectively allowing him, after 32 years of rule, to be president for life.[7] At the end of this chapter, I briefly compare the effects of President Hosni Mubarak's de-democratizing rule-of-law reforms in Egypt to those initiated by Ben Ali, underscoring how, in both cases, rule-of-law de-democratization undermined public trust in state institutions.

Therefore, this driver of change, generated from the top down, had unexpected medium-term consequences. As the autocratic leaders of the region changed term limits, built new loyalist institutions, or restricted civil liberties "legally," they eroded public trust in the fairness of the electoral system, the police, judiciary, and other institutional authorities.[8] In the fifteen years before the Arab Spring, Middle Eastern autocrats increasingly employed de-democratizing rule-of-law reforms in an effort to limit competition and protect their rule. The prevalence of this strategy led many citizens to conclude that a sitting autocrat would never genuinely oversee the fair, even if incremental, expansion of political rights and civil liberties. As a result, many concluded that only radical, discontinuous change and a complete change of leadership would be necessary to achieve political freedom and human rights.[9]

Defining De-democratization through Rule-of-Law Reform

While most existing theories of political change envision, at least theoretically, a one-directional movement toward greater liberalization or democratization, there are no such guarantees. In the West, the spread of rules of law establishing and guiding elections; structuring parties, nongovernmental organizations, and detention procedures; and protecting the press and individual freedoms, as well as constitutional documents themselves, for the most part emerged in order to protect the civil liberties and procedural political rights of individuals. Yet over the past twenty years, some authoritarian leaders of the Middle East and North Africa, and elsewhere in other regions as well, have considered rules of law as means to limit the contestation of elections, freedom of expression, and participation in political and civil societies. In many nondemocracies, judiciaries are largely composed of regime loyalists, who ensure that newly passed laws are implemented in a way that shrinks the space for political opposition, limits civil liberties, or restricts civil society.

De-democratizing rule-of-law reform here refers to the state-initiated, deliberate contraction of individual political rights and civil liberties by passing new laws. For example, in the 1990s and 2000s constitutional revisions in often modified parliaments, adding an upper chamber to a previously unicameral legislature. In many cases, the upper chamber would be composed of regime-appointed loyalists or regional governments, who could neutralize policies promoted in the lower parliamentary chambers.[10] Other examples of de-democratization involve frequent revisions to electoral laws establishing party eligibility, candidate eligibility, voting systems, or district sizes and numbers. In August 1993, days after dissolving the existing parliament, Jordan's King Hussein revised his country's electoral law in order to increase the chances that any newly elected parliament would be composed of a greater number of tribal loyalists.[11]

In the 1990s and 2000s, many regional autocrats found constitutional revisions to be a particularly useful way to reorganize the political rules of the game in their favor and in particular to minimize the chance of any genuine challenge to executive rule. From 1990 through 2010, there were sixteen instances of constitutional revisions in the region, within both monarchies and presidential republics.[12] From 2001 to 2010 alone, autocrats initiated constitutional revisions or promulgated new constitutions in Yemen, Algeria, Tunisia, Egypt (twice), Bahrain, and Qatar. While many of these revisions reduced electoral competition and helped to solidify the institutional privileges of the incumbents, most of the new texts combined a modicum of liberalizing or democratizing features with additional de-democratizing measures. Most of these constitutional revisions were subsequently submitted to a popular referendum vote—a means to earn the public's imprimatur, even though in almost every case the referendum vote itself was subject to the same flawed electoral standards of presidential and parliamentary elections.

In some cases, rule-of-law reforms initiated in the Middle East and North Africa during this period were unambiguously "de-democratizing." For example, the Tunisian reforms discussed in this chapter are all unequivocal cases where Ben Ali deliberately took preemptive measures to limit putative challengers, whether opposition actors or presidential candidates. Other cases of new rule-of-law reforms were enacted with greater nuance (e.g., the Bahraini constitution of 2002), with some provisions expanding and some contracting political rights and civil liberties. As a result, regional analysts writing about this phenomenon in the 2000s called rule-of-law reforms in the region "half measures," because they reflected the authorities' efforts to respond to opposition demands partially and strategically, without ceding any control.[13] That is, many reforms included *both* de-democratizing or illiberal provisions and some measures intended to placate opposition demands that were liberalizing. Many of these compromise rule-of-law reforms, whether enacted to change political parties, elections, or judicial independence, or press freedoms, often included elements consonant with international legal norms. As discussed in Chapter 1, for instance, some regimes responded to demands for greater free expression by partially revising the state's press codes, which in many cases both limited the criminal offenses for libel and other violations and asserted stricter oversight mechanisms on free speech and press. In other instances of these compromise or half measure reforms, autocrats in Tunisia, Yemen, Jordan, Egypt, and elsewhere changed electoral laws to allow for multiparty elections—expanding the scope of political participants even as other aspects of the electoral process remained unfree (e.g., flawed voter districts, rigged tabulations).

This chapter does not focus on rule-of-law reforms that included some combination of democratizing and de-democratizing, liberalizing and illiberal elements. Instead, it focuses only on those rule-of-law reforms that were unambiguously de-democratizing—reforms that Daniel Brumberg called a "trap" intended to bolster the autocratic rule. The subject of this chapter is de-democratizing reforms that, in Brumberg's words, "hinder[ed] the emergence of an effective political society."[14] In some cases, some constituencies might have been pleased by these regime-initiated de-democratizing rule-of-law reforms, but overall, these reforms by any objective standard, including international legal standards, diminished political rights and civil liberties.

Why Use the Rule of Law to De-democratize?

Earlier generations of autocratic rulers countered their challengers by rounding up opposition members and jailing, torturing, or exiling them.

For hundreds of years, autocratic regimes suppressed citizens' rights, often using violent repression and martial law. Even in the twentieth and twenty-first centuries, autocrats routinely rigged elections, intimidated voters, or limited nongovernmental activity by stationing police or informants near public squares and meeting places.

It was therefore counterintuitive and novel when autocrats, by the late twentieth century, had begun to complement these traditional means of repression by initiating de-democratizing rules of law, which they considered strategic opportunities.[15] Many of these new laws fomented conflict and confusion among members of once-unified opposition movements.[16] Even the most illiberal and undemocratic legal revisions traditionally divided the opposition—between those factions who responded with indifference and those factions, outraged by the regime's manipulations, who were driven further away from any willingness to accommodate. In most cases, the negative response or outcry to the measures was greatest among politically inclined, elite circles, whereas more violent, traditional repressive tactics, such as detaining journalists or activists, typically enraged a broader cross section of the public. In Jordan, as discussed above, King Hussein used new electoral laws passed immediately prior to elections to ensure favorable electoral outcomes.[17] Many Jordanians were aware of these legalistic maneuvers—particularly if their party affiliates had instructed them to boycott the parliamentary elections in response—yet these rule-of-law reforms rarely triggered mass popular anger or protest movements. In Algeria, when President Bouteflika revised the electoral law in 2007 in order to limit the eligibility of parties fielding candidates in local elections, the public responded, but those most vehemently rejecting this measure were the opposition parties themselves.[18]

De-democratizing by promulgating complex laws also helped to neutralize international critique as well. In the twenty-first century, across the Middle East, leaders understood that global norms regarding governance standards were consolidating. Rather than try to defend repressive tactics, it was far easier to point to constitutional revisions, new parliamentary laws, and new systems of judicial selection—even if each of these changes limited individual political rights—when faced with foreign governments or increasingly vocal transnational human rights organizations inquiring about democratic norms.

As Lisa Wedeen argued, many Middle Eastern autocrats ruled through a series of charades and performances.[19] For an authoritarian regime, especially for the moderates among the regime elite, "appearing democratic" helped to ease the normative disconnect between the expectations of the international community in the twenty-first century when it came to democracy and the reality that their regimes were unelected and often deeply illegitimate in the eyes of their people.[20] Over the course of the 2000s, some leaders in the region adopted the "democracy language" particularly when interacting with foreign donors.[21] The "democracy language" was even more important when kings and presidents traveled to international fora, whether to United Nations meetings or to elite conferences such as Davos, and were confronted with questions about their domestic political institutions. The rulers could point to their revised constitutions, which the public had no doubt overwhelmingly endorsed, to underscore how the rule of law undergirded their political systems. Of course, not all Middle Eastern rulers felt compelled to adopt the Western democracy discourse or defend their system in these terms. The rulers of Libya and Saudi Arabia proudly defended their systems of government, contrasting them favorably to Western democracies and rejecting pressures to establish institutions such as representative parliaments or secular courts.[22]

Over the past fifteen years, authoritarian regimes outside of the Middle East and North Africa similarly adopted rule-of-law strategies to deflect opposition demands while consolidating their rule. To the Kyrgyzstani president and the Burmese junta, constitutional revisions, in 2003 and 2008, respectively, offered strategic benefits, including expanding presidential powers in the first case and enshrining military prerogatives in the second. In both cases, the constitutional changes prompted a modicum of international critique and considerable domestic concern. International criticism was much gentler, however, as compared to the global reactions when these same regimes used violent force to suppress opponents—in the Saffron revolution of 2007 (Burma) and the Tulip revolution of 2005 (Kyrgyzstan).

Over the past two decades, to many Middle Eastern autocrats, de-democratizing by using rule-of-law reform not only made strategic sense, but also, in the short term, seemed to be working. Yet by 2010 this strategy steadily eroded the credibility of the entire institutional framework undergirding many regimes, particularly the presidential republics where the ruling party and the president himself had no historical or traditional sources of credibility. If an autocrat could hijack a constitution by imposing unilateral revisions, for example, why should the opposition bother to bargain in order to improve the electoral laws or the laws governing free expression incrementally? In short, after years of steadily diminishing political rights and civil liberties through rule-of-law reforms, many regional leaders convinced their mainstream political opposition and many elites that they had no intention of gradually opening up the political systems. Citizens may have also arrived at the conclusion that trying to extract greater rights and protections from entrenched autocrats only interested in regime survival would be futile. This crisis of confidence had important ramifications for the Arab Spring, as many citizens and opposition leaders came to the realization that only radical, discontinuous change would afford them greater rights and freedoms.

Ben Ali's Initial Promises of Change

In the immediate wake of his 1987 bloodless coup against the increasingly repressive and erratic Habib Bourguiba, Ben Ali announced a new direction for the country. At the time, some Tunisia analysts argued that Ben Ali's aspirations for a *changement* (change) were genuine.[23] Ben Ali promised that institutions would "guarantee the conditions for a responsible democracy, fully respecting the sovereignty of the people."[24] As a symbol of the new era, Ben Ali revised the constitution to eliminate the core provision that had enabled Habib Bourguiba's "presidency for life"—for over thirty years. He renamed the ruling party the Democratic Constitutional Rally (RCD) and immediately legalized many opposition parties banned by Bourguiba. He adopted a law to ease restrictions on the press.[25] Finally, Ben Ali canceled the state security laws that had been used by Bourguiba to prosecute Islamists, communists, and other opposition members and announced an amnesty for hundreds of political prisoners.[26] Analysts outside of Tunisia proclaimed this small Mediterranean country on the brink of the Arab world's first democratic transition.[27]

Tunisian opposition leaders of all stripes rallied around Ben Ali, convinced by his vision of a new Tunisia defined by the rule of law and an end to the arbitrary repression rife under Bourguiba.[28] As a sign of reconciliation, dozens of political parties, including members of the moderate Islamist En-Nahda Party, issued a National Pact "to define a common denominator and a maximum of principles on which all Tunisians can agree and that can be adopted as a basis for political action and development."[29] Secular liberal parties cheered Ben Ali's promise of a transition toward a secular multiparty democracy and urged new elections. En-Nahda members celebrated the presidential coup and considered the new regime's tolerance an opportunity to express their brand of populist Islamist politics after decades of repression under Bourguiba. Many En-Nahda members returned from exile, clamoring to participate in what they believed to be a new era of pluralistic politics. Though his regime did not officially recognize En-Nahda as a party, Ben Ali allowed individual politicians affiliated with the group the freedom to organize and to express their views, as long as they committed to a policy of nonviolence. Support for the new president among the Islamists was so great that En-Nahda chief Rachid Ghannouchi declared in 1988 that Tunisian Islamists had complete confidence "in God, above all, and then in president [Ben Ali]."[30]

In 1989, Ben Ali held both presidential and parliamentary elections. In the presidential elections, Ben Ali (the only candidate on the list) won 99.27 percent of the vote. In the parliamentary elections, although Ben Ali's RCD party won all 141 seats, independent lists of candidates affiliated with En-Nahda did better than expected in some districts, garnering 14 to 25 percent of the popular vote. (The official numbers suggested the former, though most claim the latter.) The new president felt threatened by the clear popularity of the Islamist movement and its candidates. Many of the secular elites who surrounded him worried that the Islamists' popularity would undermine the secular ethos that had guided Tunisian political life and state building since independence, including the state's progressive governmental policies toward women.

It is still unclear to what extent Ben Ali had been genuinely interested in a pluralistic, inclusive political system upon coming to power. Regardless of the depth or authenticity of his original commitments to democratization, the results of the 1989 election—held less than two years after the beginning of his rule—definitively ended the early experiment with a more expansive political system.[31] Though Ben Ali had tried a tentative conciliatory approach toward En-Nahda as a way to co-opt its members, after the elections he returned to the brutal tactics his predecessor had used against the group. In 1991, when a handful of Islamists possibly linked to En-Nahda attacked an RCD office in Tunis, setting it on fire and claiming one life, Ben Ali seized upon the incident as a rationale to launch a campaign of repression against En-Nahda.[32] By the fall of 1991, the authorities had arrested eight thousand of the movement's members. Forty En-Nahda members died after being tortured in detention. Threatened with repression, Ghannouchi fled to exile.[33] For two years, the regime arrested, threatened, and tortured all opposition members suspected of identifying with the Islamists.

Neutralizing the Grassroots

Ben Ali was now in a bind. By early 1991, he had declared an all-out war on En-Nahda, and his crackdown led to clashes on the streets between En-Nahda supporters and security forces. Yet this campaign of repression against the Islamists belied Ben Ali's initial promises of a new era characterized by human rights and democratization. He tried desperately to maintain his reputation as a "defender of civil society and women," justifying his violence against En-Nahda with the mantra "no democracy for the enemies of democracy."³⁴ Ben Ali argued for En-Nahda's elimination in the name of human rights and pluralism, even while he was turning inward, rebuilding the security forces and fortifying his new Carthage palace. To add to the tension between his actions and his earlier promises, Ben Ali began to undermine or marginalize all of the independent voices among Tunisia's once vibrant grassroots. Eva Bellin and others have written about Ben Ali's successful co-optation in the early 1990s of the strong labor movement and business networks, groups that had traditionally balanced the regime as independent actors.³⁵ In addition, Ben Ali attempted to appeal to and ally with many of the feminist and women's rights groups, using the threat of the Islamist position on women to solicit their support for his regime.³⁶

However, Ben Ali also had to contend with the most powerful civil society organization (CSO) in Tunisia—the Tunisian League for Human Rights (the League). The oldest independent CSO in the Arab world, the League had been founded in 1977 and had assiduously monitored trials, investigated rights abuses, and advocated for prisoners during the Bourguiba era. Throughout the 1980s, the League had lobbied for a reform of the security court system and the Interior Ministry, as well as the abolition of the practice of pretrial detention.³⁷ Throughout the country, well-respected judges and lawyers were members of local League chapters.

During the first two years of his rule, Ben Ali worked together with the League to implement some of the human rights reforms he had promised upon coming to power. For example, Ben Ali agreed to limit the practice of pretrial detention, which was associated with the torture and abuse of political prisoners under Bourguiba. At the League's recommendation, he also canceled some of the state security laws used by Bourguiba to prosecute Islamists, communists, and other opposition members.³⁸ Ben Ali appointed two prominent members of the League to cabinet positions in his new government.[39] Yet, by the early 1990s, League members grew increasingly wary of Ben Ali's rule, particularly his repressive campaign against the Islamists. At first, the League tried to maintain a balanced position, critiquing some of En-Nahda's positions, particularly regarding pluralism and women's rights, while also criticizing the state's abuse of power in its crackdown against En-Nahda members.[40] Members of the League disagreed internally regarding how strongly to protest the state's repression against the Islamists, and rifts developed within the organization.[41]

With secular political parties weakened after losses in the 1989 elections and with En-Nahda activists jailed or exiled, by 1991 the League emerged as among the last independent voices criticizing the president and the RCD's expanding powers. League members represented an elite cadre who could effectively communicate with a base at home and with important players abroad. For instance, in 1992 the League issued a communiqué raising concerns about the Interior Ministry's detention procedures regarding En-Nahda prisoners.[42] The communiqué announced the League's plans to investigate the deaths of individual prisoners in custody after "its numerous and repeated appeals to the government during this crisis have born few fruits."[43] Ben Ali and the Interior Minister grew alarmed when they saw the communiqué appearing in major newspapers throughout Europe. The Interior Minister hastily called for a government-sponsored commission to investigate the League's charges, led by retired diplomat Rachid Driss.[44] The subsequent Driss Commission report, however, spoke only in generalities about the cause of the deaths and failed to acknowledge the regime's systematic abuse in treating, detaining, and torturing prisoners.[45] Though the government had temporarily countered the League's critiques by establishing the Driss Commission, the League's contacts abroad were actively publicizing critical details describing the deplorable detention procedures and the torture the Ben Ali regime was using in its crackdown against Islamists.

The Legal Battle to Restrict the League

In January 1991, the police interrogated League president Moncef Marzouki for more than two hours about remarks he had made to the foreign press regarding Tunisian human rights abuses.[46] While the regime began initiating limited repressive tactics such as this one to intimidate League members, by 1992 they decided to take a new, legalistic approach: The regime introduced a new law of association stipulating that individuals could not simultaneously hold a leadership position in a general association as well as be a member of a political party. The law also stipulated that all associations had to register as either professional syndicates or general associations, with the latter type of association prohibited from maintaining exclusive membership.[47] The new law would force the League, one of the country's few legally-defined "general associations," to accept thousands of new members—RCD members and government loyalists who would influence the organization's agenda.[48] Although forty-one out of Tunisia's five thousand associations were nominally affected by the new law, the League activists believed that they were the intended targets. The Ministry of Interior denied that the law was "directed against anyone . . . which should answer the worries of certain groups, notably the Tunisian League for Human Rights."[49] Members of the League debated how to respond to the new law but could not reach agreement, which led to the decision to dissolve the organization in 1992.

In 1994, former League members who had subsequently joined the RCD took control of the League leadership, reconstituted the organization, and—as the new law had intended—ensured that any criticism of the regime was muted. Throughout the 1990s, regime allies led the League and ensured that it kept mum in the face of Ben Ali's increasingly draconian policies toward opponents, including the deteriorating human rights situation.[50] The organization grew increasingly marginal.

In 2000, however, League members succeeded in regaining their independence, reconstituting the organization autonomously by electing leadership officials who were not RCD loyalists and holding the first League Congress since 1994.[51] Deprived of its internal mechanism to control the membership and leadership of the organization, the RCD leadership and its allies in the courts restarted the campaign to limit the League's activities.[52] For most of the 2000s, the League was divided between pro-RCD and independent factions, with the former faction filing petitions against independent League activists. The pending court cases meant that authorities would prohibit the League from holding meetings.[53] League officers were forced to fight their own legal battles, and they were thus left with insufficient time or resources to investigate and publicize the regime's human rights abuses. Police monitored the League's activities and closely watched all of the individuals who entered the downtown Tunis office of its president. In 2005 and 2006, when the League again tried to convene its annual congresses, police lined the streets, blocking activists from entering the building, on the basis that the ongoing legal claims rendered an associational congress inappropriate.[54] Finally, the government continued to infiltrate the League by sending RCD loyalists to join its regional branches. Outside of Tunis, almost all League chapters were led by pro-government members, thus preventing any potential antigovernment critique within the organization.[55]

Ben Ali had every opportunity to shut down the League and arrest its key leaders—both in the early 1990s and after 2002. Instead, he waged a relentless and complex campaign of legalistic maneuvers to ensure it existed in name but was paralyzed. Many League members attributed this decision to his concern regarding the international reaction should authorities shut the organization down.[56] Ben Ali, they argued, feared an outcry, particularly from former League officers influential abroad.[57] Instead, by using convoluted laws to ensure that his loyalists headed the League and later by limiting the organization's activities, Ben Ali could avoid the sharpest rebukes.[58]

Moreover, allowing the League to exist in name created a façade in support of the regime's human rights rhetoric. Ben Ali could point to the League as an example of an independent Tunisian civil society group, even as his police prevented the organization from conducting independent activities and while his courts prevented the organization from receiving much of its foreign funding. Since the early 1990s, Ben Ali's regime had dedicated remarkable energy to cultivating an image of respect for human rights while simultaneously doing its utmost to wage a war of attrition against its venerated and effective CSOs.[59] The 1992 law of associations was the first of dozens of administrative, bureaucratic, and legal maneuvers used by the Tunisian government in the 1990s to frustrate and undermine CSOs.[60] Nonetheless, even as the conditions facing independent CSOs in Tunisia deteriorated over the course of the decade, the government grew increasingly vocal in defense of its human rights and women's rights record, as well as marketing it.[61] In 2007, the government officials boasted of the country's eight thousand CSOs, when in fact fewer than a dozen at most were truly nongovernmental, given the leading role played by RCD loyalists in almost all of these organizations.[62] Of these CSOs, only five or six, including the Tunisian Association of Democratic Women (ATFD) and the League, managed to function independently.[63]

Solidifying Authority: The 2002 Constitutional Reform

Throughout the 1990s, Ben Ali promulgated a series of new laws intended to weaken and co-opt his nongovernmental opponents, as well as to undermine his opponents in non-RCD political parties. For instance, 1998, Ben Ali changed the electoral law governing parliamentary elections: now 75 percent of the 189 seats would be given to the party that obtained a simple majority in the elections and 25 percent to all other "official" opposition parties based on their share of the votes. While this law allowed token opposition parliamentarians to serve in the Chamber of Deputies, creating the appearance of pluralism, the law also solidified the RCD's majority status. The supermajority required to dismiss a minister would be a mathematical impossibility in a chamber where the RCD would automatically claim 75 percent of the seats.[64]

In 1999, Ben Ali announced that he would amend the presidential electoral law to allow multiple candidates to run in presidential elections in order to allow greater "freedom and representation for opposition parties."[65] At the same time, however, all presidential candidates had to be affiliated with legal, recognized political parties, a select group of parties carefully certified by the government. Furthermore, many potential challengers were disqualified under a 1988 law requiring candidates to be younger than seventy years old in order to run. (While originally this law had been part of Ben Ali's efforts to prevent a president for life, by 1999, when some of the key potential challengers to Ben Ali were older than seventy, his 1988 law became conveniently self-serving.)[66]

Ben Ali's decade-long effort to de-democratize using the rule of law reached a zenith in 2002. With a series of new constitutional revisions, the president abandoned the last vestiges of his 1987 changement platform by reversing one of his most important initial promises—abolishing the presidency for life. As was noted earlier, shortly after seizing power, in 1988, Ben Ali had amended the constitution to eliminate a clause that Bourguiba had used to justify his decades-long rule. While the 1988 constitution retained the extensive authority of the president and the cabinet, it had established a presidential term limit of three terms of five years—considered at the time an unprecedented check on presidential power in the Arab world. Many Tunisians had initially rallied around Ben Ali precisely because of his efforts to institute presidential term limits.

The 2002 constitutional changes, however, reversed the 1988 ones, drastically expanding executive power and enabling Ben Ali to run for a fourth term. He also raised the upper age limit of presidential candidates to seventy-five (Ben Ali was sixty-five years old in 2002). Together, these two revisions allowed Ben Ali to run again in the 2004 and 2009 presidential elections.[67] The revised constitution also gave the RCD-appointed Constitutional Council the right to determine if the president remained fit to govern (Article 57); this right had previously been granted to the prime minister. Ben Ali, as prime minister, had deposed Bourguiba on the grounds of this original Article 57, given Bourguiba's advanced age. The newly revised Article 57 granted this power of determining presidential fitness to the regime loyalists, thus ensuring that Ben Ali's prime minister, Mohamed Ghannouchi, could not push him aside.[68]

Finally, the 2002 constitutional revisions created a bicameral legislative institution by establishing a new upper chamber, the Chamber of Councilors. Local officials would appoint some of the new councilors and Ben Ali would choose the rest, creating an upper legislative chamber filled with regime loyalists. Constitutional revisions overseen by the kings of Morocco (1996) and Bahrain (2002) followed the same design, establishing a smaller upper chamber primarily reserved for government-appointed loyalists. The Chamber of Deputies passed the constitutional changes with only six abstentions in late May 2002. The subsequent public referendum on the new text passed with 99.52 percent of the vote, with 96.5 percent of the public participating, according to the highly suspect official figures.[69]

Promoting the Constitutional Reversal

Ben Ali realized that the 2002 constitutional amendments represented a dramatic reversal from the original promises and expectations on which he had founded his presidency. He thus began an intense marketing campaign to lobby for "the Republic of Tomorrow," proclaiming that the new constitution would allow Tunisia "to make a quantum leap in our political system" and "entrench the spirit of democracy and the multiparty system."[70] The RCD endorsed the changes as a "necessary constitutional step . . . to ensure Ben Ali would be the rally's candidate at the forthcoming presidential election" of 2004.[71] At the same time, at the RCD annual Congress meeting, members publicly denied any return to "presidency for life"— realizing this notion evoked the oppressive Bourguiba era.[72] This inconsistency reflected the normative bind: while insisting it was preserving the

1988 abolition of presidency for life, the RCD was advocating a constitutional fix to enable Ben Ali's fourth term.

To help in the marketing of the 2002 constitutional text, Ben Ali added
new, vague language on human rights.[73] The new constitution included a
section in its preamble guaranteeing "fundamental freedoms and human
rights in their universal, comprehensive application."[74] In his November 7,
2001, and May 27, 2002, speeches, Ben Ali justified the need for a new
constitution on the grounds of "expanding" human rights.[75] He also compared his new constitution to those constitutional designs that favored executive power promulgated in other presidential republics, such as the
constitution adopted by the French Fifth Republic in 1958.[76] Nonetheless,
few at home or abroad in Tunisia were convinced by President Ben Ali's
spin campaign, including his promotion of the new constitution on human
rights grounds. Most Tunisians considered the 2002 constitution a dramatic, irrevocable reversal of the 1987–1988 changement. The new constitution not only guaranteed Ben Ali a fourth and fifth term, but also codified
the entrenched authoritarianism that had become the daily reality.

The Delegitimization of the Tunisian Political Realm

By 2002, Ben Ali had successfully ensured the dominance of his ruling
party, the RCD, and systematically weakened all other forms of political
opposition. By 2002, the RCD claimed two million members (out of a population of ten million) and 7,800 branches nationwide. It held 152 of the
189 seats in parliament and 4,098 of 4,366 seats on local councils. Those
Tunisians who joined the RCD or tacitly accepted its dominance did so
largely because they approved of the party's successful economic policies,
which, by the end of the 1990s, had helped to build a large middle class and
attracted foreign investment by strengthening the Tunisian private sector.[77]
Moreover, the average Tunisian relied on the tangible benefits conferred by
RCD membership, such as educational and housing subsidies, small business permits, and waivers on zoning restrictions.[78]

Ben Ali had engineered a decade-long campaign to marginalize all independent political and civil society opposition while increasing the resources
and purview of the RCD.[79] By 2002, En-Nahda was the only credible opposition party that could have challenged the RCD's hegemony, yet most of
its members were in jail or in exile. In fact, En-Nahda could muster only a

weak response to the 2002 constitutional changes, faxing a communiqué of condemnation from London. The center-left Mouvement des Démocrates Socialistes (MDS) might also have campaigned against the constitutional reforms, as it had once been among Tunisia's most powerful parties.[80] In 2002, the legally recognized wing of MDS held fourteen of the non-RCD seats allotted to the opposition in the Chamber of Deputies. All fourteen MDS deputies supported the 2002 constitutional changes, however. They had backed Ben Ali in the 1999 presidential elections and would do the same in 2004.[81] Over the course of the 1990s, MDS leaders began to accept Ben Ali's rule, in part because they believed the RCD's economic policies could modernize the country.[82]

A few smaller political opposition groups such as the Democratic Progressive Party (PDP) and the Democratic Forum for Labor and Liberties (FDTL) mobilized to protest the constitutional revisions. The FDTL organized a boycott of the referendum, though most Tunisians were uninterested in voting anyway. In July 2002, human rights lawyer and former League president Moncef Marzouki created a new political party, the Congrès pour la République (Republican Congress), explicitly to condemn the constitutional revisions and to call for greater civic and political freedoms through an overhaul of the political system.[83] To Marzouki and other CPR founders, the constitutional revisions were so blatantly antidemocratic that they necessitated a return to a basic set of demands by the Tunisian political opposition. From now on, according to Marzouki, the opposition should advocate for a new constitution in order to protect citizens' rights. The founding of CPR helped to shape the thinking of many in the political elite over the course of the 2000s, and reflected the increasing consensus that Ben Ali's rule had become irredeemable.[84]

Moreover, by 2002 Tunisian civil society—once the envy of the Arab world—had been reduced to a few lone activists unable to challenge the constitutional revisions. The Tunisian government claimed the country hosted thousands of CSOs, but fewer than a dozen were independent of the RCD or the government itself. The regime and the RCD had co-opted what had been some of the strongest democratic activists, such as the women's rights groups, and had all but paralyzed other groups, such as the League. By 2002, the League published a short report outlining the troubling aspects of the new constitution, but few at home or abroad responded to its critiques.[85] By some estimates, no more than two hundred activists throughout the country rallied to protest the constitutional revisions. This weak response was not, according to many, a reflection of the public's acceptance of the constitutional changes, simply a manifestation of the deep fear among many Tunisians of registering dissent.[86]

Therefore, by 2002 after undermining the political opposition parties or banning them outright, deliberately suppressing the formal civil society, and co-opting many once independent actors, Ben Ali emerged without any challengers. He could now change the term limits and limit the competitiveness of the presidential elections by promulgating de-democratizing constitutional revisions. He took advantage of his new liberties. In 2008, for instance, Ben Ali revised the electoral law to stipulate that only an individual who had headed a political party for at least two years could run. Given this new eligibility criterion, only three qualified candidates contested Ben Ali in the October 25, 2009 presidential elections. Two other more serious challengers were deemed ineligible to run.[87] One candidate, Ahmed Brahim, secretary general of the Movement for Renewal (Ettajdid), attempted to run a legitimate campaign. The other two candidates publicly acknowledged that their campaigns intended solely to make a point about the importance of contested elections, recognizing the odds they faced.[88] Unsurprising, Ben Ali won a fifth presidential term in the October 2009 elections with 89.6 percent of the vote, according to the official numbers.[89]

Yet by 2009, most Tunisians had come to disregard the validity of the electoral process anyway. Tunisia's formal political institutions, including the parliament and the judiciary, were considered instruments of the president and his ruling party. As one Tunisian political scientist argued, "political competition" in Tunisia had been turned "into an administrative process wherein the Interior Ministry pulls all the strings throughout all stages of the elections, from registering voters to announcing the results. Unlike in liberal electoral systems, the legal code does not even explicitly outlaw electoral fraud."[90]

The constitutional revision of 2002 marked a significant turning point, after which political institutions would cease to be meaningful to most Tunisians. According to one Bourguiba-era ambassador who had become a member of the opposition,

The 2002 reform took away any last hope that there would be a democratic transition. Since the 2002 referendum, any confidence we had held since 1987 of a future democratic transition is gone. Since 1987 there had been a gradual evolutionary decrease in our freedom, but 2002 was a dramatic revolutionary turning point: it unveiled the Pouvoir's [the Power's] intentions—which are not to transition to democracy. Since 2002 the intelligentsia is no longer considered or consulted. The Pouvoir no longer even pretends to consult or respond to public opinion. The Pouvoir is no longer beholden to any groups or interests in society.[91]

By 2002, rule of law had become an instrument of authoritarian control, protecting the Ben Ali regime rather than the Tunisian people.[92] Nonetheless, in the lives of average Tunisians, these legalistic regime machinations were certainly less egregious than violent repression, although instances of brutality at the hands of authority still occurred. For the rest of the decade, many Tunisians grew disenchanted with politics.[93] Ben Ali's frequent public statements about reform and democratization rang hollow for Tunisians frustrated with the de-democratizing trend and the complex set of reforms, laws, and constitutional revisions that had served to solidify executive rule. Ultimately, as the political edifice underlying Ben Ali and the RCD's rule grew, many concluded that the political structure would need to be cleared in order to create any legitimate "changement." This sentiment became evident during the last days of Ben Ali's rule, in January 2011, as he futilely clung to power by promising to end media censorship. One Tunisian, summarizing the past decade of life under Ben Ali's rule, told the *New York Times*, "These are the same promises he made last week, that he made a few years ago, that he made in 1987, but on the ground it is always the same."[94]

Neighborhood Effects

Although it is difficult to determine exactly whether Ben Ali and his neighbors actively shared regime maintenance strategies among themselves or simply observed each other's decision making, by the late 1990s and early 2000s other regional leaders began introducing de-democratizing rule-of-law reforms that were similar to those initiated in Tunisia.[95] In the 2000s, the leaders of Algeria, Egypt, Jordan, and Yemen announced changes to electoral laws that had the effect of narrowing the playing field of electoral contestants and ensuring the hegemony of the ruling parties or the parties considered loyal to the king.

Promulgating new constitutions or revising existing ones proved to be a particularly attractive strategy—one replicated with great success by non-democratic regimes in the Middle East and beyond. Within the Middle East and North Africa, President Hosni Mubarak initiated two sets of constitutional revisions in the mid-2000s. Although Mubarak had not chosen to revise the constitution over the course of the first two decades of his rule, in late February 2005 he announced that he would modify Article 76 of the Egyptian constitution to allow multiparty candidates to run in the September 2005 presidential election.[96] On its surface, the 2005 constitutional change appeared to be an unprecedented regime concession to a new coalition of opposition groups that had unified in opposition to a potential Mubarak fifth term.[97] Three months earlier, leftists, Islamists, and intellectuals had joined together to oppose Mubarak's continued rule, uniting as the Egyptian Movement for Change (EMC, also known as Kefaya). While the constitutional revisions met the protestors' chief demand of multiparty elections, the new text also imposed eligibility limitations for the presidential candidates and changed the registration requirements for political parties, thus protecting Mubarak and the ruling National Democratic Party. Despite these latter provisions, the EMC and other opposition parties considered the 2005 constitutional reform a limited success.[98]

After the 2005 constitutional reforms, Mubarak decided he could no longer afford to respond to an opposition demand for constitutional change thrust upon him from grassroots activists. Taking a page from Ben Ali's playbook, he decided to preemptively reform the constitution again—this time to shore up the position of the ruling National Democratic Party (NDP). Less than two years after Mubarak's first constitutional reform, in January 2007, he submitted thirty-four amended constitutional articles to the People's Assembly, which promptly approved the reforms, although the 20 percent of the deputies representing the opposition parties boycotted the vote. Weeks later, Mubarak submitted the constitutional revisions to a national referendum, and 75 percent of Egyptians endorsed the reforms, according to official figures.[99]

The 2007 constitutional changes allowed Mubarak to maintain the procedural trappings of multiparty elections while reducing the competitiveness of future People's Assembly elections even further. The president wanted to limit the electoral successes of candidates affiliated with the Muslim Brotherhood, whose unexpected gains in the 2005 parliamentary election (20 percent of the seats) had set off alarm bells. The proposed constitutional amendments banned political parties with a religious "frame of reference," thereby preventing the Egyptian Muslim Brotherhood from registering legally as a recognized party. The amendments also introduced a new electoral system—combining both party and single-candidate lists—to minimize the Muslim Brotherhood's future electoral successes.[100]

The 2007 constitutional revisions also limited the increasingly independent judicial branch from interfering in the executive control over the election procedures. Since 2000, judicial oversight of the elections by the semi-independent Supreme Constitutional Court had led to a relatively more transparent electoral process, especially during the 2005 parliamentary elections, even though electoral fraud and electoral intimidation persisted. The 2007 amendments created a new supreme supervisory committee to oversee elections instead of the Supreme Constitutional Court, consisting of members appointed by the president himself. Finally, the 2007 constitutional changes gave the president and the security forces unprecedented power to search, investigate, and arrest terrorism suspects. The president could now refer any such suspects to military courts without any judicial process. The despised security services were free to conduct arrests, search homes, and place wiretaps without a warrant.[101]

While the first constitutional reform of 2005 was mixed in its effect on political rights, the second constitutional revision of 2007 significantly narrowed the opportunity for political participation and contestation. As one popular columnist wrote at the time, "One can only feel frightened and humiliated by the contents of the constitutional amendments. One must be afraid in particular of the persons who would draft such amendments. Egypt will never again know honest elections."[102]

All of the Egyptian opposition groups opposed the 2007 constitutional revisions. Because the NDP enjoyed a comfortable majority in the People's Assembly, however, the ruling party could ensure the passage of the new text. The 2007 revisions in Egypt, like the 2002 Tunisian constitutional revisions, marked a key turning point in the de-democratization of Egypt's political institutions. Almost every area of Egyptian law—from the constitution to the electoral laws to the laws governing due process—now served the interests of President Mubarak and his party. The president, as he aged, was increasingly interested in solidifying power and limiting the operating space afforded to his opponents. The 2010 parliamentary elections were the most fraudulent and restricted of any in Egypt's recent history.[103] The de-democratization of the political sphere left many frustrated and disillusioned. Neither the public nor the political opposition could realistically hold out hope that incremental reforms—initiated by a sitting autocrat presiding over a one-party state—would genuinely offer Egyptians greater rights.[104]

Short-Term Strategic Success

It is hard to gauge the extent to which the region's autocrats, including Ben Ali and Mubarak, watched and learned from each other's successes and failures using rules of law to de-democratize.[105] The fact that such similar reform strategies emerged in the Middle East and North Africa around the same time does, in fact, suggest some degree of regional mimicry. Many of the region's leaders may have perceived rule-of-law de-democratization to be strategic and beneficial, at least in the short term. What they did not consider, however, was how this driver of change would set in motion a series of unintended consequences, which would eventually endanger regime stability over the medium term.

In the late 1990s and 2000s, among the most interesting convergent decisions made by regional leaders was the choice to de-democratize and consolidate power using complex rules of law and institutions—in addition to the tried-and-true methods of violent repression. As the case of Tunisia exemplifies, de-democratizing by using rule-of-law reforms might have appeared to confer considerable benefits. First, relying on rule-of-law de-democratization, in addition to traditional repressive measures of arrest and intimidation, seemed, at least in the short term, to divide, co-opt, confuse, and marginalize domestic opposition.[106] In Jordan, Egypt, and Tunisia, rule-of-law reforms, whether those with some liberalizing and democratizing components or those that were entirely de-democratizing, generated ambivalent responses among different oppositionists.[107] In most cases, elite opposition actors were outraged, but the de-democratizing reforms rarely mobilized party constituencies, labor movements, or other types of mass public protest movements.

De-democratizing reforms typically sowed disagreements about how to respond—among political parties and movements and civil society groups, but also within them—fragmenting and therefore weakening once-unified opposition coalitions. De-democratizing reforms created a wedge between the moderates willing to "give the reforms a chance" and the holdouts immediately suspicious of any autocrat-initiated measure. This split was particularly pronounced when the reforms themselves had some redeeming qualities, such as the constitutional reforms initiated by King Hamad al-Khalifa in Bahrain discussed in the next chapter. In the Bahraini case, the restoration of parliamentary life was attractive to some elements of the opposition, while others wanted to boycott the entire proposition, on the grounds that the limitations on the restored parliament's powers rendered it ineffective and subject to the whims of the ruling family. Even in situations in which the regime reform was entirely de-democratizing, constraining political rights or civil liberties, typically opposition groups and elites were divided about how best to respond. For example, even when faced with an illiberal civil society law, some members of the Tunisian League advocated acquiescing to the law's stringent restrictions, creating a split within the League's leadership.

Second, it is possible that some regional rulers preferred employing rules of law—rather than brute force—to solidify power, in part to diminish international criticism. While it is unlikely that these leaders genuinely believed that their international critics would be fooled by de-democratizing rules of law, solidifying power by using apparently legal means, rather than violent or repressive ones, tended to limit the negative response of the international community. While Western governments recognized how some autocratic constitutional revisions or electoral laws could constrain the participation of political opponents and the political rights afforded citizens, often the diplomatic response to these reforms tended to be measured. For example, U.S. Secretary of State Condoleezza Rice initially expressed tepid "concern and disappointment" in response to Mubarak's 2007 de-democratizing constitutional revisions. When the Egyptian government reacted negatively to her already calibrated statements, she immediately backtracked, saying, "I have made my concerns known as well as my hopes for continued reform here in Egypt. I think what I said is the process of reform is one that is difficult. It is going to have its ups and downs, and we always discuss these things in a way that is mutually respectful."[108] To political opponents in Egypt, this response seemed to reward Mubarak's strategy, by legitimizing the constitutional revisions and accepting them at face value. When Ben Ali visited the White House in 2005, President Bush expressed some concern regarding the limited press freedoms in Tunisia, but kept mum regarding the constitutional machinations that had helped Ben Ali secure his fourth presidential term.

In contrast to their limited response to de-democratizing rule-of-law reforms, international actors, including the UN, almost always respond more forcefully, and sometimes punitively, to coups, martial law, or the violent abrogation of election results. For instance, when a military junta instigated a coup in Mauritania in 2008, Secretary Rice "condemned the anti-democratic action" and immediately cut off all nonhumanitarian U.S. aid to Nouakchott.[109] In 2008 in Kenya, Western diplomats responded to postelection violence by publicly demanding significant political reform, and by threatening to impose travel bans on those Kenyan officials impeding reform efforts.[110] The international community sent the former UN secretary general to negotiate a power-sharing agreement between the two candidates.

By contrast, the efforts to consolidate power legalistically as described in this chapter were and continue to be far more subtle and measured than overt power grabs or violent contestations of power. De-democratizing rule-of-law reforms reengineer constitutions, electoral laws, and courts, often in a way that is hard for most outsiders to understand. Legalistic de-democratization, therefore, rarely prompts strong responses from the international community. Transnational organizations such as Freedom House or the Committee to Protect Journalists publish press releases criticizing the reform, or mention of it might find its way into annual governmental publications such as the U.S. State Department's annual Human Rights Report, but there are rarely consequences of being criticized in these annual compendiums. There is no international mechanism—or even a set of norms—guiding the international response to autocrats who cleverly restrict democratic rights and civil liberties by employing rules of law, as opposed to utilizing violent tactics. As a result, de-democratizing rule-of-law reforms are a far more appealing strategy to those rulers who are trying to avoid international condemnation.[111]

The Unintended Consequences

Over the course of the 1990s and 2000s, many nondemocratic leaders across the Middle East and North Africa deliberately diminished their citizens' procedural rights and civil liberties, but they used legalistic means to do so. This de-democratizing driver of change, epitomized by the measures initiated by the Tunisian regime but embraced enthusiastically elsewhere in the region, could neutralize and divide domestic opponents and potentially limit international criticism. This approach offered Ben Ali strategic benefits, at least in the short term. The 1992 civil society law targeting the freedom of membership of the Tunisia Human Rights League limited the ability of Tunisia's most important CSO to challenge state policies. The 2002 Tunisian constitution limited competitors from challenging the ruling party or the president himself and institutionalized authoritarianism by dissolving term limits. While these reforms limited any opposition to Ben Ali in the short term, over time these laws, and other similarly de-democratizing reforms, had the effect of eroding the legitimacy of institutions such as the presidency, constitution, courts, and parliament. These measures not only quashed the once-vibrant Tunisian political opposition and civil society but also drove both communities to the conclusion that the changement Ben Ali had promised could never come into fruition under his presidency.

Tunisia might have represented an extreme, a regional apotheosis of rule-of-law de-democratization. By the late 2000s, however, neighboring states were quickly imitating Ben Ali's reforms. As a result, by the 2000s, "rule-of-law reform" began to take on a different meaning in the Middle East and North Africa for both rulers and the ruled than it did to many Western governments and nongovernmental organizations. As Chapter 4 discusses, outside actors, particularly from the West, encouraged rule-of-law development within existing authoritarian regimes, hoping that autocrats might gradually initiate democratizing or liberalizing reforms, either because they were instinctively committed to reform as a means to advance national development or because they felt compelled to do so by the imperatives of economic development.[112] Yet, as the Tunisian case demonstrates, despite the persistent hopes of many outsiders, few autocrats approached rule-of-law reform in an enlightened manner. Nowhere in the Middle East and North Africa did a leader commit to a serious, long-term path of gradual reforms to augment political freedom, even as a mechanism to enhance economic growth. Instead, to many rulers in the region, rules of law were typically opportunistic, self-serving instruments.

Academics and policy makers searching for political change in the Middle East and North Africa in the 1990s and 2000s were typically looking in only one direction. Yet, few autocrat-initiated reforms in the region moved the states in a liberal or democratic direction. Instead, many rules of law promulgated by Middle Eastern autocrats offered a means to drive political change in the opposite direction, bolstering executive power while marginalizing, weakening, or co-opting opponents. De-democratization by nominally "legal" means, through reforms and constitutional changes, appealed to many regional autocrats, particularly because of the short-term benefits at home and abroad. What the autocrats such as Ben Ali or Mubarak did not realize, however, was the unintended consequences of this approach: by eroding the meaning and substance of institutions such as constitutions and elections, the regime would progressively convince even opposition moderates to abandon any hopes for a genuine liberalization or democratization process. As regional leaders increasingly hijacked state institutions and legal frameworks to consolidate personal power, citizens came to the conclusion that only a complete regime change could advance their rights.

Chapter 3

New Sons and Stalled Reforms

Chapter 2 addressed a political change born of the deliberate, top-down contraction of political rights and civil liberties. This chapter argues that some rulers of the Middle East and North Africa over the past two decades introduced limited liberalizing reforms that advanced educational, economic, and social rights. In a few cases, these reforms expanded political participation and representation. Many of these liberalizing reforms, like the de-democratizing measures discussed in the previous chapter, were codified in the legal system.[1] While throughout the twentieth century and even earlier, Middle Eastern and North African rulers had intermittently experimented with liberalizing reforms, the fifteen years before the Arab Spring commenced saw a new wave of such reforms in the region. In part, this trend resulted from the leadership shift in many states. Between 1995 and 2006, a cohort of new leaders in Morocco, Jordan, Qatar, Syria, Bahrain, Kuwait, and Saudi Arabia succeeded their fathers or half brothers. In most cases, these new leaders, here called the "sons," immediately initiated liberalizing reforms upon their accession to power, largely to signal the start of a new era to the public.[2]

The "fathers" had ruled for decades in part by relying on repressive tactics to confront opposition challengers. While the sons did not dismantle the coercive apparatuses sustaining regime control, including repressive state security forces, they did introduce limited liberalizing reforms, the substance of which reflected the particular interests of each son and the regime he had inherited. The majority of these reforms focused on neoliberal economic measures, educational and institutional reforms, economic development, human rights and women's rights, and—in a few, select cases—the expansion of political participation and contestation, short of democratization. Select, strategic reforms could signal the change of leadership at home, allay and sometimes co-opt domestic opposition actors, and help the new leaders to burnish their image as responsive rulers on the international stage. Social and economic reforms offered the opportunity to build new networks of patronage and support for many of the sons who had succeeded to power without traditional power bases.[3] While in some cases regional rulers introduced liberalizing reforms in the 1990s and 2000s without a leadership transfer—including Hosni Mubarak—overall there was a high correlation between states that became known as "liberalized autocracies" and those states where succession had occurred.[4]

While most of the transitions took place among the region's monarchies, the impulse to initiate liberalizing reforms during the first years of rule was not a pattern embraced only by kings.[5] Throughout the twentieth century, presidents such as Habib Bourguiba, Anwar Sadat, Zine el Abidine Ben Ali, and Ali Abdullah Saleh had also used liberalizing reforms immediately upon assuming power, and Seif al-Qadhafi and Gamal Mubarak would have almost certainly taken a similar approach had they been given the opportunity to succeed their fathers.[6] During the first years of Egyptian Anwar Sadat's presidency in the 1970s, he introduced a series of economic reforms as part of a political program often dubbed "de-Nasserification." In the late 1980s, the new President Ben Ali, as discussed in Chapter 2, announced a series of institutional, constitutional, and human rights reforms as part of his changement policies and to differentiate his rule from that of his successor, Bourguiba. In fact, the numerous hereditary successions on the horizon in many other presidential republics, such as in Egypt, Libya, Tunisia, and Yemen, proved destabilizing in their own right, as discussed in the conclusion to this chapter.

Scholars studying the Middle East concluded that the liberalizing reforms enacted by the region's rulers were for the most part strategic, that is, they helped to solidify the regime's rule.[7] None of the reforms touched on sensitive areas that challenged the fundamental rule of the executive. In the few instances when the sons did experiment with reforms to constitutional and parliamentary institutions or to political party and electoral law, the changes were carefully crafted, and often very limited in their impact.

Nonetheless, even though the liberalizing reforms offered clear strategic benefits to the new sons, for a few years in the early 2000s it appeared to many citizens in these countries that this cohort's efforts to expand women's legal rights (Morocco), build new educational institutions (Qatar and Saudi Arabia), or institute constitutional reform (Bahrain and Qatar) were genuinely motivated and generating tangible results. Some in the region hoped that these limited reforms might augur the beginning of a long-term process that could eventually open up the economic and political systems, following the transition template away from authoritarianism that had occurred in other countries as part of the third wave of democratization.[8] And while it is impossible to ascertain the motives catalyzing each of the son's reforms, there is evidence that the particular selection of the substance of the reforms—such as the choice to focus on women's rights or educational advancement—derived from the personal interests of each new ruler and an individualized, genuine vision regarding how to advance his country's development.[9]

Ultimately, as the 2000s progressed, it became clear that the liberalizing reforms initiated by each son would be modest in scope.[10] And, to varying degrees, in some cases, entrenched elites tried to derail the new economic and political reform measures.[11] In most of the cases where a son had succeeded his father, by the end of the decade the new leader's resolve and enthusiasm for enacting reforms had slowed. By 2010, certain segments of the elite and public grew dissatisfied—and in some cases disillusioned—with the lackluster outcomes of the limited reform approach.

The new leaders of the Middle East and North Africa chose limited liberalizing reform agendas during the first years of their rule, to build their personal credibility, attract new allies, and signal the start of a new era to their people. The liberalizing reform programs did not go far enough, however, and in some cases stalled or reversed, generating frustration among the public, the opposition, and key elites—those whom the reforms had been intended to mollify. Even in the case of Syria, the new leader, Bashar al-Assad, briefly experimented with reforms. Upon confronting opposition from old guard elites, however, he quickly abandoned his reform efforts, returning to the repressive strategies employed by his father.

The main focus of the chapter is Bahrain, a case that exemplifies both the genuine initial reform impulses of the sons and the limits of their willingness to follow through on truly inclusive reforms. The Bahrain case also depicts how a new, untested generation of autocrats tried to shore up domestic supporters while looking over their shoulders, aware of the normative pressures exerted by the international community. In the Bahraini case, King Hamad bin Isa al-Khalifa's initial conciliatory gestures raised expectations among the Shia opposition for genuine political reforms that would offer them greater representation and participation. These high expectations, however, were not met by the end of the 2000s, creating a political stalemate between the opposition and the regime that would have dire consequences.

Public opinion data could help to confirm the central argument made here. Yet the regimes in question carefully controlled public opinion polling during this time period, particularly regarding citizens' attitudes toward their government. Instead, I rely on a single, critical case to exemplify the chapter's arguments. On one hand, the context for King Hamad's reform program was unique, in that the unstable political environment he confronted upon his succession differed from the other new leaders' situations. King Hamad was trying to redress deep grievances and political disenfranchisement that had led to episodic but significant protests for decades. He recognized that political and constitutional reforms would be necessary to signal a new era and an interest in reconciliation with the opposition movements and the public, in addition to a series of social and economic reforms. On the other hand, Bahrain serves as an important exemplar of the general pattern inherent in the sons' succession patterns, as well as a case that was often neglected in the study of Middle Eastern politics in the twenty-first century, before 2011. Bahrain is also a case where the intensity of the 2011 popular protests caught many by surprise, despite the deep political impasse that had intensified by 2010, in part due to the stalled reform agenda initiated a decade earlier.

Succession of the Sons

In the seven cases of familial succession that occurred in the Middle East and North Africa between 1995 and 2006, at the moment of the father's death, the heir apparent had already been chosen, mitigating the possibility of a power vacuum and leadership crisis. Many of the autocratic fathers or half brothers had begun preparations for this power transfer years earlier, and all seven successions occurred in a smooth, orderly fashion. Academic studies of hereditary successions have empirically shown the greater propensity for regime instability in the immediate wake of the transition.[12] Yet in these seven cases, the moments of transition themselves did not trigger significant dissent from disgruntled elites, potential military or political challengers, or the public. Even the most contentious familial succession of the seven, following the death of the Kuwaiti Emir, Shaykh Jaber III al-Ahmad al-Jaber al-Sabah, after twenty-nine years of rule, was resolved peacefully.[13] As Michael Herb has argued, the dynastic monarchies of the Middle East have developed robust mechanisms to distribute the benefits of power among the family members, particularly around the time of succession.[14]

Each new leader initiated a series of high-profile reforms during the first few years of his rule, such as augmenting women's rights (Morocco, 2004), eliminating repressive political detention laws (Morocco, 1991; and Bahrain, 2001), abolishing censorship laws (Qatar, 1995), or privatizing various industries (Jordan, 1999, 2000). A few sons introduced limited political reforms, such as promulgating a new constitution (Bahrain, 2002; and Qatar, 2003).

Explanations for the wave of reforms initiated by the sons varied. The first explanation, often relayed by those closest to the leaders themselves, noted the genuine interest of each ruler in developing his country economically and socially. By all accounts, the substance of the reforms chosen in each country did reflect the particular predilections of each new leader. For example, many close to King Mohammed VI attested to his genuine commitment to women's rights.[15] Saudi King Abdallah enacted a series of educational, judicial, institutional, and religious reforms, including the establishment of the first non-gender-segregated university, challenging the religious establishment's monopoly over the educational system. In January 2003, when he was still crown prince, Saudi King Abdallah had published a "charter to reform the Arab stand" in *Asharq Alawsat* in order to articulate the key reforms that the Arab world would have to undertake domestically, including the promotion of political participation.[16] At the same time, the Saudi ambassador to London said publicly that "reforming the kingdom is not a choice, it is a necessity."[17] Interviews given by Saudi King Abdallah immediately before and after his succession suggest his longstanding belief in the necessity of socioeconomic and societal development within Saudi Arabia.[18]

Second, as analysts of the region's politics argued at the time, initiating reforms offered rulers opportunities to co-opt and divide opposition groups, attract new elites, and perpetuate their rule.[19] Indeed, empirical research suggests that all autocrats, regardless of how they achieved their office, are at their weakest during their first two years of rule, when they have to prove their strength, neutralize challengers, and build a coalition.[20] While overt political challenges to newly transitioned leaders have been rare in the region, often the new leaders are viewed suspiciously, given their deficit in leadership experience. Globally, empirical research reveals that autocratic leaders who can survive the first two years of office are two to three times more likely to survive after that.[21] Liberalizing reforms initiated by new leaders in the Middle East helped them to obtain elite supporters at the beginning of their tenure, including important constituents such as economic technocrats or women. These reforms also helped to satisfy some of the demands of the opposition. Liberalizing reforms, therefore, are good politics for new, untested, nondemocratic leaders.

Those Middle Eastern and North African states ruled by the sons constituted the majority of the systems that by the early 2000s had come to be known as "liberalized autocracies"—hybrid regime types characterized by "guided pluralism, controlled elections, and selective repression."[22] Daniel Brumberg, surveying the landscape of liberalizing reforms initiated by the region's leaders in the early 2000s, concluded that these reforms were often a "trap," introduced to bolster the regime's rule. Brumberg described liberalized autocracies as a unique type of a political system, one whose institutions, rules, and logic defied any linear model of democratization.[23] Because of the limited extent of the reforms, Brumberg argued that they made it harder for even reformers with the best of intentions to envision a different future.[24] In the words of one of Jordanian King Hussein's key advisors during this period, liberalization was intended to invite more "guests into the living room for 'coffee talk,' with a few welcome to stay for dinner. None were to be invited into the kitchen, though, and certainly none were welcome in the rest of the house."[25]

Third, some scholars argued that reforms were a response to two types of international pressure. The first type of pressure was implicit, deriving from the fact that familial succession did not comport with the twenty-first-century global norms for governance. Certainly the new Syrian president, who succeeded his father in a country with no history of familial succession, but even the new monarchs of Morocco, Jordan, and Qatar as well likely recognized the extent to which dynastic familial rule was anathema to twenty-first-century standards. The sons were familiar with democratic institutions and processes—many had spent years living abroad and participated frequently in international fora. They were thus aware that the international community, like their people, might question the legitimacy of a monarch's rule, and that they would be held to account by institutions such as UN human rights organizations and nongovernmental organizations monitoring their records and actions.

A second type of international pressure was explicit: many of the new Middle Eastern and North African leaders came to power immediately before or after September 11, 2001. They understood how undertaking liberalizing reforms could buy them additional foreign patronage and approbation, particularly by a more activist United States interested in promoting democratization and liberalization in the Middle East in the early part of the twenty-first century. Responding to these international pressures, many regional leaders began to adopt "democracy language" on the international stage.[26] In the case of Bahrain, Jordan, and Morocco, the sons had so successfully created a reformist image after their first few years in power that President George W. Bush highlighted the "hopeful reform taking hold" in each state in his January 2005 State of the Union Address.[27]

Therefore, the wave of successions occurring in the Middle East and North Africa at the turn of the twenty-first century contributed to the conclusion reached by many scholars studying the region at the time, who noted that "liberal reforms are on the increase" and that "at least economic and social rights had expanded in most Arab countries."[28] And while there was a series of explanations for this observable trend, including regional demonstration effects and international pressures associated with the aftermath of September 11, 2011, in large part, the generational transition at play—and the sons' responses to the global pressures discussed above—contributed to the proliferation of liberalizing reforms.[29] By 2009, all of those Middle Eastern and North African states that earned the label "partly free" in the 2009 Freedom House rankings were ruled by a new ruler: Bahrain, Kuwait, Morocco, Jordan (the rest earned the label "not free").[30]

The Logic of Liberalizing Reforms

Many of the sons chose similar substantive reforms upon succeeding their fathers, embracing in many cases new economic reform programs, urged on by international financial institutions and local elites interested in greater global economic integration.[31] In 2000–2001, King Mohammed VI of Morocco introduced structural adjustment and financial sector reforms and outlined a broad national development plan.[32] In part, these economic and socioeconomic reforms helped the king win favor among a new set of technocratic elites interested in economic reforms and greater global trade integration.

Only months after succeeding his father, King Abdullah of Jordan also announced an ambitious set of economic reforms prioritizing economic growth and global integration. He linked his economic reform agenda to the priorities of the sons as a cohort, claiming that "we are part of a new generation of leaders, we have taken the initiative to make free markets the only norm of resource allocation and to capitalize on our competitive advantage in human resources, modern infrastructure, and service orientation."[33] King Abdullah also recruited into his inner circle a new set of business-minded elites, individuals who had worked in the information technology, banking, finance, and industry sectors. These young economic reformers, many of whom had trained in the West, rallied around King Abdullah, celebrating his succession as an opportunity to eliminate some of the economic policies implemented during King Hussein's era.[34]

In addition to introducing economic reforms as a means of appealing to technocratic elites, the sons introduced liberalizing educational, social, and human rights reforms, many of which had wide public appeal. In Morocco—a country where a significant percentage of the population was living in poverty—the new king's National Initiative for Human Development (NIHD) was good politics.[35] By emphasizing economic equality, development, and an end to corruption, King Mohammed VI quickly earned the nickname "king of the poor."[36] In order to signal a symbolic break with the ways of his repressive father, King Mohammed also enacted a series of human rights reforms during the first three years of his reign. In the early months after his succession, the king ousted the notoriously repressive Interior Minister Driss Basri.[37]A series of important human rights reforms followed, most notably the launch of the Equity and Reconciliation Commission (IER), a formal independent inquiry established to investigate the human rights offenses committed under King Hassan's rule and to compensate the victims.[38]

During the first few years of his reign, King Mohammed pushed the revision of the personal status code, or moudawana, in order to grant women greater social and legal rights with regard to marriage, divorce, and child custody. Initially, the king faced some popular and elite opposition to the proposed revisions. But King Mohammed was not deterred, and the Moroccan parliament formally adopted the reform in 2004. There are many explanations for Mohammed's persistence and focus on reforming the controversial personal status code as one of his very first priorities, particularly his own personal commitment to the status of women.[39] Yet many within

Morocco argue that the revision to the moudawana also offered the king the opportunity to bolster his popularity—"a marketing strategy approach to build legitimacy."[40] It is likely that Mohammed was genuinely committed to women's rights, as well as human rights, which he associated publicly with core Islamic beliefs and teachings. Mohammed spoke of a "new concept of authority" with respect for human rights, the rule of law, and religious tolerance.[41] Nonetheless, these reforms offered the additional benefit of rallying important constituencies to the side of the new monarch, including women, liberal and secular political party affiliates, and other reformers.

Stalled Reform Agendas

In regions beyond the Middle East and North Africa, when nondemocratic leaders set out to make limited reforms, in many cases, they had often spiraled beyond the intended limits, leading to unintended reforms and the end of the regime's rule. "Transitologists" who had studied this phenomenon of liberalizing reforms in other democratic transitions concluded that while transitioning authoritarian rulers were anything but genuine democrats, their reforms—often part of strategic, self-serving negotiations with regime opposition members—were often hard to control and could lead to their own demise.[42] As a result, these scholars believed that "liberalizing autocracies" would be an inherently temporary, unstable stage of political development as countries transitioned to democracy. To Adam Przeworski, for instance, liberalization was a transient stage because the "melting of the iceberg of civil society" would overflow "the dams of the authoritarian regime," This conclusion reflected, to a large extent, the empirical fact of how authoritarian regimes had handled political change from the 1970s to the 1990s. Przeworski assumed that a crack of open political space would immediately allow latent student associations, unions, and other political actors to emerge, generating either demand for greater liberalization (South Korea) or brutal repression and a reversal toward greater authoritarianism (Tiananmen Square).[43] Similarly, to Samuel Huntington, the examples of the reforms initiated in the late 1980s by South African President P. W. Botha and by Soviet leader Mikhail Gorbachev suggested that autocratic systems could not withstand "the halfway house" of liberalizing reforms. Protests, societal upheaval, or mass violence would immediately follow any

liberalization measures, while liberalizers within the ancien régime would
be empowered to press for a democratic transition.[44]

Yet, as the first decade of the twentieth century progressed, it became
clear that the sons' reform programs would be limited. As the sons designed
their liberalizing reforms, they tried to prevent a Pandora's box from opening. The liberalizing reforms introduced by the sons and other Arab leaders
in the 2000s never opened the flood gates, and rarely led to unexpected
outcomes that challenged or exceeded the state's carefully calibrated strategy.[45] The sons most likely did not consider their liberalizing reforms as a
transitional stage on the path toward a democratization process. Rather,
the reforms were attractive because they might help them *avoid* democratization by stanching opposition demands and also increasing patronage
from elites and Western actors willing to reward their reformist instincts.[46]
It is possible that in Jordan, Morocco, Bahrain, or Kuwait, each of the
new leaders came to power intending to continue the liberalizing reforms
introduced in the first few years and then circumstances changed. In each
case, reformist aspirations seem to have attenuated when the ruler faced
the constraints and reality of staying in power, including the material interests of the ruling clique and other entrenched status quo interests. It is
also possible that international and regional events shaped each autocrat's
trajectory. By the end of the 2000s, the global pressures to reform had
subsided, in part as a result of the civil conflict in Iraq after the 2003 war
and its effect on the enthusiasm for democracy promotion in the region. In
addition, as Chapter 4 discusses, the Bush administration grew ambivalent
about its Freedom Agenda, leading to diminished U.S. pressure and rhetoric regarding reform in the region.

As a result, in most of the states in which a son had come to power in
the late 1990s and early 2000s, a decade later the sons began to hunker
down, limiting liberalizing reforms in most cases to economic liberalization
measures and some key social reforms.[47] The citizens of the region noticed
this pattern. By the end of the decade, for instance, Moroccan oppositionists noted that King Mohammed VI, having cultivated goodwill domestically through his initial reforms, and having secured cachet with the West
through his women's rights and human rights reforms, could now afford
to maintain the status quo. In particular, he had protected himself from
having to enact any measures that might begin to devolve the immense
power consolidated around the palace. In 2007, a leading Moroccan journalist and editor commented on the degree of confidence and security

projected by King Mohammed VI and his court, observing that "nothing now can force a change to the constitution. Even 10 million people marching in the streets would only be a start; it would not ensure that the king would change the constitution. Even today if President Bush instructed him to share power, King Mohammed would not move. His power is that immense."[48]

Bashar al-Assad's Abandoned Reform Efforts

In almost all of the cases where a new son succeeded his father, following the historical patterns of new rulers, he made a series of initial reforms upon coming to power. Yet, as the decade progressed, many but not all of the sons' reform experiments stalled or attenuated. The pace and outcome of each son's reform experiment varied, however. In the Syria case, the new son's interest was only fleeting, as Bashar al-Assad flirted with the notion of reform before quickly abandoning that agenda.

During the first year of his rule, Bashar appealed in his inaugural speech to parliament for "creative thinking" and also recognized the "dire need" for constructive criticism, reform, and modernization.[49] He immediately closed the notorious Mezzah political prison—a symbol of the Hafez regime's brutality—and whittled down the number of political detainees to mere hundreds, compared to the thousands who had been detained by his father.[50] Bashar allowed the publication of three independent newspapers and even permitted a group of prodemocracy intellectuals to hold public meetings.[51] He enacted a new law allowing the establishment of private media and immediately granted 180 licenses for private press operations. The new era of political tolerance motivated a group of prominent civic figures—parliamentarians, businessmen, academics, and former opposition leaders—to publish a "Statement of 1,000" in January 2001. The statement called for economic, legal, and administrative reforms and "urged Syria to face the challenges of the twenty-first century," including by replacing the one-party system with a multiparty democracy.[52]

However, the stirrings of the opposition movement's political activism startled the powerful old guard members of the Hafez al-Assad regime, who had retained their positions after the succession.[53] Worried that the increased demands for civil liberties and political rights would escalate beyond their control, these hard-liners pressured Bashar to put an end to his reform experiments. Bashar, bereft of any of his own allies among the elites, acceded to these demands. Weeks after the publication of the "Statement of 1,000," authorities oversaw a swift crackdown against the reformers: Prominent regime officials publicly impugned the opposition's nationalist credentials, and the security services assaulted some of the regime's most vocal critics. Opposition leaders were detained on charges of treason, including the most vocal proponents of reform.[54]

Whereas most of the other sons proceeded and followed through on their limited reform agendas, at least for a few years, Bashar almost immediately abandoned course.[55] Bashar's quick experimentation with a political opening, followed by his expeditious reversal, was unusual among his generational cohort. It is possible that, without a monarchical structure, Bashar had less maneuvering room and credibility to initiate liberalizing reforms than his peers did.[56]

The quick abandonment of the Syrian reform agenda had the long-term effect of hardening the opposition's resolve and intensifying its demands. In response to Bashar's crackdown on what became known as the "Damascus spring" of 2000–2001, the Syrian opposition grew more hard-line and revolutionary. In the early 2000s, for instance, the opposition leaders repeatedly claimed that they did not seek the overthrow of the regime but rather political liberalization that would make the Syrian regime resemble Mubarak's Egypt. By 2005, however, the Damascus Declaration issued by opposition leaders took a much harsher tone, calling for democratization and blaming authorities for ripping apart the national social fabric, presiding over economic collapse, and exacerbating a range of crises. The 2005 Damascus Declaration was also signed by a much broader set of opposition leaders than earlier declarations had been—suggesting that the regime's repression had backfired, serving to unite disparate factions of the opposition.

The Succession of Shaykh Hamad al-Khalifa

Bahrain is a clear case of a son who, like many of his peers, introduced a series of reforms as a way to signal that his succession marked the start of a new era. Many of the fiercest regime opponents were willing to give him a chance, believing his commitment to greater inclusivity and opportunity for all Bahrainis to be authentic. Nonetheless, like the rest of the king's cohort, ten years after his succession, King Hamad's reform program had stalled, generating widespread frustration and disappointment that proved combustible.

Background to the Succession

By the early 1990s, Bahrain had become a closed and repressive dictatorship under the emir, Shaykh Isa bin Salman al-Khalifa. In 1975, Shaykh Isa had shut down the parliament after a brief period of parliamentary rule (1973–1975) and ruled ever since under an emergency law that prohibited dissent. In the early 1990s, the fall of the Berlin Wall and the reconstitution of the parliament in nearby Kuwait inspired the Bahraini opposition—including the Sunnimidelle class, former leftists, and Shia religious leaders—to demand greater rights from the Sunni al-Khalifa family. Whereas in the 1970s and 1980s the opposition actors had demanded the end of the al-Khalifa regime, by the early 1990s their rhetoric had moderated. As one opposition leader from the time period recalled, "While our radical demands were easy to dismiss and the opponents easy to jail, by 1990 we were calling for evolutionary, rather than revolutionary, changes—such as political development and liberalization. We no longer called for the end of the al-Khalifas. Our demands converged with the Western call for globalization and economic reforms. We were harder to ignore."[57] In 1992, the opposition sent a signed petition to Shaykh Isa calling for the restoration of parliamentary life. Shaykh Isa responded by establishing the largely symbolic and consultative thirty-person Shura Council in December 1992, which would act as an advisory body to the executive, rather than an actual legislature with elected representatives. This gesture failed to satisfy the opposition members, and they circulated a new "popular petition" in 1994. This petition gained thousands of signatures and mobilized a united opposition front of leftists and Shia clerics. When Shaykh Isa ignored the new popular petition, believing he had already successfully appeased opposition demands by establishing the Shura Council, anger against the regime intensified.

In December 1994, decades of simmering repression and mistreatment brought activists, citizens, and opposition leaders onto the Bahraini streets, where they confronted armed military and police officials.[58] The security forces beat and arrested adults and children and fired on unarmed demonstrators with live ammunition. The police sent hundreds of (mostly Shia) activists and youth to jail without trial. These abuses begot greater protests, and the grassroots confrontation escalated; the Bahrainis would eventually call the conflict their *intifada* (the shaking off). In all, thirty-eight protestors were killed by police or died in detention during the first two years of the Bahraini intifada, and hundreds more were injured. By the late 1990s, hundreds of political opponents were exiled and almost 1 percent of the population of 700,000 was imprisoned.[59] Near-daily antigovernment violence erupted from 1994 to 1998, and the government's harsh response attracted international attention to the political situation in Bahrain.[60] For instance, in September 1997 the European Parliament passed a resolution on human rights abuses in Bahrain, calling on the government to release political prisoners, to open negotiations with the opposition with a view to scheduling democratic elections, and to allow monitoring of human rights conditions by international and local organizations.[61]

Limited Political Reforms

By the time Shaykh Hamad bin Isa al-Khalifa succeeded his father as emir upon the latter's death in 1999, the continuous cycle of protests, arrests and abuse, and counterprotests had engulfed the small island country. In the wake of Shaykh Hamad's succession, though, the incidence of government-targeted violence and unrest declined as opposition leaders agreed to give the new emir "a chance."[62] Shaykh Hamad reciprocated with a series of goodwill gestures: during the first six months of his reign, he released over three hundred prisoners accused of participation in the intifada, including a leading opposition figure and important Shia cleric, Shaykh Abdul Amir al-Jamri, who had been incarcerated for three years.[63]

The new emir soon realized that his initial prisoner releases were not sufficient to defuse the political crisis. Only by reconstituting parliament could he settle opposition grievances once and for all. Moreover, Shaykh Hamad recognized that he faced a unified opposition with widespread public backing. In December 2000, he announced a committee would be established to draft a National Action Charter, to outline the "general framework of the future course of the state and [to] formulate the role of state institutions."[64] Shaykh Hamad appointed forty-six members of the government, the opposition, and independent intellectuals to draft the Charter, hoping this spirit of inclusion would signify a change of leadership and the start of the new era. Ultimately the opposition leaders on the committee persuaded the emir to hold a national referendum on the Charter in February 2001.[65]

In the weeks leading up to the Charter referendum, the main opposition movement—the Al Wifaq National Islamic Society (Al Wifaq)—sponsored public fora to debate the Charter. Bahrainis rushed to participate, filling meeting places to capacity, with hundreds turned away. The discussions sparked a spirited debate, which spilled over into the press and often included criticisms of the al-Khalifa family.[66] For the first time since the 1970s, many Bahrainis began to talk openly about a transition to "democracy."[67] Shia Bahrainis, who composed approximately 50 to 60 percent of the population, joined with Sunni citizens to air their grievances against the regime, often as part of a nonsectarian, leftist, class-based coalition. The opposition leadership rejected the first draft of the Charter on the grounds that the proposed revision of the title "emir" to "king" appeared to codify the al-Khalifa family's position as Bahrain's ultimate authority.[68] They considered insufficient the proposed law-making authority that the lower assembly would be granted, even though all of its members would be directly elected by the public.[69]

Shaykh Hamad worried that the opposition, Al Wifaq and its Sunni, leftist, secular, and nationalist allies, would successfully boycott the national referendum on the Charter. Having staked his credibility on its passage, Shaykh Hamad acceded to these opposition concerns, according to those who held closed-door meetings with him in the days before the Charter was put to a referendum. He guaranteed that the lower house would have full law-making powers and promised that any new constitution emanating from the Charter text would be drafted by a diverse constitutional committee.[70] He allayed concerns about the role of the al-Khalifa family in the new political establishment. In addition, in negotiations with the main opposition leaders, he promised a series of additional human rights reforms: Shaykh Hamad announced that the State Security Court would be abolished and the 1974 State Security Measures Law repealed; both had been key tools of his father's repressive policies. To sweeten the deal, Shaykh Hamad also declared a general amnesty—all political prisoners and detainees would be released and 108 Bahraini nationals who had been forcibly exiled in the 1990s would be allowed to return.[71] In light of these concessions, and after a series of negotiations, in January 2001 the opposition agreed to the Charter and urged the population to support it. In elections held the next month, widely considered free and fair, 98 percent of Bahraini voters supported the Charter.[72] This kind of high approval rate is rare in the Middle East, but in this case it reflected a genuine societal consensus in support for the Charter and the dialogue process that had produced it. By all accounts, most Bahrainis accepted the Charter and the process as a fair basis for reconciliation and reform.[73]

Additional Political, Economic, and Human Rights Reforms

In the months following the passage of the Charter, the regime relaxed its grip on the opposition, civil society, and political dissidents in the spirit of reconciliation.[74] Shaykh Hamad approved the establishment of the first human rights civil society organization in Bahraini history, the Bahraini Human Rights Society (BHRS).[75] While the law governing nongovernmental activity required government permission for groups interested in forming associations and banned formal political parties, in practice the emir began allowing the establishment of dozens of advocacy associations. The government allowed Amnesty International and other international human rights groups access to the country.

Shaykh Hamad was also concerned about socioeconomic equality. He ordered the rehiring of those, mostly Shia, who had been removed from state jobs because of their involvement in the protest movement. He granted citizenship to more than ten thousand *bidun* (residents without citizenship). In September 2002, the emir issued a landmark law allowing the establishment of independent labor unions. On the economic front, the government introduced new measures to reduce the country's reliance on dwindling oil reserves, including by strengthening industries such as banking, tourism, petrochemicals, aluminum smelting, and ship repair. The state eased restrictions on foreign investment and improved the distribution of social services, hoping to alleviate the economic disparities that fueled Shia disaffection.

Shaykh Hamad hoped that these economic, political, and human rights measures would signify the new regime's more enlightened approach and its interest in reform and international integration, while securing the goodwill of the Shia population and its leadership.[76] It was therefore not surprising that Freedom House, in 2003, elevated Bahrain's ranking from "not free" to "partially free," making Bahrain one of only two states to earn such a ranking that year across the entire region. In addition, Freedom House noted at the time, "Much like the introduction of reforms elsewhere in the Arab world, the political liberalization process in Bahrain has been intended to preserve the regime's grip on power. However, unlike most of its counterparts in the region, the Bahraini government appears increasingly committed to acquiring the consent of the governed and nurturing a truly democratic political culture."[77]

The Constitutional Change

Al Wifaq and the diverse set of Bahraini opposition leaders celebrated their success at securing the pluralistic Charter. Many opposition leaders believed that the new emir had turned a page on the era of repression under his father's reign, interpreting the 2000–2001 negotiations over the Charter as evidence that Shaykh Hamad sought genuine political reform and reconciliation, perhaps even a transition toward a new era of constitutional rule.[78] Yet by late 2001, signs began emerging that such high hopes were premature. The emir's cabinet reshuffle in the spring of 2001 favored the executive and provoked sectarian tensions. While Shaykh Hamad justified the shuffling on the grounds that he would bring in qualified figures, reduce corruption, and instill public trust in the government, the most important ministerial portfolios—defense, interior, foreign, and oil—remained unchanged. The five new additions to the cabinet included several key individuals implicated in the brutal repression of the Shia in 1995–1996.[79] The regime decreased the responsibilities of the Shia ministers in the cabinet while expanding the role for Sunnis in control of key ministries.[80]

Shaykh Hamad then charged a small group of al-Khalifas and loyalists to implement the National Charter by drafting amendments to the 1973 constitution. On the first anniversary of the Charter referendum, in February 2002, the emir announced the new constitutional text, which had to a large extent been written secretly behind closed doors. Although the emir claimed the new text was based on the vague Charter language, it departed from many of the compromises of the earlier document.[81] The constitution officially renamed Bahrain from an emirate to a kingdom. The emir was now King Hamad and he quickly reissued currency and redesigned the state logo to symbolize the change of status. New pictures of the king, as well as his crown prince and prime minister (his son and his uncle), appeared within weeks in all public spaces and businesses.[82] King Hamad sought the official status—and institutionalization of his

family's rule—which such a name change would offer: a Bahraini kingdom would institutionalize the role of the ruling family; with the al-
Khalifas in charge of a constitutional monarchy, the ruling family had
now become an intrinsic component of the Bahraini state.[83]

In keeping with the initial Charter, the constitutional text gave the
elected parliament, the Majlis al-Nuwaab, the power to question ministers
and hold a no-confidence vote on an individual minister.[84] Yet the creation
of a new upper chamber, the Consultative Council (Majlis al-Shura), canceled out the parliamentary rights of the lower chamber. The two chambers
had the same number of members (forty), even though the National Action
Charter had asserted that any new upper chamber should be smaller than
the parliament.[85] The Consultative Council could now keep the freely
elected parliament in check, neutralizing any possible opposition majority
in the lower house and vetoing lower house legislation. Moreover, while
King Hamad (and his successors) would not have the power to dissolve
parliament (like his father), Article 64 of the new constitution allowed the
king to defer the election of new parliamentarians "if there are compelling
circumstances whereby the Council of Ministers considers that holding
elections is not possible." In other words, the monarchy, under some circumstances, could once again rule without parliament as it had in the 1970s
through the 1990s.[86]

Thus, King Hamad had given the opposition the directly elected parliament it had requested, while keeping the opposition's power in check by
creating a new upper chamber. Some opposition leaders called the turn of
events a "constitutional coup."[87] They believed that the king had lured
them into negotiations in a spirit of compromise, soliciting their contribu-
tions to draft the National Action Charter. He had even accepted some of
their demands, revising the Charter to reflect their input before submitting
it to a national referendum. The opposition had agreed to support the
National Charter only when assured that a similarly representative body
would transform the imprecise wording of the Charter into a new constitution. Yet after winning the opposition's trust, Shaykh Hamad had essentially
institutionally rearranged and consolidated the al-Khalifas' rule through a
unilateral promulgation of a new constitution. The London-based Bahrain
Freedom Movement spoke of "a constitutional putsch even more alarming
than the 1975 dissolution of parliament."[88] The king responded adamantly
to his critics: the constitutional reform process, he insisted, was a royal
prerogative.[89]

A New Constitutional Era

While King Hamad's political reforms reestablished parliamentary life, the weakened parliament ensured that any disputes between the elected deputies and the executive branch could not result in the sort of confrontation that had led to Emir Isa's 1975 dissolution of parliament. With the upper chamber filled with regime loyalists, the king's proxies could now have the final word on all legislative disputes. To protest the new constitution, most of the opposition groups, including Al Wifaq and liberal and secular regime opponents, boycotted the first parliamentary elections held in October 2002.[90] The opposition also accused the government of gerrymandering the districts prior to these elections in order to reduce the electoral power of the Shia majority.[91] Due to the boycott, the majority of the seats went to new, untested candidates largely unaffiliated with opposition political societies. (Candidates ran as individuals but were often known as affiliates of various "political societies," which functioned like political parties, fielding candidates for elections and coalescing as parliamentary blocs.) A disproportionate number of Sunni candidates, including many affiliated with conservative Sunni Islamist societies, won seats in the new parliament. The distribution of parliamentary seats favoring Sunni conservatives further exacerbated Sunni-Shia tensions.[92]

As the 2006 parliamentary elections neared, Al Wifaq's resolve to boycott the new political process weakened. Leaders of Al Wifaq decided to participate, and candidates affiliated with them won seventeen seats. Shaykh Ali Salman, the secretary general of Al Wifaq, which became the largest bloc in parliament after the 2006 elections, told the pan-Arab *Asharq Alawsat* newspaper that he believed the elections had been fair.[93] The Shia party's participation conferred new legitimacy on the parliament. Al Wifaq's decision to engage in the political process by participating in the 2006 elections also generated internal fractionalization among the opposition, and several leading Shia figures resigned from Al Wifaq, including its vice chairman, Hassan Mushaima.[94] Less than a month later, Mushaima and other prominent oppositionist figures launched a new political movement—the Al Haq Movement for Liberty and Democracy—stating their intent to focus on "real" reforms and an abrogation of what they called the "illegal" 2002 constitution.[95] Those allied with the Al Haq movement believed it preferable to denounce the 2002 constitution and to boycott the entire political process rather than to participate in a parliament they believed would rubber-stamp executive decision making.

A POLITICAL OPPOSITION DIVIDED AND INCREASINGLY FRUSTRATED

As we saw in Chapter 2, de-democratizing rule-of-law reforms have often had the effect of dividing or fracturing the political oppositions in the region. Indeed, in Bahrain, between 2006 and 2010, the main political opposition Al Wifaq and the more radical faction Al Haq were divided based on two different approaches to the regime's constitutional maneuvers: The Al Wifaq deputies believed they could eventually redress the king's 2002 constitution by advocating for greater legislative powers and eventually, perhaps, constitutional amendments—by working within the system.[96] For instance, in late 2009, Al Wifaq's members of parliament (MPs) began negotiations with progovernment MPs, hoping to win at least the necessary twenty-one votes for a proposed constitutional amendment. In preparation for the October 2010 elections, Al Wifaq MPs hoped to prove to their base that they had made progress toward amending the constitution, as they had promised during their election campaigns.[97] The "Wifaqis" also tried to deliver jobs and other socioeconomic benefits, to ensure constituent support and to justify their contentious decision to participate in a legislature considered by many to be undemocratic.[98]

In contrast to Al Wifaq, the much smaller Al Haq movement, and its affiliated youth, women, leftist, and Islamist organizations, rejected participation in a system they considered fundamentally unfair, and instead advocated constitutional reform to transform Bahrain into a constitutional monarchy. Since the 2002 reforms, confrontation between the Al Haq movement and its partners and the government progressively intensified, with periodic outbursts of protests, arrests, and more violent protests occurring with increasing frequency toward the end of the decade. The confrontations took on a decidedly sectarian tone, compared to the more diverse protests of the late 1990s, which had included Sunnis as well. In December 2005, for example, violence erupted between Shia youth and the security services. In December 2007, a similar confrontation between police and protestors led to the death of a young man.[99]

By the fall of 2008, two dozen political prisoners remained detained from earlier protests—catalyzing yet another new round of protests. Two thousand people took to the streets of Manama in February 2009 to demand the release of an Al Haq movement leader, who had been arrested with other prominent Shia figures and accused of planning terrorist attacks.[100] On January 30, 2009, tens of thousands of Bahrainis took to the streets of Manama to protest government naturalization policies, which they claimed intended to alter the country's demographic makeup by encouraging Sunni immigration.[101] In response to the unrest, the Bahraini authorities charged thirty-five protestors with trying to promote regime change through violence, accusing them of setting up "an illegal association that opposes Bahrain's constitution and uses terrorism as a means to achieve its goals."[102] Also that month, the information minister ordered Internet service providers to block access to websites with political content that was critical of the government.[103]

By the end of the decade, Freedom House noted an escalation in the tensions between the country's Shia population and the ruling Sunni elites and, by 2010, demoted Bahrain from the "partly free" ranking it had earned in 2003 to the "not free" category. By the October 2010 parliamentary elections, popular frustration and distrust toward the government had reached a zenith. Within the parliament, the Al Wifaq deputies scrambled to prove that they were indeed trying to redress the 2002 constitution, despite the still limited procedural rights afforded the parliamentarians. In the months prior to the 2010 election, Bahraini authorities implemented the worst sectarian crackdown in years, arresting nearly 250 clerics, students, members of human rights organizations and charities, and opposition activists, most of whom were Shia. Some of those arrested were charged with support for terrorism, while others were held on charges of "spreading false news."[104] These arrests created a climate of distrust and suspicion even before the voting booths opened.

Although Al Wifaq won eighteen out of forty seats in the 2010 balloting, this win—conveniently just fewer than the twenty-one seats needed to pass legislation—was overshadowed by increasing tension between Shia activists and the government on the ground. Throughout the second half of 2010, though international attention had not yet focused on the political opposition in Bahrain, popular anger against King Hamad and the al-Khalifa family mounted. The king's gambit to initiate limited reforms had failed to offer a solution to the underlying political problem—the reality that the Shia of Bahrain were underrepresented politically, both in the parliament and in the government, and at times denied equal socioeconomic rights as well. Moreover, the institutional arrangement created by the 2002 constitution—welcoming the opposition into parliament while ensuring its minority status and limited say over policy making—had not succeeded in satisfying the demands for inclusion and equal rights of the majority of the Shia population and many Sunni Bahrainis as well.

As the decade following his succession progressed, Shaykh Hamad grew increasingly interested in pursuing additional political reforms, disappointing many Bahrainis who had seen in the new king a pragmatic ability to forge reconciliation and compromise. Rather, King Hamad likely believed that his reform work was done, completed early in his tenure. In a 2006 interview with a foreign journalist given from his vacation island resort, Hamad described the Bahraini reforms of 2001 and 2002 as "changes we made from the top and not the bottom," which is why "I am the most relaxed person in Bahrain."[105] The king had no reason to be so relaxed, however. A decade after his succession, political frustration—in part borne by hopes raised and then dashed—prevailed. This stalemate created a grievance that drove over one hundred thousand Bahraini protestors, both Sunni and Shia, to the streets in February and March 2011.

THE DIMINUTION OF INTERNATIONAL PRESSURE

There are many explanations for King Hamad's waning interest in liberalizing reforms over the course of his first decade in power after his initial interest in political concession and accommodation at the start of his reign. It is possible that the dwindling international attention—and therefore the lessening Western pressure on his regime—had some effect. The Bahraini intifada of the mid to late 1990s and the government's harsh response to it provoked international rebuke. Two Bahraini exile groups, the Copenhagen-based Bahrain Human Rights Organization and the London-based Bahrain Freedom Movement (BFM), worked with the European press and international groups such as Amnesty International to publicize Shaykh Isa's repressive tactics. In London, the BFM persuaded the British press to cover what was left out of the Bahraini press—the incarcerations, deaths, and torture in detentions, which escalated as the intifada continued. According to one activist, "The government was encircled by the opposition and the foreign attention we provoked. As the atrocities grew worse inside Bahrain, the international scrutiny on the state increased."[106]

As a result of the expatriate campaign, international organizations such as Human Rights Watch and the International Federation of Human Rights began to issue statements about the deteriorating human rights situation in Bahrain.[107] According to one prominent Bahraini activist, "When we faced the difficult situation in the 1990s, our allies in Europe, in the House of Lords, at the United Nations, and at Amnesty [International] were critical to our success—we transferred information to them and worked in sync. Both of us sounded the same message to our various audiences."[108] Shaykh Isa had not been entirely immune to this negative international publicity. Periodically, he attempted to respond. For example, in an October 14, 1998, note to the United Nations secretary general, the Bahraini government tried to rebut statements submitted on Bahrain by Human Rights Watch and the International Federation of Human Rights to the fifty-forth session of the Commission on Human Rights as "groundless and blatantly political allegations." (The Bahraini government, however, did not address the specific concerns raised.)[109] In response to the increased lobbying by active Bahraini exile groups in London and Copenhagen, parliamentarians in France, the United Kingdom, and the United States began discussing the Bahraini human rights situation. In particular, a handful of British parliamentarians who had grown sympathetic to the London-based BFM called officials from the Foreign Cabinet to testify to the House of Commons, questioning them about their policies in Bahrain.[110]

While international pressure and scrutiny had focused on Bahrain and the protest movement in the late 1990s, subsequent to the king's reforms in 2001, most international attention dissipated. President Clinton sent Shaykh Hamad a note in late 2000 to commend his appointment of women and minorities for the first time to the Shura Council, applauding this measure as a positive step toward strengthening democracy.[111] In the mid-2000s, U.S.-Bahraini diplomatic relations were robust, in part the result of a newly deepened security partnership.[112] President Bush's visit to Bahrain in early 2008 celebrated not only the robust security cooperation and the recently negotiated U.S.-Bahrain Free Trade Agreement, but also King Hamad, who the president said was "on the forefront of providing hope for people through democracy."[113] King Hamad had successfully secured Western support and approbation and, aside from isolated Western nongovernmental organizations, few noticed to what extent King Hamad's initial, well-intentioned efforts to strike a grand bargain with the opposition had failed or how the stalled reform process was generating potentially combustible public disaffection.

MISCALCULATION

The third driver of political change discussed in this chapter, the initiation of liberalizing reforms, raised public expectations for greater opportunity, participation, and representation. Yet over the first decade of the twenty-first century, it became clear that the new sons' reform programs would be limited in scope. As reform programs stalled across the region, the public and oppositions grew increasingly angry and disappointed in the new leaders who had raised their hopes a decade earlier.[114] To a large extent, this pattern held when it came to economic reforms as well. In Tunisia and Egypt, technocratic elites with ties to both ruling regimes oversaw significant economic reforms in the 2000s. Though the reforms spurred economic growth in both countries, the benefits were spread unevenly, enriching in some cases a small clique while failing to reach the broader public and diverse regions of the countries.[115]

Ten years after the succession of the first wave of sons, political stalemate and frustration prevailed.[116] Across the region, hopes had been dashed that the transition to a new set of leaders would usher in a different era. Nowhere were these frustrations more pronounced than in Syria and Bahrain. Of all the hereditary successions that had occurred in the Middle East and North Africa at the turn of the twenty-first century, in these two states frustration and disappointment were particularly salient. In Syria, the son's early reform experiments had been promptly abandoned, and in Bahrain the son had offered genuinely liberalizing reforms but failed to follow through on the spirit as well as the letter of these measures.

Bashar al-Assad was the only son among the first wave of autocratic successions from 1995 to 2006 to succeed his father in a presidential republic, as opposed to a monarchy. And yet the pattern of new autocrats experimenting with reforms upon their accession was not a pattern limited to the monarchies of the region. As discussed above, previous Middle Eastern presidents, including Mubarak and Ben Ali, had also initiated liberalizing economic and political reforms upon coming into office. And by 2010, a new wave of hereditary successions in Arab presidential republics seemed imminent in Libya, Yemen, and Egypt. In Tunisia, many talked openly about Ben Ali's desire to pass the presidency to his wife or son-in-law—both considered corrupt, unworthy and generally disdained by the Tunisian public. None of these four republics had any tradition of familial power transfer; power had always transferred through a revolution (Libya, Egypt), war (Yemen), or coup (Tunisia). Yet by the late 2000s, the aging fathers in all four states seemed to be laying the groundwork for unprecedented, risky transitions—a prospect that infuriated their people.

In Egypt, Hosni Mubarak was trying to groom his son Gamal to succeed him, and like many of the sons discussed in this chapter, the younger

Mubarak had seized upon liberal economic reforms as his central platform. In the mid-1990s, Gamal returned home after years in London with Bank of America. In September 2002, Gamal was appointed to be the general secretary of the Policy Committee of the ruling party, charged with the vague mandate of promoting economic reform. He began to accompany his father on official visits abroad and to attend cabinet meetings, much to the collective irritation of the established, though aging, cabinet and military elite.[117] Gamal subsequently courted the country's wealthy business community, which included many young Egyptians focused on economic reform.[118] Indeed, Gamal Mubarak's public statements in the late 2000s suggested that if he had been able to succeed his father, he too would have initiated economic reforms, if not other reforms, upon coming to power.[119] By the late 2000s, Gamal's presence, let alone his platform, generated deep public unease, with Egyptian protestors regularly shouting "no to inheritance [of power]" to underscore their deep opposition to any hereditary succession.[120]

Indeed, the patterns described in this book, including the desire on the part of new nondemocratic leaders to secure their rule, win allies, and appeal to international pressures, were not lost on the aging leaders of the region. As Mubarak, Saleh, Qaddafi, and Ben Ali considered their own succession plans, they likely understood the fluidity and unpredictability—the real risk—involved in managing an authoritarian transition, particularly a hereditary succession in a presidential republic without a history of such power transfers. In all four countries, Western analysts were focused on assessing the status quo authoritarianism. What outside observers failed to adequately consider was the extent to which the looming succession crises were proving to be destabilizing, even while the aging fathers were still alive.

The sons' limited liberalizing reforms over the course of the 2000s pleased certain constituencies (e.g., women, some human rights defenders, and some economic elites). Many of the reforms derived from genuine substantive commitments and many made a significant impact on their countries' economies and social development. Yet the incremental, limited, and exclusive nature of the liberalizing reform approach overall failed to satisfy regime opponents and the public. Liberalization in these states did not open Pandora's box, triggering the slippery slope toward democratization, as predicted based on the trajectory that had marked the transition out of authoritarianism in other regions of the world.

Instead, many sons initiated a spate of rule-of-law reforms upon first coming to power and then, by the late 2000s, rested on their laurels. In so doing, they miscalculated the degree to which their initial reforms had secured sufficient public and opposition support. They had grown perilously complacent.

Chapter 4

The Drivers of Change and the U.S. Response

This book has argued that three macro-level drivers of change transformed domestic politics in the Middle East and North Africa over the past two decades, changing the interaction between regime authorities and the public. None of these political changes alone independently "caused" any one particular Arab Spring revolution, and in many countries some, but not all, of these drivers were resonant. However, the combination of these factors explained the willingness of such large numbers of the region's citizens to take to the streets in protest. In some cases, such as Egypt and Bahrain, a combination of these three drivers converged, as citizens began enjoying new freedoms to express themselves and air their grievances over the course of the 2000s. At the same time, their governments had enacted de-democratizing rules of law or failed to make further progress on liberalizing reforms, with the effect of increasing public frustration and diminishing trust in the process of gradual, institutional expansion of political rights and civil liberties.

As this book has argued, many of the factors that shaped the drivers of change were particular to the 1990s and the 2000s, such as the expansion of the media environment enabled by new technologies and the rise of a new generational cohort of sons. The region's leaders either were involved in introducing the changes themselves from the top down (such as the de-democratizing rule of law) or were trying to actively respond to the political changes originating from below (such as the demand for greater freedom of expression). They believed their efforts were strategic and would help protect their own interests, and likely did not foresee any of the unintended consequences of the changes that were afoot. Despite the conventional wisdom regarding the cleverness of Middle Eastern authoritarian regimes when it came to staying in power, even those who had survived for decades were still subject to miscalculation about social forces, particularly the unintended consequences of slowly progressing political change.

Of course, in addition to the three macro-level drivers of political changed discussed in this book, other factors were at play. A set of particular local circumstances and macroeconomic trends played an important role, contributing to the exact circumstances surrounding each local and national protest movement, as well as likely shaping the timing. In Syria, despite the mass public disaffection with the regime, it took a group of teenagers arrested for spray painting antiregime graffiti—and the heavy-handed regime response—to trigger a wave of popular protests that launched the Syrian uprising. It is unclear why this particular injustice by the security services—as opposed to countless other instances of regime repression—provided the necessary spark to mobilize popular protests throughout Syria.[1] But it reflected to some extent the element of randomness contributing to the start of the Arab Spring protests. A series of important macroeconomic, demographic, and socioeconomic explanations for the Arab Spring were also key, but they lie outside the scope of this book and will certainly be the subject of academic debate for years to come.[2]

This chapter builds on the three drivers of change to discuss the challenges policy makers will confront in the wake of the Arab Spring, as they continue to encourage genuine processes of democratization and liberalization in the majority of the Middle Eastern states that remain nondemocratic. U.S. and other policy makers, like academics, were taken by surprise by the upheaval of 2011.[3] During the first decade of the 2000s, U.S. policy makers assumed that—whether presidential republics or monarchies—the region's regimes were robust and the leaders resilient in their ability to stay in power. The fact that Middle Eastern states significantly lagged behind global standards on measures of free elections, free press, and economic openness suggested a regional "freedom deficit" in the eyes of some policy makers.[4] Like the academic community, the policy community, until 2011, also widely assumed the authoritarian status quo would endure. Because of the widespread belief in the resilience of the leaders in the region, policy makers assumed that only incremental, evolutionary political and economic change was possible and that such change would have to be undertaken with at least the tacit consent of the region's leaders, if not at their behest.

After the revolutions of 2011, policy makers will continue to face a series of challenges as they continue to promote democratic rights regarding free elections, fair institutions, economic or social changes, and civil liberties, such as freedom of the press, speech, and association. This chapter lays out these challenges, which are informed by the three drivers of change. They include (1) supporting the local advocates of free expression, through both private and public diplomacy initiatives, including those that might involve the U.S. Congress; (2) confronting de-democratizing rule-of-law reforms and treating them as a challenge to democratic norms; (3) rewarding reformers with U.S. approbation in a way that encourages sustained implementation, rather than one-off reform announcements; and (4) seizing the opportunity provided by dynamic authoritarian successions, particularly moments of fluidity before and after such transitions.

Key Caveats

A few caveats frame this chapter's discussion: First, any assessment of democracy promotion in the region post-2011 must begin with the principle of differentiation: the states of the Middle East and North Africa have become increasingly dissimilar. Although they still share cultural, historical, and linguistic ties, the political systems in the region range from struggling transitioning democracies to retrenched authoritarian ones, monarchies in flux, and states consumed by civil conflict.

As a result, international actors will have to embrace a case-by-case approach, even if certain key principles such as the importance of rule of law and democratic participation and contestation apply across the region.[5] Because of the difficulty in generalizing among the political structures of the region, this chapter focuses primarily on policy lessons relevant to a subset of the current states in the region—those nondemocratic systems that have survived the Arab Spring. Some of the discussion, however, remains pertinent to states such as Egypt, Tunisia, and Libya, given the unknown trajectories of the tentative democratic transitions under way in each state.

Second, the chapter primarily addresses U.S. policy making, although the discussion here applies to other international actors devising policies and crafting strategies for engagement with Middle Eastern and North African states, whether the EU, individual European states, or international institutions, such as the United Nations or the World Bank. Third, most discussions of this kind do not honestly assess the limited impact of international democratization pressures when compared to domestic pressures for change.[6] Indeed, international forces and international actors played only an indirect role in shaping the three drivers of change discussed in this book.

Finally, this chapter brackets the discussion of whether policy makers *should* focus on promoting democratization and liberalization in the region and how and why it might be in their interest. Over the past thirty years, many academics and U.S. policy makers have debated the relevance of political reform in the Middle East and North Africa to core U.S. security and economic concerns in the region. While nearly every U.S. administration since the end of the Cold War has—to varying degrees—encouraged reform in the Middle East and North Africa, scholars and practitioners have offered convincing arguments for and against the proposition that encouraging greater civil liberties and democratic procedural rights in the region would advance other U.S. national security goals over the long term.[7] This chapter is geared toward those already convinced that the U.S. should promote these rights and liberties in the Middle East and North Africa but remain unsure about how they might do so more effectively, given the limited successes of past efforts, the deep stigma and suspicions associated with U.S. activities in the Middle East, and a reshaped region after 2011.

The Limited Role for External Democracy Promotion

Three drivers of political change in the region over the past fifteen years have changed the relationships between the ruling authorities and the citizens. At the same time that these drivers were emerging, U.S. intervention (and military presence) in the region was also increasing, first in the form of the 2003 Iraq War and subsequently during a brief period of more forward-leaning, proactive democracy-promotion policies, which explicitly linked the unfree domestic politics in the Middle East to U.S. national security imperatives.[8] Yet there is little evidence to suggest any causal relationship between the short-lived U.S. democracy-promotion emphasis during the mid-2000s and the outbreak of the Arab Spring.[9] While it is true that during the two decades addressed in this book policy makers in Washington, as well as in Paris, Brussels, and elsewhere, were focusing with renewed interest on the region's democracy deficit and therefore individual states' domestic politics, this heightened scrutiny and public rhetoric had an unclear impact. U.S. efforts did not directly precipitate any of the drivers of change discussed in this book, even though U.S. foreign policy makers did reward many of the sons in the early 2000s, in some cases bestowing upon them approbation and credibility for their limited reforms. Some activists on the ground argued at the time that the 2003 Iraq War and other U.S. policies in the 2000s in fact undermined prospects for political change in the region.[10]

Despite limited evidence of any systemic impact, from the end of the Cold War, Western policy makers and international institutions such as the World Bank have grown increasingly enamored of the idea that they should promote rule of law and other democratic reforms in the Middle East and North Africa.[11] During the 1990s and 2000s, U.S. policy makers intermittently issued public critiques of the human rights conditions in select countries in the reign though more rarely of key partners such as Egypt and Jordan.[12] Simultaneously, international financial institutions, such as the World Bank and the International Monetary Fund, adapted their approach to foster economic reform and good governance throughout the region.[13]

In the mid-2000s, the Bush administration championed a short-lived "Freedom Agenda"—a renewed focus on promoting political reform and democracy in Arab states in the name of U.S. national security interests. The agenda itself actually involved a few notorious speeches, as well as new institutional and programmatic initiatives, such as the Middle East Partnership Initiative (MEPI), the Middle East Free Trade Agreement (MEFTA), and the Broader Middle East and North Africa Initiative (BMENA).[14] The policy and programmatic approach of this Freedom Agenda seemed to vary by country, however: While promoting freedom required regime change in Iraq, elsewhere the U.S. sought to work on gradual bottom-up change by supporting local civil society activists and certain pro-Western movements. In Egypt, the United States briefly increased its public and private pressure on the Mubarak regime, pushing him to expand political rights and civil liberties. Washington went so far as to punish the Egyptian government for jailing leading opposition figure Ayman Nour by canceling Secretary Condoleezza Rice's planned visit to Cairo in 2005.[15]

By 2006, some U.S. proponents of the Freedom Agenda realized that external democracy promotion would be a more complex endeavor than they had imagined. To many, the agenda grew more complex when a new wave of elections in the region yielded triumphant Islamist victors, such as

Hezbollah (2005) and Hamas (2006), with positions directly antithetical to U.S. foreign policy interests.[16] Even in Egypt, the relatively more permissive elections of 2005 enabled victories by Muslim Brotherhood–allied candidates. By 2006, some within the United States began reassessing the merits of the Freedom Agenda, increasingly ambivalent about the fact that freer elections would empower political actors with positions considered at odds with U.S. regional interests.[17]

Other policy makers struggling to rebuild Iraqi institutions also began to realize what some scholars had long argued: the process of democratization can instigate greater insecurity, ethnic intolerance, and sometimes even civil or international conflict in the short and medium term.[18] Some analysts reevaluated whether the short-term violence and instability were worth the longer-term advantages to regional security potentially offered by consolidated democracies. Still other critics began questioning whether the Freedom Agenda's emphasis on elections rather than institutions, courts, free press, and other civil liberties had been ill-advised.

During the mid-2000s, some (but not all) local democratic activists viewed Washington's efforts to promote change suspiciously, in part stemming from their belief that domestic, indigenous drivers of change were more important and effective forces for change than international pressures.[19] From the perspective of these local opposition leaders and civil society activists, international pressure was typically exerted too inconsistently to significantly influence local politics.[20] As one editorialist wrote in the leading pan-Arab *Asharq Alawsat*, at the height of the U.S. Freedom Agenda, "The West and the Arab states are talking more and more of reform, but precious little seems to change . . . Arab officials continue to speak of reform while emphasizing the 'specificities' of each country. The West continues to use reform as a stick with which to beat the Arab regimes. Meanwhile, the world is being transformed in a manner that makes reforms more urgent than ever."[21] Indeed, historical examples suggest that international, including Western efforts, might contribute to political change at the margins, but the central drama of democratic transitions typically unfolds via local actors and their reform movements.

Thus, this book's argument first and foremost sounds a note of caution to eager future democracy promoters: They must proceed humbly, acknowledging the limited impact and sometimes only marginal effects of their efforts.[22] As Western actors reevaluate democracy-promotion strategies in light of the 2011 revolutions, they will need to begin by ensuring that their efforts complement the domestic developments occurring in each regional state, and recognize that domestic drivers of change far outweigh international ones. They will need to take particular care to respect the indigenous nature of the 2011 revolutions—and the regional sense of pride in the bravery, nationalism, and local-level participation that contributed to the successful political mobilizations.[23] A well-intentioned outside embrace can often have the unintended effect of undermining the appeal of local, grassroots actors.

Finally, outside actors—including U.S. policy makers—will need to acknowledge that democratization and liberalization processes are long-term, gradual, and nonlinear. As discussed in the Introduction, both processes are long-term endeavors, and can appear in tandem, separately, or not at all. A full democratic transition and the liberalization of political life will take decades, whether in states such as Egypt and Tunisia, which have already embarked on their founding elections, or in Jordan or Morocco, where the monarchies remain in place, with the kings pursuing new reform programs.

Post–Arab Spring Challenges:
Lessons from the Three Drivers

Supporting Free Expression

The citizens of the Middle East and North Africa will continue to demand greater free expression even after the Arab Spring. Heated public debate will be a condition of political life in those states transitioning to a tentative democratic system, whether Egypt, Libya, or Tunisia, as well as states where rulers who have survived the Arab Spring continue to initiate reforms. Though the policy goals are clear—to support the diverse, unaligned champions of free expression—the strategic dilemma remains how to do so in nondemocratic systems even more cautious and wary after the 2011 upheaval underscored the danger to regime stability generated by new greater free discourse. Some of the rulers who have survived the Arab Spring will be particularly sensitive and wary of seemingly innocuous bloggers and independent journalists, particularly those championing themes such as universal rights. Moreover, most of the remaining nondemocracies are long-standing U.S. allies, who partner with the United States to advance mutual security interests. Diplomats will continue to weigh carefully how the United States should respond, if at all, to the internal crackdowns that will inevitably continue against bloggers and journalists, similar to the ones described in Chapter 2. A response based on universal principles will likely be weighed against other aspects of the bilateral relationship.

Given these constraints, two potential shifts in approach could allow the United States to more effectively support independent journalists, bloggers, and activists who are under attack by authorities seeking to restrain the burgeoning public sphere: first, delineating consistent U.S. red lines regarding the violation of free expression and, second, institutionalizing a greater role for the U.S. Congress.

Consistency in Naming and Shaming Strategies

U.S. policy makers must begin to establish their own red lines regarding the violation of free expression in the Middle East and North Africa. Leaders in the region should know—and be made to anticipate—the extent to which their repressive measures against journalists and bloggers in particular will trigger a strong negative response from Washington, in public and in private. The standards would be more effective if they were consistent across the region (and the world). For example, senior U.S. diplomats often privately discuss media freedom and freedom of speech with senior government officials within the region. The United States also publicly raises concerns about these issues in the form of statements and through press briefings. For both public and private messaging, there should be a standard determining when U.S. diplomats raise with local government officials incarceration or fines against journalists, Internet censorship, and other regime measures targeting free expression that violate international norms. One challenge that would arise in developing such a standard is the need to objectively analyze when and where the attacks against bloggers or journalists are clearly politically motivated, which can often require understanding and rendering judgment on complex domestic legal processes.

Private diplomacy has been and will continue to be a critical tool to confront governments intent on limiting free expression. Every effort should be made, however, to create a more systematic process for public messaging. Over the past two decades, the United States has tended to respond inconsistently when authorities jail or fine independent journalists and bloggers, leaving the systematic watchdog function to transnational organizations such as Reporters without Borders and the Committee to Protect Journalists. This division of labor means that often non-governmental organizations harshly condemn jailed journalists, when the United States (and most of its allies) responds more cautiously or not at all. For example, in 2008 and early 2009, of the fifty-three press releases issued by the CPJ regarding global attacks targeting journalists, the U.S. State Department's spokesperson mentioned less than 5 percent in his daily press briefings.[24] U.S. embassy websites in the region almost never issue press releases criticizing the repression of local journalists or bloggers, events that typically captivate local political opposition movements and civil society.

In the wake of the Arab Spring, the United States can institutionalize a more systematic and consistent metric to determine when it is appropriate to criticize the repression of free expression in the region. A more systematic approach would offer support to those journalists, bloggers, and activists who have been targeted and would offer fair warning to those leaders and governments most sensitive to public, critical statements from Washington. Knowing what types of actions will trigger U.S. public critique may have a deterrent effect on those regional leaders who seek to avoid U.S. public criticism.

One way to standardize U.S. expectations is to publish a biannual summary of all violations of civil liberties in the region. Embassies might assign a public affairs specialist to work with the local independent media, bloggers, and activists and to report back to the embassy and to Washington regarding civil liberty violations. The summary of free expression violations might even be published on the U.S. embassy website for each given country, allowing visiting U.S. officials to raise the cases in their meetings with the local government.[25] The collated biannual report could be a subset of the systematic efforts by the U.S. State Department to publish annual reports on the human rights abuses occurring in regional states. The summary would have to be shorter and more frequently updated than the Human Rights Report, however. Inclusion of violations would be based on rigorous interpretations of international legal norms and local domestic law.[26]

Involving Congress

Involving the U.S. Congress as a proponent of free expression in the Middle East could underscore the American commitment to free expression at the highest levels of the federal government—and among the American people. Congressional leaders promoting free expression would be less encumbered by other diplomatic considerations than are executive branch policy makers. They would be more willing to express publicly their reservations about the domestic politics of Middle Eastern governments, including U.S. allies.

Congressional leaders are natural advocates for the region's activists, bloggers, and journalists. The opinion of Congress is important to many Middle Eastern governments because of the institution's appropriations authorities. In addition, members of Congress have traditionally led U.S. efforts to promote democratization and liberalization abroad. In the 1950s, Congress founded the Helsinki Commission to promote freedom of religion and other civil liberties behind the Iron Curtain. Both before and after 1989, members of Congress threw their support behind the civil society movements in the former Soviet bloc, by funding civil society organizations, first in Poland, Hungary, and Czechoslovakia, and then in the Baltic states and other countries of Central and Eastern Europe. In particular, the Eastern European Democracy (SEED) Act of 1989 and the Freedom Support Act (FSA) of 1991 sought to promote civil society in the transitioning democracies of Eastern and Central Europe.[27] Though it is always difficult to measure the direct effect of these U.S.-funded programs, most analysts agree that U.S. support enabled civil society to play a key role in the wake of the Central and Eastern European democratic transitions.[28]

Congress has long monitored democratization progress globally and has often taken the lead imposing sanctions against authoritarian governments, mandating restrictions on U.S. economic assistance to post-coup authoritarian governments, and limiting U.S.-funded assistance to security services involved in domestic human rights abuses.[29] Congress regularly passes resolutions applauding peaceful democratic elections and urging states to hold free and fair elections. Congress has also used resolutions to congratulate certain Middle Eastern states for discrete democratic advancements, such as the 2005 women's suffrage reform in Kuwait.[30] Between 2005 and 2008, members of Congress repeatedly tried to leverage the significant U.S. economic assistance to Egypt that is appropriated annually in order to improve the Mubarak regime's human rights and democratization record. In 2008, Congress passed a bill withholding $200 million in economic assistance to Egypt on human rights grounds.[31]

Congress is therefore well situated to oversee and issue the annual report on free expression in the region discussed above. While executive branch officials must weigh every critical word issued in light of other bilateral interests, congressional leaders are less constrained by these concerns. They are powerful representatives of both the U.S. government and, more important, the American people. While involving Congress in a response to violations of free expression need not be directly tied to assistance, congressional involvement will send a signal that those who determine foreign assistance are also carefully following freedom of expression in the region.

Confronting Rule-of-Law De-democratization

Chapter 2 argued that over the course of the 1990s and 2000s, some Middle Eastern and North African regimes used illiberal and undemocratic rule-of-law reforms to limit civil society, electoral rules, constitutions, and other institutions. This driver of change found its apotheosis under Tunisian President Ben Ali's one-party rule, but President Mubarak and others began imitating this strategy by the late 2000s. Though there was little question that such reforms contradicted the stated U.S. objectives to expand greater procedural political rights and civil liberties in the region, often policy makers responded ambivalently, with carefully qualified public messages. This response was measured compared to the more punitive response by the United States to coups and more dramatic de-democratizing power seizures.

For instance, in Yemen (2001), Bahrain (2002), Tunisia (2002), Qatar (2003), Egypt (2005, 2007), and Algeria (2002), authoritarian leaders revised their constitutions. In some of the cases, though the constitutional revisions diminished the ability of opposition groups to contest executive power and further consolidated executive power authorities, the United States (and its allies) barely responded. In particular, the U.S. government's cautious response to the Egyptian constitutional revisions of 2007 and the Tunisian constitutional changes of 2002 suggested a limited willingness to directly confront Mubarak or Ben Ali's machinations, or to get involved in complex domestic constitutional interpretation, at least publicly.

When the Mubarak regime unveiled the bundle of proposed constitutional amendments in March 2007, Amnesty International described them as the most serious undermining of human rights safeguards in Egypt since 1981, when authorities had reimposed the state of emergency.[32] While the State Department issued a press release that acknowledged problems with certain aspects of the proposed Egyptian constitutional amendments, its spokesman called the trend in Egyptian politics "positive." When asked about Egypt's de-democratizing constitutional revisions, the State Department's spokesman responded, "When you are able to look back at some point . . . you will see a general trend towards greater political reform, greater political openness, [and] a more direct correlation between . . . the will and needs and hopes of the Egyptian people and those whom they elect."[33] Only after the March 27, 2007, popular referendum on the new constitution did the State Department spokesman express skepticism, referring to the "Egyptians themselves" who have "criticized the amendments . . . as a missed opportunity to advance reform and a step backwards." He indicated that the Bush administration would continue to raise the issue of democratic reform with senior Egyptian officials.[34] Similarly, the Bush administration did not respond publicly to the constitutional reforms in Tunisia in 2002, even though this de-democratizing measure occurred at the height of the administration's Freedom Agenda.[35]

U.S. policy makers should establish a standardized public and private response should authoritarian regimes again enact de-democratizing rules of law in the region, and beyond. Over the next few years, many regional authoritarian regimes are likely to survive the Arab Spring by promising reforms that improve the quality of elections, revise constitutions, and augment the freedom afforded to political parties. While in some of these cases the proposed reforms will be genuine attempts to augment political participation or the competitiveness of elections and the transfer of power, it is likely that in some cases new rules of law will again include some de-democratizing elements in order to protect incumbent executive interests.

While it is unclear whether the United States (or any outside actor) can prevent a government from making a reform intended to buttress executive power, even if it is thinly veiled in a discourse of rule of law, Western actors must at least be prepared to respond to these measures with more forthright appraisals. They should not rush to praise all reform processes, regardless of the substance, pace, or outcome. In other words, policy makers should take pains not to fall into the public relations trap sometimes set by regional leaders interested in placating Western critics.

The international community might begin by considering de-democratizing measures initiated through rule of law as they might consider de-democratization undertaken via more repressive means. Changing term limits to allow for another presidential term is as much an affront to democratic norms as vote rigging or ballot stuffing on election day. The

United States can build coalitions of allies to jointly respond to rule-of-law de-democratization, including those third countries whose views are important to particular Middle Eastern and North African regimes.

Finally, private and public critiques of de-democratizing rules of law may be more effective when international actors are actively working to build liberalizing and democratizing rules of law. For instance, if outside actors provide technical assistance in the areas of institutional, regulatory, and legal reform, their views on the substance of local democratization reforms will carry more weight. Therefore, international actors should be prepared both to respond to de-democratizing and illiberal reforms more forcefully and to focus their programmatic support on fostering those rules of laws that are consistent with international standards.

Rewarding Sustained Reform, Rather than Reform Experiments

Over the past fifteen years, U.S. policy makers have supported and rewarded the incremental approaches to reform chosen by many leaders of the Middle East and North Africa. For example, policy makers celebrated the new young sons when they followed a limited reform agenda, whether in the economic realm or the social realm (e.g., women's rights). In fact, a large portion of the funding for the Bush administration's Freedom Agenda in practice translated into programmatic support for some of the social and economic reforms selected and implemented by the sons, including King Mohammed VI of Morocco and King Abdullah of Jordan.[36]

In their speeches throughout the 2000s, Western policy makers urged systemic transformation. In practice, the United States and others often funded projects that enabled the leaders' own agenda, particularly reforms intended to reestablish credibility, generate economic growth in support of regime priorities, and generate a new set of elite allies. In many cases in the economic and social realms, these reforms dovetailed with U.S. interests, whether economic goals such as fostering strong markets or women's rights and minority rights.

Nonetheless, after a few years, in the mid- to early 2000s, U.S. policy makers, having staked their claim on working with government reformers, were often slow and reticent to respond when some of the sons' reformist impulses withered. Not only did the sons' reforms stop short of comprehensive liberalization and democratization that would have satisfied the demands of a larger segment of the population, but in most cases even the limited reform experiments of the early 2000s stalled or reversed course. As discussed above, by the second half of the 2000s, as it became clear that the sons' reform agendas would be limited and in some cases would end entirely, many U.S. policy makers kept quiet. In some quarters, there was an overly simplistic assumption that Western-oriented leaders would eventually, at their own pace, continue to initiate reforms that were in the best interest of their people. In other cases, there was simply waning interest in Washington to monitor the follow-through and implementation by the sons. Moreover, by the time the sons' early wave of reforms ended in the mid-2000s, the United States had already publicly and privately called these sons reformers, and rewarded them accordingly. It was therefore harder to push for continued, genuine, additional reforms with allies who already had received the benefits and acclaim from Washington for their initial reform efforts in the early part of the 2000s.

REFORMS UNDER KING MOHAMMED VI

The response of U.S. policy makers to the reforms enacted by King Mohammed VI exemplifies the risks of rewarding reforming leaders too soon and the leverage abdicated by early approbation. As discussed in Chapter 1, after acceding to the throne upon the death of his father, King Mohammed VI enacted a series of strategic economic and social reforms, including economic privatization measures intended to appeal to the business community and development programs that sought to rebuild the monarchy's reputation among the disenchanted poor. In January 2004, King Mohammed VI created—for the first time in the Arab world—a national reparations committee to investigate and compensate the victims of human rights abuses by state security agencies during his father's rule. Yet the king earned the most praise from the West in 2003 and 2004, when he persistently led efforts to revise the Moroccan personal status code (or moudawana)—the first such revisions since the code's promulgation in 1957–1958. The revisions expanded the legal rights of women in matters of marriage, divorce, inheritance, legal guardianship, and custody.

The Bush administration was quick to lavish praise on the new king's flurry of economic and social reforms and in particular the reform to the moudawana. The United States was also quick to dub the new king a reformer, even as it was clear to many inside and outside of Morocco that the new king—like his father, King Hassan—had chosen these reforms at least in part based on strategic considerations. When Mohammed VI ascended the throne, he lacked the popular support enjoyed by his father. He was largely unknown, having lived abroad for many years, largely out of the public eye. Field research in Morocco conducted in 2005 and 2007 revealed that most of the reforms highly touted in Washington, even the moudawana reform to augment women's rights, also offered the king strategic benefits. At the time, many Moroccans believed that the new king's initial reforms were part of a larger public relations campaign.[37]

Nonetheless, whatever the king's motives for his initial reforms, the U.S. rewarded him: Morocco received nearly a sixth of the first round of MEPI grants, the cornerstone of the Bush administration's novel program to support political, social, and economic reform in the Middle East and North Africa.[38] Within Morocco, over a quarter of this new funding was directed toward implementation measures for the moudawana, such as educational nonprofits working in rural areas to educate illiterate women about their new rights.[39] The Bush administration responded to initial Moroccan economic reforms by accelerating the negotiation of the U.S.-Morocco Free Trade Agreement (FTA), leading to the FTA's passage through the U.S. Congress in July 2004.[40]

In public, the Bush administration embraced the thirty-six-year-old king, at times even characterizing him as a poster child for reform in the Arab world.[41] Public praise by the United States conferred greater legitimacy on King Mohammed VI and also helped to support the administration's repeated claim that "freedom [was] on the march" in the Middle East after the Iraq War.[42] In 2004, President Bush invited King Mohammed VI to the White House and the U.S. designated Morocco as a major non-NATO ally.[43] U.S. bilateral economic assistance, which had dwindled to $9.1 million in 2003 and was scheduled to be reduced further, instead increased to $27.5 million by 2008. Furthermore, in August 2007, Morocco signed a five-year compact worth $698 million in economic development assistance through the United States' Millennium Challenge Corporation (MCC).[44] Because MCC grants are given only to reward those governments "ruling justly, investing in their people, and encouraging economic freedom," the choice of Morocco, the first Arab country to earn a MCC grant, reflected the Bush administration's overall enthusiasm for King Mohammed VI's early reform interests.

King Mohammed VI's interest in reform in the early 2000s stopped at the palace's gate; while investing in economic, social, and human rights

reforms, until 2011, he avoided any meaningful political reform.[45] Moreover, even as the king initiated far-reaching human rights reforms and
women's rights reforms, he also, as Chapter 2 described, rolled back protections on free expression. The United States' quick embrace of the king's
approach occurred before policy makers could take stock of the reform
program and its impact. In part, many of the king's new reforms advanced
a careful agenda intended to shore up new allies and reach out to a wider
cross section of the Moroccan public. Although the initial reforms in Morocco had a significant impact on the population, by the second half of the
2000s King Mohammed VI became less interested in systemic liberalizing
reforms. In Morocco, U.S. policy makers might have been too generous too
soon, reducing U.S. leverage and failing to push further for greater political
reforms when King Mohammed VI's interest in advancing political rights
and civil liberties began to wane in the second half of the 2000s.

Moments of Transition

The Morocco case offers evidence that U.S. policy makers might have mis-
understood the dynamics surrounding the political fluidity before, during,
and after the successions of new leaders in particular in Bahrain, Jordan,
Morocco, and Syria. As discussed above, once the new leaders took power,
many of them were interested in reform as a mechanism to shore up their
legitimacy, and the moment offered a unique opportunity for U.S. influence. The United States had the opportunity to push these new rulers to
enact reforms beyond their chosen agendas. Instead, many in the Bush
administration assessed them to be progressive, particularly the new kings
of Bahrain, Jordan and Morocco. In part, this assessment had to do with
their Western-oriented disposition, as well as the public speeches they gave
articulating new direction for their countries, referring frequently to the
importance of human rights and democracy. Many U.S. decision makers
were naturally encouraged by these and other sons' promises of reform, so
much so that they failed to recognize how the cohort's enthusiasm for partial reforms would stall, ultimately proving to be self-defeating.

Had, in the early 2000s, U.S. policy makers understood how many sons
were attempting to secure their rule and establish patronage networks,
rather than beginning a multistep reform process, they might have been
more selective and demanding as they dispensed the rewards and acclaim
sought by these new rulers. Policy makers might have tried harder to

leverage U.S. public support and programmatic assistance, reserving these rewards only for leaders pursuing continued, sustained reform programs.

At the end of the 2000s, U.S. policy makers might have overlooked a moment of imminent leadership transition, failing to recognize the potential for instability inherent to the transitions on the horizon in Tunisia, Egypt, Libya, and Yemen. These presidential republics had no history of hereditary succession. In many of these countries, the potential for aging fathers to transfer power to their sons or other relatives was causing significant disaffection and anger among the public. Military, business, and political elites in Tunisia, Egypt, and Yemen—even those who had been loyal to the regimes for decades—had become increasingly disgruntled by the possibility that an aging father would hand over power to an undeserving and unqualified son—or worse, in the case of Tunisia, to a corrupt and widely despised son-in-law.[46]

The domestic discussions regarding potential familial transitions offered a new opportunity for the United States and other actors to exert pressure on the aging fathers. In Egypt, for example, though American officials recognized that the Mubarak regime was consumed by questions of succession, they did not fully understand the implications of the unpopularity of Gamal Mubarak for Egyptian stability. In Egypt, the notion of familial succession was anathema, even to those who had accepted Hosni Mubarak's rule. Had U.S. policy makers understood how concern about hereditary succession was generating public and elite anger against the Egyptian regime, greatly increasing the chances for potential instability, they might have approached the end of Mubarak's presidency differently.

Instead, some U.S. policy makers considered the end of an aging autocrat's life to be the wrong time to broach such topics as democratization and reform, rather than a moment of flux and dynamism when the domestic political uncertainty could implicate and even endanger shared interests. In fact, the end of an autocrat's life, as Mubarak, Ben Ali, and Saleh prepared to transfer power, may have presented an opportunity for engagement. U.S. policy makers could have exerted more pressure on Mubarak to make political reforms in anticipation of his succession, including by putting in place a more democratic succession mechanism.

The region's historical record suggests that some authoritarian fathers have been willing to take proactive steps toward reform or at least to seek a rapprochement with their opposition in preparation for their son's succession. For example, after decades of brutally repressing his opponents, including the leading leftist and nationalist political parties, in the early 1990s King Hassan of Morocco sat down to negotiate greater political rights with them, in part to create political accommodation in advance of his son's succession. Policy makers now have fair warning regarding the fluidity of future transitional moments in the region. They might consider how potential hereditary transitions in the offing (e.g., Oman, Algeria, Saudi Arabia) and elsewhere beyond the Middle East and North Africa provide opportunities and challenges to engage aging fathers and untested, insecure sons or other new leaders.

Reforms after the Arab Spring

Most policy makers subscribe to the view that incremental reforms enacted by liberalizing authoritarian rulers are worth supporting because they will make a limited impact in the short term and, over the longer term, they will build a constituency for reform. Over the past two decades, a minority expressed doubt about the merit of this approach, concluding that autocracies were "inherently in tension with both rule of law development and state-building" and therefore policy makers should not hold out hope that authoritarian systems of rule would "act as generators of rule of law development."[47] Evidence from the region over the past fifteen years reaffirms some of this skepticism.

This book has made the case that regime-initiated reforms in the 1990s and 2000s either de-democratized in the worst cases or, in the best cases, allowed new leaders to consolidate their rule and attract new allies. The sons' liberalizing reforms did very little by way of opening up the political systems, and for the most part the reform pace slowed a decade after they had assumed power. None of the reforms of the 2000s triggered a snowball effect, opening a Pandora's box and leading to more extensive and unintended reforms, as had been the case with the reforms introduced by Mikhail Gorbachev and other nondemocratic leaders.[48] In many places in the Middle East and North Africa, over the course of the two decades before the Arab Spring, rule-of-law de-democratization in fact discredited the notion of incremental or evolutionary political reform, convincing even the most moderate members of the opposition and the public that a total radical regime overhaul was necessary. In the cases where authoritarian leaders used de-democratizing reforms to buttress power, the notion of reform was entirely discredited. Even in more nuanced cases, whether in Morocco or in Jordan, it still appeared as if a sitting autocrat would not make a reform unless such a reform was personally beneficial, or at least beneficial to the ruling party or ruling elites.

It is possible that, in the wake of the Arab Spring, leaders in the Middle East and North Africa states, particularly in those nondemocracies that have survived, will now understand the risks inherent to an incremental reform approach. They may instead choose to enact more significant, far-reaching measures. On the other hand, many authoritarian leaders who have survived the Arab Spring are increasingly on the defensive, and they might be unwilling to make any reforms. Across the region, in transitioning states and those where the leadership has remained intact, there will be an impulse to focus on short-term economic and political "fixes." As this book has shown, a sitting autocrat is often reluctant to initiate reforms that involve potential economic, social, or political risks. At the same time, the United States will have to promote reforms that do not always hew to these leaders' agendas. Balancing these two constraints—finding the "soft spot"—will require using U.S. leverage to compel regimes and ruling governments to push beyond their comfort zones, to make changes that might be uncomfortable in the short term for the sake of longer term economic prosperity and political inclusivity. It will be incumbent upon skilled U.S. diplomats to explain the ways in which regional stability will require leaders to take short-term risks.

In other words, outside actors now have a role to play helping leaders of the region understand the high risks of short-term, limited reform measures. "Reform" must begin to connote changes that authorities make in the areas of the courts, political parties, electoral law, and institutional and constitutional change, understanding that these changes begin to devolve power away from the palace or presidential office. Reforms will need to genuinely satisfy reasonable opposition demands. If outside actors want to be helpful, they have to generate a set of conditions and pressures that will urge sitting rulers and regimes to make such risky changes, upsetting the often very lucrative status quo. Policy makers should recognize that pushing such changes that might upset the ossified structure is as least as risky as allowing authoritarian regimes to oversee continued limited reform processes, conducted at their own self-interested pace and discretion.

The Consequences of the Arab Spring

U.S. policy makers, like regional scholars, were so focused on the durability and strength of many Middle Eastern and North African regimes that they overlooked evidence that these systems were growing increasingly untenable. Had many of the leaders in the region understood the extent of their own vulnerabilities, they might have entered into a constructive dialogue with their opponents regarding legitimate reforms that may have undercut the widespread preference to mobilize for change on the street, rather than at the negotiating table. Neither U.S. policy makers nor the region's leaders themselves understood the high stakes and the deep risks involved in maintaining the status quo.

The Arab Spring and the revolutions it spawned have created greater diversity in the regime types of the Arab states. While some new democracies are tentatively emerging and elsewhere states are mired in civil war, many core Arab states of the Middle East and North Africa are likely to retain some semblance of their current governmental structure. Regional leaders will be preoccupied with managing change while retaining power, facing a much less secure and predictable environment than before 2011. As the region remains in flux, U.S. policy makers and the region's leaders themselves will have to engage the public's newfound voice and the citizens' willingness to confront the authorities, whether online in the public sphere or in person in the public square. The public is now willing to mobilize and make demands on their governments, whether in transitioning democratic states or in enduring nondemocratic ones.

The leaders of the region now confront a public that can and will hold in abeyance the threat to take to the streets if their demands are unmet. Fear of repression has lost its deterrent effect. It will be much harder for officials to permanently defuse an opposition movement's demands and nearly impossible to prevent popular mobilization. Even in those cases where repressive or strategic measures can temporarily limit the ability of activists, journalists, and opposition leaders to mobilize, these government measures will only be temporary. Grassroots civil society organizations and political movements will fundamentally change the nature of civil and political life in the region for the next generation.

Over the past two decades, academics and policy makers assumed that the region's leaders sought survival above all else, and made their political decisions accordingly. Where both academics and policy makers missed the mark, however, was in their failure to imagine how drivers of change could arise even as a sitting autocrat retained full power.[49] This book has begun to show how regimes cannot perfectly manage all of the consequences of drivers of political change, even drivers that they themselves initiate. Even though many of the region's leaders, over the past two decades, were desperately trying to stay in power, their strategic calculations failed to take into account not only the possibility for dramatic revolutionary change, but also, more simply, how their own management strategies could generate unintended effects. From afar, the leaders of the region were considered to be wily and strategic players. In fact, in many cases they were engaged in a high-stakes game of chicken. Even the cleverest of authoritarian leaders could not foresee, plan, or forestall the dynamism afoot, especially because most underestimated the extent and scope of the public's desire for political participation and universal freedoms.

Notes

Preface

1. The research conducted for this book and the ideas in this book do not reflect the views of the Department of State, the National Security Staff, or the United States government.

2. For a discussion of the features of hybrid regimes, see Steven Levitsky and Lucan A. Way, "The Rise of Competitive Authoritarianism," *Journal of Democracy* 13, no. 2 (2002): 51–65.

3. Freedom House's Freedom in the World annual rankings of political rights and civil liberties in 193 countries are widely used by policy makers. Academics tend to rely on the more sensitive fourteen-point Polity IV scale of democracy and authoritarianism. Middle East and North African regimes consistently cluster around the "unfree" scores in both indices.

4. Some Middle East and North Africa scholars misread authoritarian leaders' scrambling to maintain control as savvy maneuvering, suggesting the deep competency in authoritarian regimes to learn and apply new strategies, rather than a response that reflects less and less control. See, for example, Steven Heydemann, "Upgrading Authoritarianism in the Arab World" (Analysis Paper no. 13, Saban Center for Middle East Policy at the Brookings Institution, October 2007), http://www.brookings.edu/papers/2007/10arabworld.aspx.

5. An article summarizing the initial observations of the field research was published in 2010, before the Arab Spring. See Dafna H. Rand, "Drivers of Change in the Middle East and North Africa," in *Interpreting the Middle East*, ed. David S. Sorenson (Boulder, CO: Westview, 2010), 97–124.

6. There were notable exceptions, particularly (a) in the literature focused on the role of political Islam and its potential to generate political activism in the region (for a review, see Yahya Sadowski, "Political Islam: Asking the Wrong Questions?," *Annual Review of Political Science* 9 [June 2006]: 21–24, and Mona El-Ghobashy, "The Metamorphosis of the Egyptian Muslim Brothers," *International Journal of Middle East Studies* 37 [2005]: 373–395); (b) in the new crosscutting political movements (see Mona Shrobagy, "Understanding Kefaya: The New Politics in Egypt," *Arab Studies*

Quarterly 29 [Winter 2007]: 39–60); and (c) in the arguments suggesting the underestimated potential of civil society (Laith Kubba, "The Awakening of Civil Society," *Journal of Democracy* 11, no. 3 [2000]: 84–90).

7. For the clearest articulation of the resilience of the authoritarian thesis, see Eva Bellin, "The Robustness of Authoritarianism in the Middle East: Exceptionalism in Comparative Perspective," *Comparative Politics* 36, no. 2 (2004): 139–157, and Holger Albrecht and Olivier Schlumberger, "Waiting for Godot: Regime Change without Democratization in the Middle East," *International Political Science Review* 25, no. 4 (2004): 371–392.

8. See Bellin, "Robustness of Authoritarianism in the Middle East," 142. After the Arab Spring, Bellin reevaluated the viability of her original argument. She found in the pattern of events of the Arab Spring, "especially the variation observed regarding regime collapse, regime survival, and regimes in serious jeopardy," confirmation of one central insight driving her earlier argument, namely, that the "coercive apparatus, especially the coercive apparatus' varying will to repress, has indeed proved paramount to determining the durability of authoritarian regimes in the region. In every Arab country where serious protest erupted, regime survival ultimately turned on one question: would the military defect? Or, more specifically, would the military shoot the protesters or not?" See Eva R. Bellin, "Reconsidering the Robustness of Authoritarianism: Lessons of the Arab Spring," *Comparative Politics* 44, no. 2 (2012): 129–130. However, she did find that her original argument, and the research agenda it had generated, had overlooked and minimized potential generators of social mobilization.

9. See Marsha Pripstein Posusney and Michele Penner Angrist, eds., *Authoritarianism in the Middle East: Regimes and Resistance* (Boulder, CO: Lynne Rienner, 2005); Oliver Schlumberger, ed., *Debating Arab Authoritarianism* (Stanford: Stanford University Press, 2007); Nathan Brown, *Constitutions in a Non-Constitutional World: Arab Basic Laws and the Prospects for Accountable Government* (Albany: State University of New York Press, 2002); and Jason Brownlee, *Authoritarianism in an Age of Democratization* (Cambridge: Cambridge University Press, 2007).

10. Stephen King, *Liberalization against Democracy* (Bloomington: Indiana University Press, 2003), and Steven Heydemann, "The Political Logic of Economic Reform: Selective Stabilization in Syria," in *The Politics of Economic Reform in the Middle East*, ed. Henri J. Barkey (New York: St. Martin's, 1992), 11–39.

11. Ellen Lust-Okar, "Divided They Rule: The Management and Manipulation of Political Opposition," *Comparative Politics* 36, no. 1 (2004): 59–79; Ellen Lust-Okar, *Structuring Conflict in the Arab World: Incumbents, Opponents, and Institutions* (Cambridge: Cambridge University Press, 2005); Ellen Lust-Okar and Amaney Jamal, "Rulers and Rules: Reassessing Electoral Laws and Political Liberalization in the Middle East," *Comparative Political Studies* 35 (2002): 337–366.

12. At the time, there were scholars criticizing this research agenda. Lisa Anderson pointed out in 2006 that asking "why authoritarianism persists" is "little more than the inverse of the democracy question . . . many of the same factors that had been

deployed to explain democracy's fragility—the availability of external rents, the limited popular mobilization for democracy—were adduced to account for the robustness of the coercive machinery and the stability of the regimes. That there was a tautological character to this argument is not surprising; after all, 'authoritarianism' is little more than a residual category in most political science." Lisa Anderson, "Searching Where the Light Shines: Studying Democratization in the Middle East," *Annual Review of Political Science* 9 (2006): 189–214, 201.

13. There were a few important exceptions. Mark Tessler and Shibley Telhami conducted some important public opinion work. See, for example, "Islam and Democracy in the Middle East: The Impact of Religious Orientations on Attitudes toward Democracy in Four Arab Countries," *Comparative Politics* 34 (April 2002): 337–354, and Shibley Telhami, "Arab Public Opinion Poll: Results of Arab Opinion Survey Conducted June 29–July 20, 2010" (August 5, 2010), http://www.brookings.edu/reports/2010/0805_arab_opinion_poll_telhami.aspx.

14. For an example of a critical exception, see Marc Lynch, "Blogging the New Arab Public," *Arab Media and Society* 1, no. 1 (2007), http://www.arabmediasociety.com/?article_10.

15. After the Arab Spring, Arab robustness scholars acknowledged that they had underestimated this potential among the public. See Bellin, "Reconsidering the Robustness of Authoritarianism."

16. In his now infamous policy speech made on the twentieth anniversary of the establishment of the National Endowment for Democracy and cited above, President Bush said, "Sixty years of Western nations excusing and accommodating the lack of freedom in the Middle East did nothing to make us safe—because in the long run, stability cannot be purchased at the expense of liberty. . . . It would be reckless to accept the status quo" at present. Bush described it as America's historic, almost divine calling to support and catalyze the "global democratic revolution." National Endowment for Democracy, Washington, DC, November 6, 2003, available online at www.ned.org. Secretary of State Condoleezza Rice's June 2005 speech at the American University of Cairo has been reprinted here: http://www.arabist.net/blog/2005/6/20/condoleezza-rices-remarks-from-her-cairo-speech-at-auc.html.

17. Personal interview, department chair, Political Science Department, Kuwait University, Kuwait, January 7, 2008; Tamara Cofman Wittes, *Freedom's Unsteady March: America's Role in Building Arab Democracy* (Washington, DC: Brookings Institution Press, 2008).

18. "Arab Uprisings: New Opportunities for Political Science" (Project on Middle East Political Science, June 12, 2012), http://pomeps.org/wp-content/uploads/2012/06/POMEPS_Conf12_Book_Web.pdf.

Introduction

1. The transliteration of Arabic names is spelled here according to the individual's or publication's chosen English spelling.

2. Following the Western media norm, here I call the upheaval in the region the "Arab Spring," a term initially used in reference to the Prague Spring. Many in the region call the mass revolutionary change a-thawra al-arabiyya (the Arab revolution) or al-sahwah al-arabiyya (the Arab awakening). Some regional commentators, such as Rami Khouri, have criticized the use of the term "Arab Spring"; see Rami Khouri, "Drop the Orientalist Term 'Arab Spring,'" *Daily Star* (Lebanon), August 10, 2011. Academics have used different organizing principles to group the diverse states of the Middle East and North Africa, at times creating subregional sets based on geography, regime type, political economy, or ethnicity (Israeli, Persian, Arab, or Turkish). The three drivers of change discussed in this book are most relevant to the Arab-majority states, Arabic-speaking states in which regional autocrats and their security services wielded strict control until 2011. These states are Algeria, Bahrain, Egypt, Jordan, Kuwait, Libya, Mauritania, Morocco, Oman, Qatar, Saudi Arabia, Syria, Tunisia, the United Arab Emirates, and Yemen. For the sake of concision, this book uses the term "Middle East" (rather than "Middle East and North Africa") to refer to this broader set of fifteen states. This book excludes North and South Sudan, Somalia, Lebanon, Iraq, and Palestine from its analysis because, during the period discussed in the book, most of these states or semistates had highly fractious domestic politics without one central authority. Although political change was pervasive in all of these countries, domestic violence and internecine conflict—whether sectarian, regional, or ideological in nature—split or weakened the government. In post-Saddam Iraq, as in Lebanon, Palestine, and Somalia, the state's contested borders and multiple and overlapping security forces undermined the writ of the state.

3. F. Gregory Gause III, "Why Middle East Studies Missed the Arab Spring," *Foreign Affairs* 90, no. 4 (July/August 2011): 81–90.

4. For a discussion of the role of emotions in triggering the Arab Spring protests, see Bellin, "Reconsidering the Robustness of Authoritarianism." See also Michael Slackman, "Egyptians' Fury Has Smoldered Beneath the Surface for Decades," *New York Times*, January 28, 2011, http://www.nytimes.com/2011/01/29/world/middleeast/29mubarak.html?_r = 1&hp.

5. See "Freedom in the World," Freedom House annual publication, 1970–2005. The data from 1991 to 2005 are available at www.freedomhouse.org. To access the data from the Polity IV Project and its variables, see http://www.systemicpeace.org/polity/polity4.htm. For a discussion of these variables, see Monty Marshall et al., "Polity IV, 1800–1999: Comment on Munck and Verkuilen," *Comparative Political Studies* 35, no. 1 (February 2002): 40–45.

6. Guillermo O'Donnell, Philippe C. Schmitter, and Laurence Whitehead, eds., *Transitions from Authoritarian Rule* (Baltimore: Johns Hopkins University Press, 1987), and Juan Linz and Alfred Stepan, *Problems of Democratic Consolidation* (Baltimore: Johns Hopkins University Press, 1996).

7. Joseph Schumpeter, *Capitalism, Socialism and Democracy* (New York: Harper & Brothers, 1942).

8. This approach is inspired by Robert Dahl's discussion of polyarchy in *On Democracy* (New Haven, CT: Yale University Press, 1998).

9. In 2010, I published a chapter outlining these drivers of political change based on the field research conducted from 2005 through 2008. The article intended to lay down a marker and to suggest areas for further empirical research in order to investigate the effects of these drivers of change on the political status quo in the region. See Rand, "Drivers of Change."

10. For a summary of these flawed assumptions, see F. Gregory Gause III, "The Middle East Academic Community and the 'Winter of Arab Discontent': Why Did We Miss It?," in *Seismic Shift: Understanding Change in the Middle East* (Stimson Center, May 2011), http://www.stimson.org/images/uploads/research-pdfs/Full_Pub_-_Seismic_Shift.pdf.

11. By the late 2000s, experts on the region coalesced around the nearly unanimous view that autocrat-initiated liberalization measures were a "trap"—machinations to maintain and strengthen a regime's rule. Reforms offered a substitute or deflection measures, often directly derailing democratization efforts. Liberalizing reforms reinforced the position of the autocratic incumbents by increasing the scope of patronage and creating a positive but ultimately false image of the autocrat as a liberalizer. See Daniel Brumberg, "Democratization in the Arab World? The Trap of Liberalized Autocracy," *Journal of Democracy* 13, no. 4 (2002): 56–68; and Posusney and Angrist, *Authoritarianism in the Middle East*. Groups that were typically considered forces for political change, whether industrialists, labor groups, or professional unions, had been induced to support the autocrats through a system of rewards and incentives. Eva Bellin, *Stalled Democracy: Capital, Labor, and the Paradox of State-Sponsored Development* (Ithaca, NY: Cornell University Press, 2002).

12. For the best articulation of the robustness of authoritarianism view, see Bellin, "Robustness of Authoritarianism in the Middle East"; Albrecht and Schlumberger, "Waiting for Godot"; and Posusney and Angrist, *Authoritarianism in the Middle East*.

13. See Bellin, "Robustness of Authoritarianism in the Middle East," 144–147; and Jason Brownlee, "Political Crisis and Restabilization: Iraq, Libya, Syria and Tunisia," in Posusney and Angrist, *Authoritarianism in the Middle East*, 43–62.

14. Joel Benin, "The Militancy of Mahalla al-Kubra," *Middle East Report*, September 29, 2007, http://www.merip.org/mero/mero092907.

15. For a discussion of this growing anger pre–Arab Spring, see Shadi Hamid, "In Egypt, Mubarak's Regime May Be a Victim of Its Own Success," *The National*, July 29, 2010.

16. Important scholars during the 2000s chartered the effects of new media technologies on the emerging public sphere, including Marc Lynch, *Voices of the New Arab Public: Al-Jazeera, Iraq, and Arab Politics Today* (New York: Columbia University Press, 2006), and Dale Eickelman and Jon Anderson, eds., *New Media in the Muslim World: The Emerging Public Sphere* (Bloomington: Indiana University Press, 2003).

17. One important exception was Marc Lynch's article "Blogging the New Arab Public." See also Gal Beckerman, "The New Arab Conversation," *Columbia Journalism Review* (January/February 2007), http://www.cjr.org/issues/2007/1/Beckerman.asp; "The Arab Blogosphere" (Bitter Lemons International roundtable with Ammar Abdulhamid, Mona Eltahawy, Esra'a al-Shafei, and Ahmed al-Omran, February 15, 2007), http://www.bitterlemons-international.org/previous.php?opt = 1&id = 168.

18. According to Steven Heydemann, "[Arab autocrats] have developed techniques for managing and easing public access to the internet and new communications technologies that until recently were resisted as potential carriers of democratic ideas." Heydemann, "Upgrading Authoritarianism," 2.

19. Russell E. Lucas, "De-liberalization in Jordan," *Journal of Democracy* 14, no. 1 (2003): 137–144.

20. Barry Weingast, "The Political Foundations of Democracy and the Rule of Law," *American Political Science Review* 9 (1997): 245–263, and Lust-Okar, "Divided They Rule."

21. Daniel Brumberg, "Authoritarian Legacies and Reform Strategies in the Arab World," in *Political Liberalization and Democratization in the Middle East*, vol. 1, ed. Rex Brynen, Bahgat Korany, and Paul Noble (Boulder, CO: Lynne Rienner, 1995), 229–260, and Brumberg, "Democratization in the Arab World?"

22. Brumberg, in "Authoritarian Legacies and Reform Strategies in the Arab World," was one of the first to use this term. See also Lucas, "De-liberalization in Jordan."

23. See Bellin, *Stalled Democracy* and "Robustness of Authoritarianism in the Middle East"; Albrecht and Schlumberger, "Waiting for Godot"; Brumberg, "Authoritarian Legacies and Reform Strategies" and "Democratization in the Arab World?" For example, Bellin, in *Stalled Democracy*, showed how Tunisian President Ben Ali co-opted both capitalists and labor unions—natural democracy proponents in other settings—through reform measures that benefited both groups.

24. Eva Bellin argues that emotional triggers—frustration, anger, but also euphoria—inspired many individuals to join the 2011 protests. See Bellin, "Reconsidering the Robustness of Authoritarianism."

25. For instance, Dina Shehata makes the case that the Egyptian revolution was caused by "increasing corruption and economic exclusion; youth alienation; and the elections and divisions among the elite over questions of succession." See Shehata, "The Fall of the Pharaoh: How Hosni Mubarak's Reign Came to an End," *Foreign Affairs* 90, no. 4 (May/June 2011): 26–32. Other important preliminary explanations for the Arab Spring include Lisa Anderson, "Demystifying the Arab Spring," Foreign Affairs 90, no. 4 (May/June 2011): 2–7; and Kenneth M. Pollack, Akram Al-Turk, Michael S. Doran, Daniel L. Byman, and Pavel Baev, "The Arab Awakening: America and the Transformation of the Middle East" (Washington, DC: Brookings Institution Press, 2011). For a summary of Arab explanations for the protests, see Marc Lynch,

"The Big Think behind the Arab Spring," *Foreign Policy*, November 28, 2011, http://www.foreignpolicy.com/articles/2011/11/28/the_big_think.

26. See Marc Lynch, "After Egypt: The Limits and Promise of Online Challenges to the Authoritarian Arab State," *Perspectives on Politics* 9, no. 2 (June 2011), http://www.marclynch.com/wp-content/uploads/2011/06/download-Lynch-article.pdf.

27. Bellin, "Reconsidering the Robustness of Authoritarianism." Journalists and pundits immediately noticed how the antigovernment protests in early 2011 spread like contagion from country to country across the Arab world. Some noted the role of Arab world satellite television channel Al Jazeera in bringing unbiased news of the revolutions to all the countries in the region (see Shashank Joshi, "Revolutions Are Proving Contagious—But the Tyrants Are Not Beaten Yet," *Telegraph*, August 25, 2011).

28. For a description of how the Tunisian revolutionaries aided their Egyptian colleagues, see, for example, David D. Kirkpatrick and David E. Sanger, "A Tunisian-Egypt Link That Shook Arab History," *New York Times*, February 13, 2011. For the best social science arguments regarding the effects of neighborhood pressures on local democratization processes, see Scott Mainwaring and Anibal Perez-Linan, "Why Regions of the World Are Important: Regional Specificities and Region-Wide Diffusion of Democracy," in *Regimes and Democracies in Latin America*, ed. Gerardo Munck (Oxford: Oxford University Press, 2007), 199–229, and Jon Pevehouse, "Democracy from the Outside In?," *International Organization* 56 (Summer 2002): 515–549.

29. Some authors have offered general macroeconomic arguments attributing the Arab Spring to the statist nature of the region's economies, the region's lackluster private sectors, and low levels of trade. See Adeel Malik and Baseem Awadallah, "The Economics of the Arab Spring" (Center for the Study of African Economies Working Paper Series 2011/23, December 2011).

30. Human rights activist and protester Ghada Shabandar told the *New York Times*, "Egyptians are sick and tired of being corrupted and when you live on 300 pounds a month [about $51], you have one of two options: you either become a beggar or a thief. The people sent a message: 'We are not beggars and we do not want to become thieves.'" Slackman, "Egyptians' Fury."

31. Felipe R. Campante and Davin Chor, "The People Want the Fall of the Regime: Schooling, Protest, and the Economy" (Harvard Kennedy School Faculty Working Papers Series, March 2011).

32. Clemens Breisinger, Olivier Ecker, and Perrihan Al-Riffai, "The Economics of the Arab Awakening: From Revolution to Transformation and Food Security" (International Food Policy Research Institute Policy Brief 18, May 2011). The authors note that on conventional measures of economic health (e.g., GDP growth, poverty rates), most of the states of the Middle East and North Africa were doing well relative to similarly underdeveloped Asian and Latin American nations. However, the proportion of people in eleven out of twelve of the region's countries reported greater food insecurity in 2011 as compared to 2010, and in ten countries individuals reported lower living standards than in 2010.

33. Personal interview, editor of *al-Mawqef* (opposition newspaper), Tunis, Tunisia, May 21, 2007, and reporter and editorialist, *L'Expression*, Tunis, Tunisia, June 12, 2007.

34. See David D. Kirkpatrick, "Tunisia Leader Frees and Prime Minister Claims Power," *New York Times*, January 14, 2011.

35. Other authors have and will focus on the difference between presidential republics and monarchies in particular when it came to the causes of the Arab Spring, given that, in 2011, the popular protests seem to have been particularly intense in the presidential republics of Egypt, Tunisia, Libya, Yemen, and Syria. Here, I do not differentiate between monarchies and republics with regard to their susceptibility to popular protest movements. Before the Arab Spring, authors focused on the particular ways in which monarchies were more resilient than other Middle Eastern states. See Lisa Anderson, "Absolutism and the Resilience of Monarchy in the Middle East," *Political Science Quarterly* 106, no. 1 (Spring 1991): 1–15, and Michael Herb, "Princes and Parliaments in the Arab World," *Middle East Journal* 58, no. 3 (Summer 2004): 367–384. Others argued that before the Cold War, presidential regimes (Egypt, Iraq, Syria) enjoyed greater legitimacy because of the power and popularity of their pan-Arab, Nasserist ideology. However, by the 1990s, their legitimacy began diminishing as the appeal of the ideological basis for their ruling party diminished. Future researchers might consider how this shift may explain what seemed like increased popular dissent in 2011 in the one-party presidential republics, such as Egypt, Syria, and Tunisia. See Albrecht and Schlumberger, "Waiting for Godot."

36. This approach follows Jack Goldstone's argument that twentieth-century revolutions derived from a wide variety of causes, rather than one fixed cause. Explanations of revolutionary causes, he argues, require causal tracing that may be possible only in hindsight. Prediction is very difficult, Goldstone argues, although not impossible. See Jack A. Goldstone, "Predicting Revolutions: Why We Could (and Should) Have Foreseen the Revolutions of 1989–1991 in the USSR and Eastern Europe," in *Debating Revolutions*, ed. Nikki R. Keddie (New York: New York University Press, 1995), 39–61, and Jack A. Goldstone, *Revolution and Rebellion in the Modern World* (Berkeley: University of California Press, 1993). On the application of his research to the Arab Spring revolutions, see Jack Goldstone, "Understanding the Revolutions of 2011," *Foreign Affairs* 90, no. 4 (May/June 2011): 8–16.

37. This book does not operationalize or measure high or low levels of protest, nor why the Arab Spring protests proved existentially challenging to rulers in some states (Egypt, Tunisia, Libya, Syria, Yemen, and Bahrain), but not in others.

38. Personal interview, Amnesty International Tunis section chief, Tunis, Tunisia, June 7, 2007, and personal interview, former president of the Organisation Marocain des Droits de L'Hommes (OMDH), Casablanca, July 3, 2007.

39. For theories describing how regional autocrats respond to normative pressures, see Albrecht and Schlumberger, "Waiting for Godot." Some scholars have shown how autocrats are keenly sensitive to global norms and ideas as transmitted

through communicative action, argument, and moral persuasion. See Thomas Risse, Steve C. Ropp, and Kathryn Sikkink, *Power of Human Rights: International Norms and Domestic Change* (Cambridge: Cambridge University Press, 1999), and Thomas Risse, "International Norms and Domestic Change: Arguing and Communicative Behavior in the Human Rights Area," *Politics and Society* 27, no. 4 (1999): 529–559.

40. Anderson, "Searching Where the Light Shines."

41. See, for instance, the debate regarding whether ratifying international human rights treaties imposes any costs on authoritarian regimes in Emilie M. Hafner-Burton, "Sticks and Stones: Naming and Shaming the Human Rights Enforcement Problem," *International Organization* 62 (2008): 689–716.

42. Albrecht and Schlumberger, "Waiting for Godot," 376.

43. Personal interview, newspaper editor and professor, Kuwait City, January 2008, and personal interview, political science professor, Rabat, Morocco, August 2005.

44. Personal interview, political activist and former parliamentary candidate, Tunis, Tunisia, May 7, 2007.

45. Many scholars have argued that there are important regional contagion effects when it comes to democratization. See, for instance, Kristian Skrede Gleditsch and Michael D. Ward, "Diffusion and the International Context of Democratization," *International Organization* 60, no. 4 (Autumn 2006): 911–933; Pevehouse, "Democracy from the Outside In?"; and Mainwaring and Perez-Linan, "Why Regions of the World Are Important."

46. Personal interview, human rights lawyer and activist, Rabat, Morocco, July 7, 2007.

47. For a discussion of the "critical case design," case selection based on the cases' strategic importance in relation to the general problem, see Bent Flyvbjerg, "Five Misunderstandings about Case-Study Research," *Qualitative Inquiry* 12, no. 2 (April 2006): 219–245; Lee Peter Ruddin, "You Can Generalize Stupid! Social Scientists, Bent Flyvbjerg, and Case Study Methodology," *Qualitative Inquiry* 12 , no. 4 (August 2006): 797–812; and James G. March, Lee S. Sproull, and Michal Tamuz, "Learning from Samples of One or Fewer," *Organization Science* 2, no. 1 (February 1991): 1–13.

48. See Rifaat El-Said, *Al-Liberaliya al-Misriyya* [Egyptian liberalism] (Cairo: Al-Ahli, 2003), cited in Saad Eddin Ibrahim, "Arab Liberal Legacies: Full Circle" (unpublished working paper, 2004), 7. While it is true that under the reign of Kehdive Ismail, the Advisory Council of Representatives, consisting of seventy-five members, was elected for the time, the electorate included only dignitaries in Cairo, Alexandria, and Damietta, as well as village chiefs and shaykhs.

49. See Ibrahim, "Arab Liberal Legacies." For a review of the economic liberalization movements that changed the region's economies beginning in the 1970s and 1980s, see Iliya Harik and Denis Sullivan, eds., *Privatization and Liberalization in the Middle East* (Bloomington: Indiana University Press, 1992).

50. A significant body of scholarly research has attempted to substantiate the claim that in general, over time and space, with some exceptions, most autocrats have as their primarily goal regime survival, and have gone to violent means and overseen massive repression in order to do so. For a summary of this literature, see Gordon Tullock, *Autocracy* (Boston: Kluwer, 1987), who initially posited that all autocrats share the same goal of regime survival, and Stephen Haber, "Authoritarian Government," in *The Oxford Handbook of Political Economy*, ed. Barry R. Weingast and Donald A. Wittman (New York: Oxford University Press, 2006), 693–707.

Chapter 1

1. Personal interview, prominent journalist, Casablanca, Morocco, August 2005.

2. Beckerman, "New Arab Conversation," 17, and Lynch, *Voices of the New Arab Public* and "Blogging the New Arab Public."

3. "Internet Usage in the Middle East" (Internet World Stats, Usage and Population Statistics, 2010), http://www.internetworldstats.com/stats5.htm.

4. This chapter builds on earlier arguments, such as those offered before the Arab Spring about the complex but powerful effects on Arab authoritarian politics exerted by new media, including Lynch, *Voices of the New Arab Public* and "Blogging the New Arab Public"; Najib Ghadbian, "Contesting the State Media Monopoly: Syria on al-Jazira Television," *Middle East Review of International Affairs* 5, no. 2 (June 2001): 75–87; Jon B. Alterman, "Counting Nodes and Counting Noses: Understanding New Media in the Middle East," *Middle East Journal* 54, no. 3 (Summer 2000): 355; and Jon Anderson, "New Media, New Publics: Reconfiguring the Public Sphere of Islam," *Social Research* 70, no. 3 (2003): 888–906. In the wake of the Arab Spring, many academic and popular explanations for the uprisings included the role of media technologies as primary causes. See Robin Wright, *Rock the Casbah: Rage and Rebellion in the Islamic World* (New York: Simon & Schuster, 2011), and Bellin, "Reconsidering the Robustness of Authoritarianism."

5. "Freedom of the Press Index." For data from 2000 to 2010 on 195 countries, see Freedom House, http://expression.freedomhouse.org/reports/freedom_of_the_press?country = &year = 2010.

6. Ibid.

7. This book does not discuss the reasons why certain protest movements have led to regime change and others have not. Today, in Morocco, protestors affiliated with the February 20th movement continue to push the monarchy and the government toward greater reform, but the protests attract much smaller crowds than they did in 2011. The king's constitutional changes of 2011 and subsequent parliamentary elections of November 2011, in which the Islamist opposition won the majority of seats, have attenuated the intensity of the protest movement. In Egypt, the upheaval led, in relatively short order, to a quick and dramatic end to the presidency of Hosni Mubarak, even if the protest movement continues to fill Tahrir Square in an effort to

hold interim authorities to their economic and political promises. Despite this divergence in Arab Spring outcomes, however, Morocco and Egypt are both cases where the driver of change outlined in this chapter was particularly pronounced from the mid-1990s until 2010.

8. See John Milton, "Areopagatica," in *Great Essays by Montaigne, Sidney, Milton, Cowley, Disraeli, Lamb, Irving, Lowell, Jefferies, and Others*, ed. Helen Kendrick Johnson (New York: Appleton, 1904), 122, and John Stuart Mill's passionate defense of freedom of speech in *On Liberty* (1859; repr., London: Penguin, 1985). See also John Locke, *A Letter Concerning Toleration* (1689) and *The Second Treatise of Government* (1690).

9. Jürgen Habermas, *The Structural Transformation of the Public Sphere: An Inquiry into a Category of Bourgeois Society*, trans. Thomas Burger (Cambridge, MA: MIT Press, 1989), and T. C. W. Blanning, *The French Revolution: Class War or Culture Clash?* (New York: St. Martin's, 1998).

10. Pippa Norris, "The Role of the Free Press in Promoting Democratization, Good Governance, and Human Development" (paper, UNESCO meeting on World Press Freedom Day: Media, Development, and Poverty Eradication, Colombo, Sri Lanka, May 1–2, 2006).

11. Author's email exchange with *TelQuel* editor and founder Ahmed Benchemsi, January 24, 2012.

12. Ibid.

13. See "Internet Usage in the Middle East."

14. For a discussion of the new Arab blogosphere at its inception, see Lynch, "Blogging the New Arab Public." Of course, not all of these blogs offered spaces for free expression; many were run by governments or those sympathetic to the government's view. See "Mapping the Arabic Blogosphere: Politics, Culture, and Dissent" (Berkman Center for Internet and Society, Harvard University, June 16, 2009), 3, http://cyber.law.harvard.edu/node/5437.

15. Larry Diamond, "Liberation Technology," *Journal of Democracy* 21, no. 3 (2010): 69–83, and Evgeny Morozov, *The Net Delusion: The Dark Side of Internet Freedom* (New York: Public Affairs, 2011).

16. Even in Saudi Arabia, by the late 2000s blogs edited by women's rights activists had proliferated.

17. One illustrative case occurred in Algeria, where officials imprisoned journalist Hafnaoui Ghoul for several months in 2004 for criticizing a local official. He was arrested again in the fall of 2009 in connection with reporting for the Algerian League for the Defense of Human Rights. "Algerian Journalist Faces 16 Politicized Lawsuits" (Committee to Protect Journalists, October 8, 2009), http://cpj.org/2009/10/algerian-journalist-faces-16-politicized-lawsuits.php.

18. See Dafna Hochman, "The Dictator's Dilemma: Rule of law Reforms in the Middle East and North Africa, 1960–2005" (Ph.D. diss., Columbia University, 2009).

19. Regimes have tried to respond to the explosion of free expression, in part by enacting laws to limit the freedom to associate, join groups, or form civil society organizations. While some autocrats such as President Ben Ali of Tunisia relied on laws of association to constrain nongovernmental activity and limit the populist power of opponents at the grassroots level, similar laws regulating the press proliferated throughout the region and have been enacted since the early 2000s in Bahrain (2002), Egypt (1999 and 2002), Yemen (2001), and Jordan (2001). These new laws on the press codes allow Middle Eastern autocrats to preserve a veneer of legality that purports to respect the rule of law even as they introduce censorship and limits on the membership and activities of NGOs. Neither the journalists and activists affected nor the international community is fooled, however.

20. Personal interview, editor in chief of *Al-Wasat*, Manama, Bahrain, February 2008.

21. Khalid Naciri, "Lettre ouverte de Khalid Naciri à Benchemsi," *Aujhourd'hui*, November 22, 2011, reprinted at http://www.portaildumaroc.com/fr/Lettre-ouverte-de-Khalid-Naciri-a-Benchemsi.html.

22. Reflecting this trend, Freedom House began an annual "Freedom on the Net" analysis in 2009, reporting on Internet censorship around the world as a supplement to its Freedom in the World and Freedom of the Press reports.

23. Morozov, *Net Delusion*.

24. Please note, throughout this book, the transliteration of Arabic proper nouns is done to conform to the preferred English spelling of the individual, publication, or institution. If multiple standards exist, the *New York Times* spelling is used.

25. Michael M. Laskier, "A Difficult Inheritance: Moroccan Society under King Mohammed VI," *Middle East Review of International Affairs* 7, no. 3 (2003): 1–20.

26. Personal interview, vice president of the association for Moroccan human rights, Rabat, Morocco, July 2007, and Stephen O. Hughes, *Morocco under King Hassan* (Reading, UK: Garnet, 2001), 315–324.

27. See, for example, "Morocco: Human Rights in Garde-a-Vue Detention" (Amnesty International Report, February 1990); U.S. Senate, "Foreign Operation, Export Financing, and Related Programs Appropriations Bill" (Report 101-131, September 18, 1989), 47–48; and Gilles Perrault, *Notre Ami le Roi* (Paris: Galimmard, 1990).

28. Personal interview, former Minister of Human Rights, and personal interview, human rights activist, Rabat, Morocco, July 2007.

29. Personal interview, former leader of the USFP (National Union of Popular Forces), Rabat, Morocco, July 22, 2007; Abdallah Saaf and Abdelrahim Manar Al Slimi, "Morocco (1996–2007): A Decisive Decade of Reforms?," *Arab Reform Initiative Publication* (2008), http://arabreform.net/IMG/pdf/Morocco_The_State_of_Reform_Country_Report_ENG.pdf, 33.

30. Hughes, *Morocco under King Hassan*, 316.

31. Saaf and Al Slimi, "Morocco," 33, and Organisation Marocaine des Droits de l'Homme, *Liberté de la Presse et de l'Information au Maroc: Limites et Perspectives* (Rabat: OMDH, 1995).

32. In 1996, King Hassan negotiated a political settlement with the Kutla bloc, a group of opposition parties that had powerfully challenged the monarchy for two decades. See personal interview, member of the Consultative Human Rights Council (CCDH), Rabat, Morocco, August 2005.

33. Aboubakr Jamai, "Still Shooting the Messenger in Morocco," *Arab Reform Bulletin*, Carnegie Endowment for International Peace, December 20, 2004.

34. "Morocco" (Press Reference Data, 2002), http://www.pressreference.com/Ma-No/Morocco.html.

35. "Morocco: Freedom of Press 2002," Freedom House, http://www.freedomhouse.org/report/freedom-press/2002/morocco.

36. "Morocco" (Press Reference Data, 2002).

37. Mohammad Ibahrine, "Morocco: Internet Making Censorship Obsolete," *Arab Reform Bulletin*, Carnegie Endowment for International Peace 3, no. 7 (September 2005).

38. See http://www.yassine.net, quoted in ibid.

39. Personal interview, former president of OMDH, Casablanca, Morocco, July 3, 2007.

40. Laskier, "Difficult Inheritance."

41. "Truth Commission: Morocco" (U.S. Institute of Peace), http://www.usip.org/publications/truth-commission-morocco; Pierre Hazan, "Morocco: Betting on a Truth and Reconciliation Commission" (Special Report 165, U.S. Institute of Peace, July 2006), http://www.usip.org/files/resources/sr165.pdf; and "The Moroccan Equity and Reconciliation Commission: Three-Part Summary of the Final Report," The Kingdom of Morocco Justice and Reconciliation Commission, http://www.ccdh.org.ma/IMG/pdf/rapport_final_mar_eng-3.pdf.

42. "Advances and Reverses for Press Freedom during King Mohammed's First Decade" (Reporters without Borders, July 22, 2009), http://www.rsf.org/Advances-and-reverses-for-press.html.

43. Issandr El Amrani, "Morocco Loses a Beacon of Freedom," *Guardian*, January 30, 2010.

44. Driss Ksikes and Khalid Tritki, "Enquête: Le salaire du roi," *TelQuel* 156–157 (December 2004–January 2005), http://www.telquel-online.com/archives/156/couverture_156_1.shtml.

45. El Amrani, "Morocco Loses a Beacon of Freedom."

46. See, for example, Ksikes and Tritki, "Enquête," or Sanaa al-Aji, "How Moroccans Laugh at Religion, Sex, and Politics," *Nichane*, December 2006 (translation mine); Joel Campagna and Kamel Labidi, "The Moroccan Facade" (Committee to Protect Journalists, June 2007), http://cpj.org/reports/2007/07/moroccoweb.php; and Nadia Lamlili, "Enquete, Lady Salma," *TelQuel* 232 (July 1–7), http://www.telquel-online.com/archives/232/couverture_232_1.shtml.

47. See, for example, Nadia Lamlili, "Virginité: Est-ce encore un tabou?," *TelQuel*, August 3, 2007, and al-Aji, "How Moroccans Laugh."

48. Jamai, "Still Shooting the Messenger in Morocco."

49. Personal interview, human rights lawyer, Rabat, Morocco, July 7, 2007; and personal interview, former president of the Association for Moroccan Human Rights, Rabat, Morocco, July 2, 2007.

50. Quoted in Campagna and Labidi, "Moroccan Facade."

51. Campagna and Labidi, "Moroccan Facade."

52. Letter to Prime Minister Abderrahamane Youssoufi, "Morocco: Censorship, Criminal Prosecution of Journalists on the Rise" (Committee to Protect Journalists, May 17, 2000), http://cpj.org/2000/05/morocco-censorship-criminal-prosecution-of-journal.php.

53. Letter to King Mohammed VI, "Convicted of Criminal Defamation, Two Journalists Face Jail and Crippling Fine" (Committee to Protect Journalists, March 1, 2001), http://cpj.org/2001/03/convicted-of-criminal-defamation-two-journalists-f.php.

54. "Interview with King Mohammed VI," *Asharq Alawsat*, July 24, 2001, quoted in "Morocco: Study of Media Laws and Policies in the Middle East and North Africa" (Internews), http://www.pressreference.com/Ma-No/Morocco.html.

55. RTM State Television, Morocco, July 30, 2002, transcript obtained via World News Connection.

56. "Maroc: Code de la Presse," *Marrakech*, October 3, 2002, http://democratie .francophonie.org/IMG/pdf/Code_Presse_MAROC.2002.pdf.

57. The code also criminalized racial incitement in the press, as well as hatred and violence based on sex, color, ethnic origin, and religion. Ibid., and Saaf and Al Slimi, "Morocco," 33.

58. Article 42 of Morocco's press law provided for a prison sentence of between one month and one year and a fine of between $150 and $120,000 for "the publication, dissemination or reproduction by any means of false news or allegations, or inaccurate facts based on fabricated or falsified evidence attributed to third parties, when this disrupts public order or arouses fear in the public." "Morocco: Al Jazeera Bureau Chief Fined for 'Disseminating False Information'" (International Freedom of Expression Exchange, Reporters Sans Frontiers, July 12, 2008), http://www.ifex.org/morocco/.

59. "A Journalist Charged with 'Damaging the Monarchic Regime'" (Reporters without Borders, June 23, 2005), http://en.rsf.org/morocco-a-journalist-charged-with-damaging-23-06-2005,14176.html. See also "Maroc: Code de la Presse."

60. Ahmed R. Benchemsi and Mehdi Sekkouri Alaoui, "Au Coeur de Polisario," *TelQuel*, June 21–27, 2008, http://www.telquel-online.com/329/index_329.shtml.

61. "Morocco," in *Arab Political Systems: Baseline Information and Reforms* (Carnegie Endowment for International Peace and FRIDE, March 6, 2008), http://www .carnegieendowment.org/publications/index.cfm?fa = view&id = 16918.

62. Similarly, a new antiterrorism code promulgated in 2003 after the Casablanca terrorist attacks gave the government additional legal justification to curb peaceful political protests and to shut down independent newspapers. The 2003 anti-terrorism law held reporters and editors criminally liable for publishing material the government

deemed to be moral justification for terrorism. See Abdeslam Maghraoui, "Morocco's Reforms after the Casablanca Bombings," *Arab Reform Bulletin*, Carnegie Endowment for International Peace, July 26, 2003. See "Morocco: 2005" and "Morocco: 2004," Map of Press Freedom, Freedom House, http://www.freedomhouse.org/template.cfm ?page=251&year=2005, and Jamai, "Still Shooting the Messenger in Morocco."

63. "Morocco," in *Arab Political Systems*.

64. While the press code regulated local, domestic Moroccan media, the regime had even less tolerance for international media, particularly pan-Arab satellite stations such as Al Jazeera. In mid-2007, the royally appointed Higher Council of the Audio Visual Sector (HACA) withdrew the permit afforded Al Jazeera to operate its Rabat bureau. See *Bayane Al Yaoume*, July 24, 2007, http://www.bayanealyaoume.ma.

65. Whether writing about the king's health, the royal family's private affairs, or the victims of political oppression, these topics would have been considered taboo for journalists during King Hassan's reign. Aziz Douai, "Obstacles to a New Moroccan Press Code," *Arab Reform Bulletin*, Carnegie Endowment for International Peace, November 10, 2009.

66. "Morocco" (Internet Usage World Statistics), http://www.internetworldstats .com/af/ma.htm.

67. *Jeune Afrique*, November 30, 2008.

68. Ibid.

69. Florence Beauge, "Maroc: Le journalist Ali Lmrabet est interdit d'exercise de son métier," *Le Monde,* April 15, 2005, http://www.lemonde.fr/cgi-bin/ACHATS/ 896848.html. This fine was probably particularly severe because Lmrabet had had a long and combative relationship with the monarchy and the legal harassment was part of a settling of scores. In May 2003, Lmrabet had been sentenced to four years in prison for insulting the king. See Craig Whitlock, "Satirist Continues to Prove Himself a Royal Pain," *Washington Post*, April 26, 2005, http://www.washingtonpost.com/ wp-dyn/articles/A16473–2005Apr26.html, and *Jeune Afrique*, June 17, 2003, http:// www.jeuneafrique.com/Article/LIN15063maroctebarm0/Maroc—l-enigmeAliLmrabet .html. See also "Shock and Concern after Ali Lmrabet Banned from Practicing as a Journalist for 10 Years" (Reporters without Borders, April 12, 2005), http://en.rsf.org/ morocco-shock-and-concern-after-ali-12-04-2005,13186.html.

70. Conversation with leading Moroccan publisher, Washington, DC, January 24, 2012.

71. *Al Arabiya*, January 8, 2008, www.alarabiya.com.

72. "French Weekly Censored in Morocco, Tunisia, and Algeria for 'Attack on Islam'" (Reporters without Borders, November 3, 2008), http://www.rsf.org/French-weekly-censored-in-Morocco.html.

73. Al-Aji, "How Moroccans Laugh." Many marveled at what they considered to be the regime's overreaction, as the jokes highlighted in the article were well known—and not beyond the pale in terms of Moroccan humor. Campagna and Labidi, "Moroccan Facade."

74. James Liddell and Maati Monjib, "Morocco's King Mohammed VI: 10 Years and Counting" (Brookings Institution, August 5, 2009), http://www.brookings.edu/research/opinions/2009/08/05-morocco-monjib.

75. "Backsliders: The Ten Countries Where Press Freedom Has Most Deteriorated" (Committee to Protect Journalists, May 2, 2007), http://cpj.org/reports/2007/05/backsliders.php, and "Morocco: Government Confiscates Newsweeklies, Charges Publisher" (Committee to Protect Journalists, August 6, 2007), http://cpj.org/2007/08/morocco-government-confiscates-newsweeklies-charge.php.

76. Naoufel Cherkaoui, "Interview with Moroccan Blogger Mohammed Erraji," *Magharebia*, September 16, 2008, www.magharebia.com/cocoon/awi/xhtml1/en_GB/features/awi/feature s/2008/09/16/feature-02, and "2008 Human Rights Practices: Morocco" (2008 Country Reports on Human Rights Practices, Bureau of Democracy, Human Rights, and Labor, U.S. Department of State, February 25, 2009).

77. "2008 Human Rights Practices: Morocco."

78. "Confirmation en appel de la peine à l'encontre de Driss Chahtan," *La Vie Eco*, November 11, 2009, http://www.lavieeco.com/actualites/2824-confirmation-en-appel-de-la-peine-a-lencontre-de-driss-chahtan.html.

79. Jax Jacobsen, "Moroccan Newsweeklies Confiscated over Royal Poll" (Committee to Protect Journalists, August 10, 2009), http://cpj.org/blog/2009/08/moroccan-newsweeklies-confiscated-over-royal-poll.php.

80. "Interview with Moroccan Communications Minister Khalid Naciri," *Muhammed Kurayshan's Behind the News*, Al Jazeera, August 5, 2009 (translation mine), and "Moroccan Press Fear Clampdown over Reports on Ruling Monarch," *BBC Monitoring Media Analysis*, September 23, 2009.

81. "Santé du roi: Ali Anouzla poursuivi pour 'fausse information,'" *Jeune Afrique*, September 8, 2009, http://www.jeuneafrique.com/Article/DEPAFP200909 08T054051Z/-media-justice-Mohammed-VI-monarchie-Sante-du-roi-Ali-Anouzla-poursuivi-pour-fausse-information-.html. See also Mehdi Sekkouri Alaoui, "Presse: L'affaire Rotavirus," *TelQuel*, December 22, 2009, http://www.telquel-online.com/archives/389/actu_maroc1_389.shtml.

82. "Maroc: Deux journalistes condamnés à la prison avec sursis," *Jeune Afrique*, October 30, 2009, http://www.jeuneafrique.com/article_depeche.php?idarticle = 2009 1030T225456Z20091030T225417Z.

83. Personal interview, professor of political science, Rabat, Morocco, 2007.

84. Morocco's "press laws hark back to another era," wavering between repression and liberalization. Reporters without Borders, observed in 2008, quoted in Douai, "Obstacles to a New Moroccan Press Code."

85. *As-Sabah*, May 6, 2008, accessed via World News Connection.

86. "Newspaper Raided, Editors Harassed for Wanting to Write about King's Mother" (Reporters without Borders, May 2009), http://en.rsf.org/morocco-news paper-raided-editors-harassed-13-02-2009,30304.html.

87. *Almassae*, November 14, 2008, accessed via World News Connection.

88. Douai, "Obstacles to a New Moroccan Press Code."

89. Youssef Ziraoui, "Le Prince de Facebook," *TelQuel*, February 16–22, 2008, http://fr.ossin.org/index2.php?option=com_content&do_pdf=1&id=333, and "2008 Human Rights Practices: Morocco."

90. "Facebook: Le Marocain Fouad Mourtada Gracie," *L'Express France*, March 19, 2008, http://www.lexpress.fr/actualite/monde/facebook-le-marocain-fouad-mour tada-gracie_471306.html.

91. Lynch, "After Egypt."

92. "Facebook Usage: Factors and Analysis," *Arab Social Media Report*, Dubai School of Government 1, no. 1 (January 2011).

93. Wright, *Rock the Casbah*; Bellin, "Reconsidering the Robustness of Authoritarianism"; Ethan Zuckerman, "The First Twitter Revolution?," *Foreign Policy*, January 14, 2011, http://www.foreignpolicy.com/articles/2011/01/14/the_first_twitter_revolu tion.

94. Adel Iskander, "Egypt's Media Deficit," *Georgetown University Journal of International Affairs* 7, no. 1 (Winter 2006): 17–23.

95. Kamel Labidi, "The Paradox of Press Freedom," *Arab Reform Bulletin*, Carnegie Endowment for International Peace, June 19, 2007.

96. J. Hunter Price, "The New Media Revolution in Egypt: Understanding the Failures of the Past and Looking towards the Possibilities of the Future," *Democracy and Society* 7, no. 2 (Spring 2010): 1–7.

97. "Egypt, 2008," Freedom of the Press, Freedom House, http://freedomhouse .org/template.cfm?page=251&year=2008.

98. Sahar Khamis and Katherine Vaughn, "Cyber-activism in the Egyptian Revolution: How Citizen Journalism and Civic Engagement Tilted the Balance," *Arab Media and Society*, no. 13 (Summer 2011), http://www.arabmediasociety.com/?article =769.

99. Hussein Ibish, "Is Bahrain Creating a New Terrorist Threat?" *Foreign Policy*, April 14, 2011, http://www.foreignpolicy.com/articles/2011/04/14/is_bahrain_creat ing_a_new_terrorist_threat.

100. Timur Kuran, "Now Out of Never: The Element of Surprise in the East European Revolution of 1989," *World Politics* 44, no. 1 (1991): 7–48; Susanne Lohmann, "The Dynamics of Informational Cascades: The Monday Demonstrations in Leipzig, East Germany, 1989–91," *World Politics* 47, no. 1 (1994): 42–101.

101. "Morocco Protesters Demand Political Change," BBC World News Africa, February 20, 2011, http://www.bbc.co.uk/news/world-africa-12518116, and Marc Champion, "Morocco Joins in, Defying Predictions," *Wall Street Journal*, February 21, 2011, http://online.wsj.com/article/SB10001424052748703498804576156180408970252 .html?mod=googlenews_wsj.

102. "Feb. 20 Maroc Protest et la revolution," http://www.youtube.com/watch ?v=mZm750joM0U.

103. Ahmad Zaki Osman, "Egypt and the Demand for Free Expression: Second Generation Internet Users and Political Change in Egypt" (Sada blog, Carnegie Endowment for International Peace, May 12, 2008), http://carnegieendowment.org/2008/08/12/second-generation-internet-users-and-political-change-in-egypt/6bou.

104. Lynch, "After Egypt" and "Arab Uprisings: New Opportunities for Political Science."

105. "Egypt, 2008," Freedom of the Press, http://www.freedomhouse.org/report/freedom-press/2008/egypt.

106. Ibid.

107. Osman, "Egypt and the Demand for Free Expression."

108. Imane Belhaj, "Moroccan Bloggers Create First Association," *Magharebia*, April 30, 2009, http://magharebia.com/cocoon/awi/xhtml1/en_GB/features/awi/features/2009/04/30/feature-02. RBM is affiliated with the Paris-based World Association of Newspapers, which has promised to advocate for a "legal framework to ensure [the RBM's] rights and recognition."

109. Al Jazeera, July 10, 2007, accessed via World News Connection.

110. Lynch, "Blogging the New Arab Public."

111. Ahmed Benchemsi, "Morocco and Press Freedom: A Complicated Relationship" (Nieman Reports, Fall 2011), http://nieman.harvard.edu/reportsitem.aspx?id=102679.

112. Habermas argues that the key to emancipation is to be found in communication, free moral discourses between individuals, and deliberative discourses among equal citizens. See Jürgen Habermas, *The Theory of Communicative Action*, trans. Thomas McCarthy (Cambridge: Polity, 1984–1987).

Chapter 2

1. In November 1987, then prime minister Zine el-Abidine Ben Ali (Ben Ali) initiated a bloodless coup and swiftly wrested power from the aging president Habib Bourguiba, who had ruled since Tunisia's 1956 independence. Justifying the regime change, Ben Ali immediately called for a new era of political reconciliation, a "changement," in which the institutions would "guarantee the conditions for a responsible democracy, fully respecting the sovereignty of the people." See Ben Ali, "Discours de monsieur le president de la république a la Chambre des Députes a l'occasion de l'anniversaire du 7 novembre," *Le Pacte National*, 1988, 6. See also "Lettre d'Ismail Khelil au President de la République," *Le Renouveau*, August 5, 1988; Khalil Zamiti, "La Societe Tunisienne: Absolutisme et democratie après la deposition du president a vie," *Peuples Méditerranéens*, no. 47 (1989): 125–135.

2. "2008 Human Rights Practices: Tunisia" (2008 Country Reports on Human Rights Practices, Bureau of Democracy, Human Rights, and Labor, U.S. Department of State, February 25, 2009), http://www.state.gov/g/drl/rls/hrrpt/2008/nea/119128.htm.

3. "A Textbook Case in Press Censorship for the Past 20 Years" (Reporters without Borders, November 5, 2007), http://en.rsf.org/tunisia-a-textbook-case-in-press-05–11–2007,24264.html. The Tunisian government controlled the country's web portals and filtered web pages critical of the government and its human rights record extensively. "Internet Filtering in Tunisia" (Open Net Initiative, April 7, 2009), http://opennet.net/sites/opennet.net/files/ONI_Tunisia_2009.pdf.

4. Although the strategy included both de-democratizing and deliberalizing elements, both are called "de-democratization" for short, because the majority of the measures aimed to contract political rights and narrow the space for the contestation of political and civil society.

5. Mouldi Jendoubi, the second in command of Tunisia's trade union, told the *New York Times* in January 2011 after the installation of an interim government made up of some members of the ousted president's political party, "We want the resignation of the whole [former] government to form a new government." James D. Kirkpatrick, "Protesters Say Ruling Party in Tunisia Must Dissolve," *New York Times*, January 21, 2012, http://www.nytimes.com/2011/01/22/world/africa/22tunis.html?ref=tunisia.

6. Personal interview, Tunisian democracy activist and constitutional expert, Tunis, Tunisia, June 5, 2007.

7. "Amendment could make Yemen's Saleh life-president," *Agence France Presse*, December 29, 2010, http://english.ahram.org.eg/NewsContent/2/8/2863/World/Region/Amendment-could-make-Yemens-Saleh-lifepresident.aspx.

8. Personal interview, lawyer and human rights activist, Rabat, Morocco, July 7, 2007.

9. Personal interview, former Tunisian ambassador to the United Nations under President Habib Bourguiba, Tunis, Tunisia, May 23, 2007; personal interview, Freedom House representative and civil society leader, Tunis, Tunisia, May 23, 2007.

10. Personal interview, Moroccan political scientist and scholar, Washington, DC, August 2005.

11. Glenn E. Robinson, "Defensive Democratization in Jordan," *International Journal of Middle East Studies* 30, no. 3 (1998): 398.

12. See Hochman, "Dictator's Dilemma."

13. Brumberg, "Democratization in the Arab World?"; Posusney and Angrist, *Authoritarianism in the Middle East*; Brumberg, "Authoritarian Legacies and Reform Strategies."

14. Brumberg, "Democratization in the Arab World?," 66.

15. Robinson, "Defensive Democratization in Jordan"; Brumberg, "Democratization in the Arab World?"; and Daniel Brumberg, "Beyond Liberalization?," *Wilson Quarterly* 28, no. 2 (Spring 2004): 47–55.

16. Lust-Okar, "Divided They Rule."

17. Robinson, "Defensive Democratization in Jordan."

18. Freedom House, *Countries at the Crossroads 2007: A Survey of Democratic Freedoms* (Lanham, MD: Rowman & Littlefield, 2008), 21–23.

19. Lisa Wedeen, *Ambiguities of Domination: Politics, Rhetoric, and Symbols in Contemporary Syria* (Chicago: University of Chicago Press, 1999).

20. During this period, many of the states in the region built quasi-governmental human rights commissions or ministries at home. In Bahrain, Morocco, Egypt, and Algeria, for instance, consultative bodies played a key role in mediating between the international human rights community and the regime and in consulting with local civil society organizations.

21. Albrecht and Schlumberger, "Waiting for Godot," 376, and Anderson, "Searching where the Light Shines."

22. By contrast, Libya's leader Muammar Qadhafi eschewed Western-style democracy, going so far as to argue that multiparty democracy led to bloodshed in Africa. See, for example, "Gaddafi Condemns Africa Democracy," *BBC News*, February 4, 2009.

23. L. B. Ware, "Ben Ali's Constitutional Coup in Tunisia," *Middle East Journal* 42, no. 4 (Autumn 1988): 87–601; Dirk Vandewalle, "From the New State to the New Era: Toward a Second Republic in Tunisia," *Middle East Journal* 42, no. 4 (Autumn 1988): 602–620; Lisa Anderson, "Political Pacts, Liberalism, and Democracy: The Tunisian National Pact of 1988," *Government and Opposition* 6, no. 2 (April 1991): 244–260; Paul Delaney, "New Tunis Chief Begins Democratic Changes," *New York Times*, December 13, 1987.

24. Larbi Sadiki, "Ben Ali's Tunisia: Democracy by Non-democratic Means," *British Journal of Middle Eastern Studies* 29, no. 1 (2002): 63.

25. Vandewalle, "From the New State to the New Era"; Anderson, "Absolutism and the Resilience of Monarchy in the Middle East"; and Zamiti, "La Societe Tunisienne."

26. Vandewalle, "From the New State to the New Era"; Anderson, "Absolutism and the Resilience of Monarchy in the Middle East"; and Christopher Alexander, "Authoritarianism and Civil Society in Tunisia," *Middle East Research and Information Project* 27 (October–December 1997), http://www.merip.org/mer/mer205/authoritarianism-civil-society-tunisia.

27. Lisa Anderson's early optimism about the 1988 Tunisian pact, which included a diverse array of political opposition groups, including the Islamists, exemplifies these academic views (see Anderson, "Absolutism and the Resilience of Monarchy in the Middle East"). To Anderson's credit, she subsequently revised her earlier position on Tunisia's democratic potential, most notably in Lisa Anderson, "Politics in the Middle East: Opportunities and Limits in the Quest for Theory," in *Area Studies and Social Science: Strategies for Understanding Middle East Politics*, ed. Mark Tessler, Jodi Nachtwey, and Anne Banda (Bloomington: Indiana University Press, 1999), 1–10.

28. Mohammed Charfi, who led the Tunisian League for the Defense of Human Rights and who was imprisoned by Bourguiba, told the *New York Times*, "I am absolutely certain of Ben Ali's good will." James M. Markham, "Tunisia Is Pulling a Democratic Rabbit Out of a Dictator's Hat," *New York Times*, April 10, 1989.

29. Ben Ali, "Discours de monsieur," and "Lettre d'Ismail Khelil."

30. Kamel Labidi, "Tunisia: Independent but Not Free," *Le Monde Diplomatique*, March 2006.

31. Email correspondence with leading Tunisian journalist, February 2012.

32. The government claimed that a well-organized plot to overthrow the government necessitated the raid. See "Tunisia," *Annual Register: A Record of World Events* (1991): 236–237.

33. "Tunisia: Update on Amnesty International Concerns" (Amnesty International, November 30, 1991), and Zakya Daoud, "Chronique Tunisienne," *Annuaire de L'Afrique du Nord* 20 (1990): 794–795.

34. Olfa Lamloum and Luiza Toscane, "The Two Faces of the Tunisian Regime: Women's Rights but Only for Some," *Le Monde Diplomatique*, July 1998.

35. Bellin, *Stalled Democracy*.

36. Lamloum and Toscane, "Two Faces"; and Nikki R. Keddie, "The Islamist Movement in Tunisia," *Maghreb Review* 11, no. 1 (January–February 1989): 26–39. Personal interview, president of the Tunisian Association for Women's Rights, and personal interview, editor of *Réalités* magazine, Tunis, Tunisia, May 20, 2007.

37. See Zyad Limam, "Contre-pouvoir ou contre le pouvoir?," *Jeune Afrique*, no. 1762, August 13–19, 1994.

38. "Tunisia: Law of Associations"; personal interview, president of the League, Tunis, Tunisia, August 2007; and Zuhayr al Mazfar, *Al-Thawra al Hadi'a* [The quiet revolution of November 7] (Tunis: Muassasat Abdal-karim Ben Abdallah, 1992).

39. Susan Waltz, *Human Rights and Reform: The Changing Face of North African Politics* (Berkeley: University of California Press, 1995), 176.

40. Ibid.

41. Personal interview, president of the League.

42. The League's communiqués on the human rights abuses against the Islamists in 1991 led to three important reports published by international human rights groups: "Tunisia: Prolonged Incommunicado Detention and Torture" (Amnesty International, March 1992); "Tunisia: Heavy Sentences after Unfair Trials" (Amnesty International, October 1992); and "Tunisia: Military Courts That Sentenced Islamists Leaders Violated Basic Fair-Trial Norms" (Middle East Watch, October 1992).

43. Ligue Tunisienne des Droits de l'Homme, "Communique," June 14, 1991; and "Les Droits de l'homme en Tunisie," *Réalités*, no. 304 (June 28–July 4, 1991).

44. "Les Droits de l'homme en Tunisie."

45. Waltz, *Human Rights and Reform*, 182.

46. Moncef Marzouki became president of Tunisia in 2011. See "Precision," *Réalités*, no. 335 (February 14, 1992): 10, and "Human Rights Developments 1992, Tunisia" (Human Rights Watch, 1992), http://www.hrw.org/reports/1993/WR93/Mew-10.htm#P558_261205.

47. Waltz, Human Rights and Reform, 184.

48. "Bataille Autour D'une Reform," *Réalités*, no. 341 (March 27, 1992): 12.

49. Waltz, *Human Rights and Reform*, 184.

50. Personal interview, professor of law, University of Tunis, Tunis, Tunisia, May 17, 2007.

51. Immediately after the October 2002 League internal elections, five members of the League who were also loyal RCD members lodged formal complaints that they had been barred from participating in the Congress. They claimed the League Congress elections had not been clean. The government complained that the League election results did not reflect regional representation.

52. Personal interview, vice president of the League, Tunis, Tunisia, June 2007; and "The Lawsuit Against the Human Rights League, An Assault on All Human Rights Activists," *The Observatory* 13, no. 3 (April 2001): 1–28.

53. Personal interview, vice president of the League, Tunis, Tunisia, June 2007.

54. Conversation with prominent Tunisian journalist, February 2012.

55. This last tactic was replicated with much success within other Tunisian civil society organizations, including the once-independent magistrates and lawyers' professional association. Personal interview, president of the League, Tunis, Tunisia, May 23, 2007.

56. Personal interview, vice president of the League; and personal interview, political activist and political oppositionist, Tunis, Tunisia, May 7, 2007.

57. See Waltz, *Human Rights and Reform*, and "Lawsuit Against the Human Rights League."

58. Personal interview, editor of *al-Mawqef*, Tunis, Tunisia, May 21, 2007.

59. Sihem Ben Sedrine and Omar Mestiri, *L'Europe et ses despotes: Quand le soutien au "modèle tunisien" dans le monde arabe fait le jeu du terrorisme Islamiste* (Paris: La Découverte, 2004), and "Human Rights Developments 1992, Tunisia."

60. "Lawsuit Against the Human Rights League."

61. "Tunisia also polished its image: English-language publications distributed by its embassies regularly insist on the Tunisian government's commitment to human rights." Waltz, *Human Rights and Reform*, 201.

62. Personal interview, External Relations and Communications Bureau, government of Tunisia, Tunis, Tunisia, June 17, 2007.

63. The rest—thousands of organizations—constituted a labyrinth of nongovernmental organizations with either direct or indirect links to the government or the ruling party, the RCD. Many of these organizations had few if any substantive programs on the ground in Tunisia. Some of these organizations could be relied upon to issue indignant joint communiqués in response to criticism of Tunisia from international human rights organizations. Personal interview, head of the Tunisian Association for Women's Rights, Tunis, Tunisia, July 2007.

64. *Al-Hayat*, August 25, 1999, accessed via World News Connection.

65. Brown, *Constitutions in a Non-Constitutional World*, 78.

66. Personal interview, deputy (member of parliament) of the Mouvement des Démocrates Socialistes (MDS) Party, Tunis, Tunisia, August 2007.

67. Personal interview, Tunisian democracy activist employed by the U.S. government, Middle East Partnership Initiative (MEPI) specialist, MEPI headquarters, Tunis, Tunisia, June 5, 2007. See also "Les principaux amendements a la constitution approuves par referendum," *Agence France Presse*, May 27, 2002.

68. Personal interview, retired professor, law faculty, University of Tunis, Tunis, Tunisia, August 2007. In January 2011, when Ghannouchi did ultimately serve as an interim president, there was some debate as to whether he was doing so extra-constitutionally, given Article 57.

69. See "Référendum sur le projet de la réforme constitutionnelle en Tunisie: Résultats définitifs du référendum au niveau national" (RCD, May 26, 2002), http://www.rcd.tn/index1.html.

70. "Le President Ben Ali Lance La Campagne Referendaire," *Réalitiés*, no. 855 (May 16–22, 2002): 8, and "Discours du Président Zine El Abidine Ben Ali," February 27, 2002, www.carthage.tn.

71. "Ruling Party Congress Urges President to Stand for Third Term," Tunisia Radio, Tunis, September 26, 2001.

72. For more on the RCD's motion that "rubber-stamped" Ben Ali as its presidential candidate for 2004, see the special online edition of *Le Renouveau*, "Ben Ali candidat du RCD aux prochaines élections présidentielles," September 27, 2001.

73. Personal interview, MEPI specialist; personal interview, party director, Progressive Democracy Party (PDP), Tunis, Tunisia, June 7, 2007.

74. The Constitution of Tunisia (updated in 2002), University of Richmond Constitution Finder, http://confinder.richmond.edu/admin/docs/Tunisiaconstitution.pdf.

75. "Un Oui Massif," *Réalités*, no. 857 (May 2002): 10. Yet Ben Ali's new constitutional text ignored the specific language offered by the League, one of the few outside groups consulted during the parliamentary debate over the constitutional amendments. The new text ignored the League's recommended provisions to prohibit political detention and civil rights abuses. Instead, the text vaguely stated that "Tunisians have the right to preserve their independence and their sovereignty." Personal interview, MEPI specialist. See also "La Position de la LTDH sur la Reforme de l'a Constitution," communiqué, Ligue Tunisienne pour la Defense des Droits de l'Homme (LTDH), Tunis, Tunisia, March 15, 2002.

76. "Un Oui Massif."

77. Economic Intelligence Unit, "Politiqua Forces," Tunisia, August 2007. See also Rhida Kefi, "Pourquoi le 'oui' l'a emporte?," *Jeune Afrique, l'Intelligent*, no. 2160 (June 3–9, 2002). Personal interview, MEPI director, Tunis embassy, Tunis, Tunisia, May 8, 2007; and personal interview, former Al Jazeera correspondent (before Al Jazeera was banned locally) and the former head of the (now disbanded) journalists' union, Tunis, Tunisia, June 7, 2007.

78. Personal interview, MEPI director, Tunis embassy, Tunis, Tunisia, May 8, 2007.

79. Personal interview, former Al Jazeera correspondent and former head of the journalists' union, Tunis, Tunisia, June 7, 2007.

80. Personal interview, professor of law, University of Tunis (Campus), Tunis, Tunisia, September 2007.

81. Explaining his party's position on the constitutional revision, one MDS deputy said, "I have no problem with Ben Ali continuing to be president for life. I want Ben Ali to advance Tunisia. He is a good for us. He will continue to make progress in Tunisia—the current progress is all due to him. People complain about human rights, but you know, it is also a human right to travel, have an education and to support ourselves." The deputy argued that "[o]ur economy is dependent on the resources of our people. We are extremely endangered by globalization, because our resources are our people, we have no gas or oil. If Europe and America want to help our human rights, they can help the fact that we are endangered by globalization." Personal interview, deputy representing the MDS party, Tunis, Tunisia, June 12, 2007.

82. Ibid.

83. Personal interview, president of the League, Tunis, Tunisia, May 23, 2007.

84. The head of the CPR party, Moncef Marzouki, would become the country's first post-transition president. In his inauguration speech, Marzouki lamented the state of Tunisia during Ben Ali's rule: "The dictatorship, with its oppression and corruption, [which] turned our country into a place from which people flee, instead of a place to which people escape." See "Tunisian President Moncef Marzouki, in Inauguration Speech, Vows to Lay the Foundation for a Civil Democratic Republic and a Pluralistic Society" (Middle East Media Research Institute, December 13, 2011), http://www.memritv.org/clip_transcript/en/3239.htm.

85. "La Position de la LTDH."

86. Personal interview, president of the League, Tunis, Tunisia, May 10, 2007.

87. The 2008 amendment to the electoral code passed months after Ahmed Nejib Chebbi, former secretary-general of the opposition PDP, announced his candidacy for the 2009 election. The revisions disqualified him, since Maya Jribi took over as the party's secretary-general in 2006. On October 10 Tunisia's Constitutional Council declared the candidacy of another challenger, Mustafa Ben Jaafar, invalid on the basis of the 2008 change. See Hamadi Redissi, "Do Elections Have Meaning," *Arab Reform Bulletin*, Carnegie Endowment for International Peace, October 6, 2009, http://www.carnegieendowment.org/sada/2009/10/06/do-elections-in-tunisia-have-meaning/6bsn.

88. "Tunisia: Elections in an Atmosphere of Oppression," Human Rights Watch Report, October 23, 2009, http://www.hrw.org/news/2009/10/23/tunisia-elections-atmosphere-repression. While the state-controlled television offered each candidate limited air time to address the public, Ben Ali claimed disproportionate exposure as the sitting president. The government also restricted print media for all of the candidates aside from Ben Ali. On October 10, the authorities seized the weekly publication of the Ettajdid party, Ettarik al-Jadid, which contained the campaign manifesto of one

of Ben Ali's competitors, on the grounds that it came out before the October 11 official opening of the campaign.

89. John Thorne, "Tunisian President Wins Fifth Term," *National*, October 26, 2009, http://www.thenational.ae/news/world/middle-east/tunisian-president-wins-fifth-term.

90. Redissi, "Do Elections Have Meaning?"

91. Personal interview, with former Tunisian ambassador to the United Nations under President Habib Bourguiba, Tunis, Tunisia, May 23, 2007.

92. Before the fall of the Ben Ali regime, few public opinion polls were allowed in Tunisia, and none were permitted to ascertain public political views. This conclusion relies on interviews conducted in 2007 and 2008.

93. Personal interview, professor of law, University of Tunis (Campus), Tunis, Tunisia, September 2007.

94. David D. Kirkpatrick, "Behind Tunisia Unrest, Rage over Wealth of Ruling Family," *New York Times*, January 13, 2011.

95. Personal interview, Freedom House representative and civil society leader, Tunis, Tunisia, May 23, 2007.

96. "Arab Political Systems: Baseline Information and Reforms—Egypt" (Carnegie Endowment for International Peace, January 24, 2012), www.carnegieendowment .org/files/Egypt_APS.doc.

97. Amira Howeidy, "Tipping the Balance," *Al-Ahram Weekly*, no. 732 (March 2005).

98. Amr Hamzawy and Nathan J. Brown, "Can Egypt's Troubled Elections Produce a More Democratic Future?" Policy Outlook, Carnegie Endowment for International Peace, December 2005, http://www.carnegieendowment.org/files/PO24.brown .hamzawy.FINAL1.pdf, and Nathan J. Brown, Michele Dunne, and Amr Hamzay, "Egypt's Controversial Constitutional Amendments: A Textual Analysis" (Carnegie Endowment for International Peace, March 23, 2007), http://www.carnegieendow ment.org/files/egypt_constitution_webcommentary01.pdf.

99. Even the government conceded that voter participation was particularly low, estimated at 27 percent voter turnout. The civil society organizations that monitored the referendum claimed that turnout had not exceeded 3 percent. See "Results of the Monitoring of the Public Referendum over the Constitutional Amendments" (press release, Egyptian Organization for Human Rights, March 26, 2007), www.eohr.org.

100. Amr Hamzawy argued at the time that "the revisions changed the electoral process from a candidate-centered system to a mixed one that depends mostly on party lists, leaving only a small unspecified margin for independent seats. This minimizes the Muslim Brotherhood's chances. As an outlawed organization that is not allowed to form a political party, the Muslim Brotherhood has depended on the candidate-centered system for fielding candidates in parliamentary elections over the years." See Amr Hamzawy, Opinion, *Washington Post*, April 2, 2007.

101. Ibid.

102. Column by Islamist-leaning columnist Fahmy Howeidy, *Al-Masri al-Youm*, March 25, 2007. The column was initially written for *al-Ahram*, but the leading state newspaper refused to run it. Cited in "Egypt's Muslim Brothers: Confrontation or Integration?" (International Crisis Group Report, Middle East/North Africa Report no. 76, June 18, 2008), 14.

103. At the time, Human Rights Watch reported widespread ballot stuffing, voter intimidation, and violence. Forty-four-year-old Mustafa Nashar, a spokesman for an independent candidate, told Human Rights Watch, "[O]ne of the officers verbally abused me and hit me on my shoulder, saying, 'There are no elections today.'" "Egypt: Elections Marred as Opposition Barred from Polls" (Human Rights Watch, November 29, 2010), http://www.hrw.org/news/2010/11/29/egypt-elections-marred-opposition-barred-polls.

104. One researcher at the Brookings Institution told the London *Guardian* at the time, "Egypt has joined the ranks of the world's most autocratic countries. Now we're talking full-blown, unabashed dictatorship." See Jack Shenker, "Egypt's Rulers Tighten Grip amid Claims of Election Fraud and Intimidation," *Guardian*, November 30, 2011. The Muslim Brotherhood, the primary victim of the election fraud, boycotted the runoff election in a gesture of protest. "Egypt's Muslim Brotherhood to Boycott Runoff Vote," *CNN Wire*, December 1, 2010.

105. For evidence that autocrats learn from each other's successful and failed strategies, see William J. Dobson, *The Dictator's Learning Curve: Inside the Global Battle for Democracy* (New York: Doubleday, 2012). See also Mainwaring and Perez-Linan, "Why Regions of the World Are Important," and Pevehouse, "Democracy from the Outside In?"

106. Brumberg, "Authoritarian Legacies and Reform Strategies" and "Democratization in the Arab World?" The large literature on elite interaction in the Middle East and North Africa finds that elites are not usually committed to the autocrat's persona or ideology, but rather have a personal stake in the regime's persistence over time. Most elite loyalists find it easier to defend a regime at least purporting to abide by the rule of law, and one that justifies its policies in the name of human rights and democratization. Volker Perthes, ed., *Arab Elites: Negotiating the Politics of Change* (Boulder, CO: Lynne Rienner, 2004). For example, in Tunisia, some of the RCD senior leadership and the other elites who supported the regime were once active opponents of the Bourguiba regime and rallied around Ben Ali in the name of democratization and pluralism. Over time, as the RCD's powers expanded, these elites had such a stake in the regime's endurance that they took some comfort in at least the veneer of elections and constitutional revisions, even if they understood how meaningless these institutions had become.

107. Robinson, "Defensive Democratization in Jordan"; Brumberg, "Authoritarian Legacies and Reform Strategies" and "Democratization in the Arab World?"; and Lust-Okar, "Divided They Rule."

108. "U.S. Tones Down Criticism of Egypt's Constitutional Changes," *Voice of America*, March 27, 2007.

109. "Rice Condemns Military Coup in Mauritania," *Agence France Presse*, August 6, 2009.

110. Ted Dagne, "Kenya: Current Conditions and the Challenges Ahead" (Report to Congress, Congressional Research Service, December 9, 2010).

111. International legal scholars have addressed the related question of why authoritarian leaders are interested in signing international treaties, including human rights treaties. See Oona A. Hathaway, "Why Do Countries Commit to Human Rights Treaties?," *Journal of Conflict Resolution* 51, no. 4 (August 2007): 588–621, and Emilie M. Hafner-Burton and Kiyoteru Tsutsui, "Human Rights in a Globalizing World: The Paradox of Empty Promises," American Journal of Sociology 110, no. 5 (March 2005): 1373–1411.

112. Thomas Carothers argues that "rule of law development and autocracy (liberal or otherwise) go poorly together. Key elements of the rule of law directly threaten autocratic rule. An independent judiciary will be a source of power and authority beyond the executive's reach. Impartial adjudication, fair and equal treatment of all persons before the law, and respect for political and civil rights—all these essential components of the rule of law—restrict or remove the tools that autocrats typically employ to control political life and stay in power. Autocrats tend to block or at least truncate the rule of law as a result." He concludes, "Thus, the idea that rule of law development under autocracy is a natural precursor to democracy gets the story backwards. It is the lack of democracy—that is, the persistence of autocracy in many countries—that is a fundamental obstacle to rule of law development." See Carothers, "How Democracies Emerge: The Sequencing Fallacies," *Journal of Democracy* 18, no. 1 (2007): 12–27.

Chapter 3

1. The definition of liberalizing reforms versus democratizing reforms used here is based on the definitions of liberalization and democratization offered in Chapter 1. Liberalization refers to the expansion of civil liberties, both individual rights such as freedoms of press, speech, and assembly/association and group rights affecting women and minority groups. Democratization refers to the expansion of political rights and freedoms, particularly the right to contest and participate in a governing structure. Democratization might be preceded by liberalization, but democracy is never the assured outcome of any liberalization experiment. While liberalization opens up "space" for individual or group action, democratization changes the structure of "authority." O'Donnell, Schmitter, and Whitehead, *Transitions from Authoritarian Rule* and Linz and Stepan, *Problems of Democratic Consolidation*.

2. Larbi Sadiki, "Like Father, Like Son; Dynastic Republicanism in the Middle East," *Policy Outlook* 52, Carnegie Endowment for International Peace, November 2009, http://www.carnegieendowment.org/publications/index.cfm?fa = view&id = 24

226, and Kristina Kausch, "Managed Successions and Stability in the Arab World" (FRIDE, 2010).

3. It is possible that a deficit in political legitimacy motivated the sons' reformist impulse. Since Michael Hudson's bold statement that the "shortage of this indispensable political resource largely accounts for the volatile nature of Arab politics and the autocratic . . . character of all present governments," regional scholars have been cautious to measure, judge, or assess the decrease or increase in legitimacy of the region's leaders or states. See Michael C. Hudson, *Arab Politics: The Search for Legitimacy* (New Haven, CT: Yale University Press, 1977), 2. Some authors have argued that while the fathers, particularly in presidential republics such as Syria, Iraq, Yemen, Libya, and Egypt, based their legitimacy on the ideology of their ruling parties and their pan-Arab nationalist credentials, the sons did not have this ideological basis for legitimacy. See Albrecht and Schlumberger, "Waiting for Godot." It is nearly impossible to measure a perceived decrease in public legitimacy of the sons over time, however, without public opinion data or similar verification measures.

4. For a discussion of liberalized authoritarianism in the Middle East and North Africa, see Brumberg, "Authoritarian Legacies and Reform Strategies" and "Democratization in the Arab World?"

5. The difference in the legitimacy of Arab monarchies and presidential republics has been and will continue to be a key source of academic research on the region. Prior to the Arab Spring, for example, Daniel Brumberg contended that monarchies had more durable controls on legitimacy and credibility, and thus more leeway than dictators had to initiate reform and expand political rights. Daniel Brumberg, "Democratization versus Liberalization in the Arab World: Dilemmas and Challenges for U.S. Foreign Policy" (Strategic Studies Institute, July 2005), and Daniel Brumberg, "The Trap of Liberalized Autocracy." Lisa Anderson suggested that monarchs were particularly resilient because their personalist, centralist, and absolutist characteristics are well suited for overseeing their states' modernization process. In the post–Arab Spring context, many authors continue to argue that the monarchies in the region are inherently more legitimate and credible among their publics, thus explaining why, for the most part, they escaped (thus far) the greatest brunt of the protests. Anderson, "Political Pacts, Liberalism, and Democracy." See Michael Herb, "The Arab Spring and Political Science, May 23, 2012," in Lynch, "Arab Uprisings: New Opportunities for Political Science," 27.

6. For a discussion of how the aging autocrats were grooming their sons in Egypt and Libya for a hereditary succession upon their deaths, see Kausch, "Managed Successions and Stability." For an indication of the reforms that Seif al-Qadhafi and Gamal Mubarak might have implemented had they succeeded their fathers, see "Qaddafi Son Says Libya Wants to Invest in U.S.," *Associated Press*, November 21, 2008, and Daniel Williams, "Clearing the Path for a Scion of Egypt: Hosni Mubarak's Son Climbs Party Ranks as Country's Leaders Undercut His Rivals," *Washington Post*, March 10, 2006.

7. See Brumberg, "Authoritarian Legacies and Reform Strategies" and "Democratization in the Arab World?"; and Albrecht and Schlumberger, "Waiting for Godot."

8. For the seminal transitions paradigm, see O'Donnell, Schmitter, and Whitehead, *Transitions from Authoritarian Rule*, and for a summary of the "findings," see Barbara Geddes, "What Do We Know about Democratization after Twenty Years?," *Annual Review of Political Science* 2 (1999): 115–144.

9. Personal interview, president, Centre Morocain Des Etudes Strategiques, Rabat, Morocco, June 27, 2007.

10. Liddell and Monjib, "Morocco's King Mohammed VI."

11. Lucas, "De-liberalization in Jordan."

12. In most cases, regime elites will accede to the ruler's choice of heir apparent. Because the economic well-being of many of these elites depends on their relationship with the ruler, they often support and encourage hereditary succession—it offers a low-risk way to keep their preferential relationships and status with the former ruler intact with a new generation. Jason Brownlee, "Hereditary Succession in Modern Autocracies," *World Politics* 59, no. 4 (July 2007): 597; John H. Herz, "The Problem of Successorship in Dictatorial Régimes: A Study in Comparative Law and Institutions," *Journal of Politics* 14 (February 1952): 19–40; and Gordon Tullock, *Autocracy* (Boston: Kluwer Academic Publishers, 1987).

13. Shaykh Jaber al-Sabah's heir apparent, Shaykh Saad al-Abdullah al-Sabah, was ailing. The Kuwaiti National Assembly stepped in, averting a possible succession crisis by invoking a 1964 succession law. The deputies in the Assembly voted unanimously to remove Shaykh Saad from the line of succession for health reasons and instead appointed Shaykh Sabah al-Jaber al-Ahmad al-Sabah, the next in line, as the new emir. Emir Shaykh Sabah then named the crown prince and prime minister from his own branch of the family. Thus the other branch, to which Shaykh Saad belonged, which has generally alternated rule with the Shaykh Sabah and Shaykh Jaber's branch, found itself holding none of the top three posts of emir, crown prince, and prime minister. This side of the family is now dominant. See "The Kuwait Succession Crisis and the New Leadership," *The Estimate*, February 27, 2006; Hassan M. Fattah, "Kuwait Moves to Strip Power from Ill Emir," *New York Times*, January 22, 2006; and Michael Slackman, "Death of Kuwaiti Emir Raises Long-Term Leadership Worries," *New York Times*, January 16, 2006.

14. Michael Herb found that dynastic monarchies in the region persist through a form of power sharing that placates would-be successors and prevents fissures among the ruling elites. Those members of the royal family who are not tapped as heirs apparent are invested in the regime's survival because they hold top cabinet posts including the prime ministership, the ministry of defense, the ministry of foreign affairs, and the ministry of the interior. The family bands together when succession nears rather than risk an internecine feud. Michael Herb, *All in the Family: Absolutism, Revolution, and Democracy in the Middle Eastern Monarchies* (Albany: State University of New York Press, 1999), 8.

15. Personal interview, member of the Human Rights Coordinating Council, Berber rights activist, and former deputy, Moroccan parliament, Rabat, Morocco, July 6, 2007.

16. Crown Prince Abdallah, "Charter to Reform the Arab Position," *Asharq Alawsat*, January 13, 2003 (translation mine). After the crown prince issued this call, later that month 104 Saudi Arabian citizens sent a charter titled "Vision for the Present and the Future of the Homeland" to Crown Prince Abdallah. The charter urged comprehensive reforms including guarantees of freedom of expression, association, and assembly, and requested the release of or fair trials for political prisoners. A second petition followed in September 2003. See "Arab Political Systems: Baseline Information and Reforms—Saudi Arabia" (Carnegie Endowment for International Peace and FRIDE, 2007), www.carnegieendowment.org/arabpoliticalsystems.

17. "A Conference on 'Saudi Arabia and the West and the Impact of September 11, 2001,'" *Ain-al-Yaqeen*, March 28, 2003, http://www.ainalyaqeen.com/issues/20030328/feat8en.htm (translation mine).

18. Roel Meijer, "Reform in Saudi Arabia: The Gender Segregation Debate," *Middle East Policy Council*, http://www.mepc.org/journal/middle-east-policy-archives/reform-saudi-arabia-gender-segregation-debate?print.

19. See Lust-Okar, "Divided They Rule" and *Structuring Conflict in the Arab World*; Albrecht and Schlumberger, "Waiting for Godot;" and Posusney and Angrist, *Authoritarianism in the Middle East*.

20. See Bruce Bueno de Mesquita, Alastair Smith, Randolph M. Siverson, and James D. Morrow, *The Logic of Political Survival* (Cambridge, MA: MIT Press, 2003); Henry Bienen and Nicolas van de Walle, *Of Time and Power: Leadership Duration in the Modern World* (Palo Alto, CA: Stanford University Press, 1991); and Alexander Baturo, "Presidential Succession and Democratic Transitions" (Institute for International Integration Studies no. 209, March 2007).

21. This is often because an autocrat's coalition is relatively unstable at first since its members fear exclusion. However, as the learning process continues, it becomes increasingly unlikely that supporters will be replaced, and so their fear of exclusion diminishes and the loyalty norm strengthens. See Bruce Bueno de Mesquita, James D. Morrow, Randolph M. Siverson, and Alastair Smith, "Political Institutions, Policy Choice and the Survival of Leaders," *British Journal of Political Science* 32, no. 4 (October 2002): 559–590.

22. Brumberg, "Democratization in the Arab World?"

23. Brumberg, "Democratization versus Liberalization in the Arab World."

24. Brumberg predicted in 1995 that there was unlikely to be any change to the liberalization trap until the United States pressed its "Arab Allies to transcend [their] convoluted gradualism." See Brumberg, "Democratization in the Arab World?," 66. Thomas Carothers makes a similar point, calling on Western democracy promoters to acknowledge the strategic liberalization processes in the Middle East and North Africa

that were sustaining autocratic rule. See Thomas Carothers, "The End of the Transition Paradigm," *Journal of Democracy* 13, no. 1 (2002): 5–21.

25. See Russell Lucas's interview with Adnan Abu Odeh, former chief of the Royal Hashemite Court, Amman, Jordan, March 9, 1998, cited in Lucas, "De-liberalization in Jordan," 144.

26. Albrecht and Schlumberger, "Waiting for Godot," 376. The outcome of the Iraq War of 2003 to a large extent made some democratization advocates in Washington cautious, and might have actually dissuaded or slowed down democratization efforts in the region, particularly after Iraq's first free elections led to bloody civil conflict. See Lawrence White Oxford, "Losing the Force? The 'Dark Side' of Democratization after Iraq," *Democratization* 16, no. 2 (2009): 215–242.

27. See "Text of President Bush's 2005 State of the Union Address," *Washington Post*, February 2, 2005.

28. In 2000, Laith Kubba, a Middle East expert at the National Endowment for Democracy, wrote that progress had been made in the Middle East on social and educational fronts, with the achievement of high literacy and education rates, gains for women in terms of equal opportunities and political participation, and the modernization of public administration. See Kubba, "Awakening of Civil Society."

29. There are additional explanations for the spike in regional reforms and liberalization experiments in the early 2000s. U.S. policy shifted after September 11, as policy makers began pressuring Arab regimes to make domestic reforms.

30. See "Freedom in the World 2009: Global Data," Freedom House, http://www.freedomhouse.org/reports.

31. The leaders of the region also understood to what extent neoliberal economic reforms could enhance their external relations, especially by increasing patronage from the United States. See Bellin, "Robustness of Authoritarianism in the Middle East."

32. See Saloua Zerhouni, "Morocco: Reconciling Continuity and Change," in Perthes, *Arab Elites*, 61–86.

33. Francesca Ciriaci, "King Abdullah Presents Jordan's Economic Reform Plan, Warns of Widening 'Digital Gap' between Rich and Poor; 'Global Reality Brings Both Promise and Peril,' King Tells Davos Gathering," *Jordan Times*, January 31, 2000. Like that of the other sons, King Abdullah's willingness to enact neoliberal economic reforms stemmed from a combination of personal commitments, pressure from international actors such as the International Monetary Fund, and demands of a clique of Western-educated technocrats with neoliberal economic views.

34. André Bank and Oliver Schlumberger, "Jordan: Between Regime Survival and Economic Reform," in Perthes, *Arab Elites*, 35–60, and Rami Khouri, "Jordan First? Internal Politics and the Approaching Iraq War" (transcript of the briefing to the Brookings Institution, Saban Center for Middle East Policy, January 23, 2003), http://www.brookings.edu/comm/events/20030123saban.html.

35. The NIHD was a five-year plan for sustainable socioeconomic and political development through projects for building infrastructure, employment, and social services, particularly in rural areas.

36. Liddell and Monjib, "Morocco's King Mohammed VI."

37. Laskier, "Difficult Inheritance."

38. By the end of 2007, this first truth and reconciliation commission in the Arab world had paid out $85 million in individual compensation to victims and victims' family members. An institutional mechanism was established to manage the implementation of communal reparation programs to affected regions of the country. "Truth Commission: Morocco." In November, 2005, the Moroccan Equity and Reconciliation Commission submitted its final report to King Mohammed VI. The report was based on a comprehensive investigation of the violations in Morocco that occurred between 1956 and 1999. See "Morocco's Truth Commission Experience: One More Step toward Truth and Justice" (press release, International Center for Transitional Justice, November 10, 2005). See also "Synthèse du rapport final" (Commission national pour la vérité, l'équité et la réconciliation, Royaume du Maroc, Instance Equite et Réconciliation, 2007).

39. Less than a year after his succession, in March 2000, King Mohammed VI and the Yousoufi government unveiled a national action plan to give Moroccan women more social, political, and legal rights. The plan followed the publication of an alarming report on the marginal status of women and its social consequences. The report found for example, that every six hours a Moroccan woman dies in childbirth and that 28,000 acts of domestic violence against women were reported between 1984 and 1998. Abdeslam Maghraoui, "Political Authority in Crisis: Mohammed VI's Morocco," *Middle East Report* 218 (Spring 2001), www.merip.org.

40. Personal interview, Moroccan political scientist, Rabat, Morocco, August 16, 2005.

41. His modern political discourse was matched with disdain for certain archaic protocols. He shied away from public displays of servitude and released all women from the Royal Harem, taking only one wife and even appearing with her in public. See Liddell and Monjib, "Morocco's King Mohammed VI."

42. For the seminal articulation of these theories, see O'Donnell, Schmitter, and Whitehead, *Transitions from Authoritarian Rule*; and Samuel P. Huntington, *The Third Wave: Democratization in the Late Twentieth Century* (Norman: University of Oklahoma Press, 1991).

43. Adam Przeworski, *Democracy and the Market: Political and Economic Reforms in Eastern Europe and Latin America* (Cambridge: Cambridge University Press, 1991), 58.

44. Huntington, *Third Wave*; and Carothers, "End of the Transition Paradigm."

45. Brumberg, "Authoritarian Legacies and Reform Strategies" and "Democratization in the Arab World?"; Marina Ottaway and Julia Choucair-Vizoso, eds., *Beyond the Façade: Political Reform in the Arab World* (Washington, DC: Carnegie Endowment for International Peace, 2008); and Carothers, "End of the Transition Paradigm."

46. Brumberg, "Democratization in the Arab World?" and "Democratization versus Liberalization in the Arab World.

47. Campagna and Labidi, "Moroccan Facade."

48. Personal interview, editor of *TelQuel*, Casablanca, Morocco, July 22, 2007.

49. "President Bashar al-Assad's Address to the People's Council," July 17, 2000, http://www.presidentassad.net/SPEECHES/BASHAR_ASSAD_2000_INAUGURATION_SPEECH.htm, and Alan George, *Syria: Neither Bread nor Freedom* (London: Zed Books, 2003), 31–32.

50. "Syria Human Rights Advocate Welcomes New Leader's Reforms," *New York Times*, December 17, 2000, and "Syria to Free Thousands of Non-political Prisoners," *Associated Press*, November 23, 2000. The prisoners released included members of the Muslim Brotherhood, a group against which Hafez had waged a brutal war for two decades. See David Ethan Corbin, "Like Father, Like Son: Personalized Succession; Bashar Asad and the New Challenges to the Ba'athist State," *Al Nakhlah: The Fletcher School Online Journal for Southwest Asia and Islamic Civilization* (Fall 2008): 6.

51. "Profile: Syria's Bashar al-Assad," *BBC News*, March 10, 2005.

52. "The One Thousand Statement Calls for Democracy and the Revival of the Civil Society in Syria," *Arabic News*, January 12, 2001, http://www.arabicnews.com/ansub/Daily/Day/010112/2001011212.html.

53. Ellen Lust-Okar, "Reform in Syria: Steering between the Chinese Model and Regime Change," in Ottaway and Choucair-Vizoso, *Beyond the Façade*, 73.

54. Corbin, "Like Father, Like Son," and Flynt Leverett, *Inheriting Syria* (Washington, DC: Brookings Institution, 2005).

55. Fouad Ajami, "The Lost Bequest of Hafez Assad," *Newsweek*, January 23, 2012.

56. Recognizing the elite distrust of political reforms, Bashar began to pursue limited economic reforms, passing a 2001 law to permit the privatization of Syrian banks. Bashar's economic reform agenda, though gradual, also confronted suspicious elites trying to protect the state-run economic system. Eyal Zisser, "Does Bashar al-Assad Rule Syria?," *Middle East Quarterly* 10, no. 1 (Winter 2003): 15–23. See Corbin, "Like Father, Like Son."

57. Personal interview, Shia oppositionist, Manama, Bahrain, February 2008.

58. Munira Fakhro, "The Uprising in Bahrain: An Assessment," in the *Persian Gulf at the Millennium: Essays in Politics, Economy, Security, and Religion*, ed. Gary Sick and Lawrence G. Potter (New York: Macmillan, 1997), 167.

59. Mark Pellas, "Bahrein: Un Simulacre de Democratie," *Le Monde Diplomatique*, March 25, 2005.

60. As a result of the awareness campaign and political activism of Bahraini expatriates, international organizations such as Human Rights Watch and the International Federation of Human Rights began to issue statements about the deteriorating human rights situation in Bahrain. Personal interview, former opposition leader, now parliamentarian, Manama, Bahrain, January 2008.

61. Joe Stork, *Routine Abuse, Routine Denial: Civil Rights and the Political Crisis in Bahrain*, Human Rights Watch–Middle East (New York: Human Rights Watch, 1997).

62. "Anti Government Clashes in Capital," *World Markets Analysis* (World Markets Research Center, November 15, 1999).

63. Personal interview, former opposition leader, now member of parliament, Manama, Bahrain, January 20, 2008.

64. The committee was chaired by the Minister of Justice, Shaykh Abdullah Ben Khalid al-Khalifa. See J. E. Peterson, "The Promise and Reality of Bahraini Reforms," in *Political Liberalization in the Persian Gulf*, ed. Josh Teitelbaum (London: Hurst, 2009), 161–162.

65. Personal interview, former opposition leader and Al Wifaq member of parliament, Manama, Bahrain, January 20, 2008.

66. Personal interview, former Shia opposition leader and member of the Charter Committee, Manama, Bahrain, January 2008, and personal interview, president, National Democratic Action Society, Manama, Bahrain, January 20, 2008.

67. J. E. Peterson, "Bahrain's First Steps toward Reform under Amir Hamad," *Asian Affairs* 33, no. 2 (July 2002): 221.

68. *Gulf News*, December 11, 2000. Six new members were added to the committee, apparently to replace an equal number who were said to have resigned in protest of the possible change of Bahrain's status from emirate to kingdom. In response to the rumors of their resignation, the minister of state for the Amiri Court, Shaykh Khalid Ben Ahmad al-Khalifa, told the press on December 6, 2000, that a monarchical system had existed in Bahrain since the constitution was adopted in 1973. *Gulf News*, December 13, 2000, cited in Peterson, "Bahrain's First Steps."

69. Moreover, the opposition opposed the fact that the charter excluded long-standing opposition demands—for the legalization of political parties and labor unions, for acceptance of the Shia into sensitive government and security positions, for the return of deported opposition leaders, and for the release of all political prisoners. Economic justice and the "Islamicization" of public life were not addressed. Nadeya Sayed Ali Mohammed, "Political Reform in Bahrain: The Price of Stability," *Middle East Intelligence Bulletin* 4, no. 9, September 2002, http://www.meforum.org/meib/articles/0209_me1.htm.

70. Personal interview, former opposition leader, Manama, Bahrain, January 2008.

71. "Bahrain: General Amnesty Welcomed—But Legislation Should Be Amended" (Amnesty International, February 7, 2001), http://www.amnesty.org/en/library/asset/MDE11/002/2001/en/e80afff0-dc42-11dd-a4f4-6f07ed3e68c6/mde110022001en.htm.

72. Mohammed, "Political Reform in Bahrain."

73. Personal interview, professor of political economy and former parliamentary candidate, Manama, Bahrain, January 14, 2008.

74. Personal interview, former political prisoner and current blogger, Manama, Bahrain, January 13, 2008; and Pellas, "Bahrein: Un Simulacre de Democratie."

75. "Bahrain Annual Report 2001" (Amnesty International, February 2002). The first objective of the BHRS was to help those who had been forcibly exiled during the 1980s and 1990s to recover their Bahraini citizenship.

76. Ibid. Moreover, Shaykh Hamad had a strategic interest in granting citizenship, particularly to Sunnis—he sought to counter the demographic Sunni-Shia split—which made the ruling family part of the Sunni minority.

77. "Bahrain: Freedom in the World, 2003," Freedom House, http://www.free domhouse.org/report/freedom-world/2003/bahrain.

78. Personal interview, former member of the 1973 parliament and former political prisoner, Manama, Bahrain, January 22, 2008.

79. Mohammed, "Political Reform in Bahrain."

80. Personal interview, member of the 1973 parliament, Manama, Bahrain, January 2008.

81. "Bahrain's Sectarian Challenge" (International Crisis Group Middle East/North Africa Report 40, May 6, 2005), 5, and Gerd Nonneman, "Political Reform in the Gulf Monarchies: From Liberalization to Democratization? A Comparative Perspective" (Sir William Luce Fellowship Paper 6, Durham Middle East Papers 80, June 2006), 8–9.

82. Personal interview, former political prisoner and popular blogger, Manama, Bahrain, January 13, 2008.

83. Mohammed, "Political Reform in Bahrain," and "The Kingdom of Bahrain: The Constitutional Changes," *Estimate* 15, no. 4 (February 22, 2002), http://www.the estimate.com/public/022202b.html.

84. A minister can be forced to resign if two-thirds of the Chamber votes for a no-confidence measure. The prime minister, however, always a senior member of the al-Khalifa family, cannot be subjected to a no-confidence vote. "Kingdom of Bahrain: The Constitutional Changes," and Government of Bahrain, "The Constitution of 2002," www.e.gov.bh.

85. "Kingdom of Bahrain: The Constitutional Changes."

86. Ibid.

87. Alain Gresh, "'Bandargate' et tensions confessionnelles," Nouvelles d'Orient blog, *Le Monde diplomatique* French website, October 19, 2006, http://blog.mondediplo .net/2006–10–19-Bandargate-et-tensions-confessionnelles, and Abdulhadi Khalaf, "The King's Dilemma: Obstacles to Political Reform in Bahrain" (paper, Fourth Mediterranean Social and Political Research Meeting, Florence and Montecatini, March 2003). For a discussion regarding the new constitution from the government, see Government of Bahrain, "The Explanatory Memorandum to the Constitution of Bahrain," February 14, 2002.

88. Anoushiravan Ehteshami and Steven Wright, *Reform in the Middle East Oil Monarchies* (Reading, UK: Ithaca Press, 2011), 100n9.

89. Khalaf, "King's Dilemma," and Nonneman, "Political Reform in the Gulf Monarchies."

90. The Democratic Action Society, a liberal/secular society, the National Assembly Society, also a liberal society, and the Islamic Action society, a Shia Islamic group, all boycotted. Boycotting unfree and unfair elections is a common method of protest

in the Middle East. Opposition groups in Jordan, Algeria, Bahrain, Iraq, Egypt, and Jordan have boycotted elections over the past twenty years.

91. A. A. Mohamoud, "The Role of the Constitution-Building Process in Democratization: Case Study Bahrain" (Working Paper, International IDEA Democracy Building and Conflict Management, 2005), http://www.idea.int/conflict/cbp/, 20; Personal interview, former opposition leader and Shia leader, Manama, Bahrain, January 2008.

92. The overlap of political conflict with sectarian tensions makes for a combustible mix. See "Bahrain's Sectarian Challenge."

93. *Asharq Alawsat,* November 28, 2006, http://www.aawsat.com/english/news.asp ?section = 3&id = 7176. See also Salman Dossari, "Roundup: Bahraini Elections 2006," *Asharq Alawsat,* November 28, 2006.

94. Abd Al-Nabi Al-Ekry, "Bahrain: Al Wifaq and the Challenges of Participation," *Daily Star,* May 18, 2007, reprinted by the Bahrain Center for Human Rights, http://www.bahrainrights.org/en/node/1233.

95. Personal interview, al-Haq leader, Manama, Bahrain, February 2008.

96. Mansoor al-Jamri, "Are Constitutional Amendments Possible?," *Arab Reform Bulletin,* Carnegie Endowment for International Peace, April 2, 2009.

97. Ibid. Al Wifaq deputies are also trying to amend the controversial Public Gatherings Law, which prohibits full freedom of association and is the pretext for the frequent arrests at Bahraini opposition protests. See "Arab Political Systems: Baseline Information: Bahrain" (Carnegie Endowment for International Peace and FRIDE, 2008), www.carnegieendowment.org/arabpoliticalsystems.

98. Personal interview, professor of political economy and former parliamentary candidate, Manama, Bahrain, January 14, 2008.

99. "Bahrain Charges Dozens with Attempted Murder, Rioting after Shiite Protests," *Associated Press,* December 27, 2007.

100. "Protests in Bahrain over Jailed Shiite Activists," *Associated Press,* February 20, 2009.

101. "Police in Bahrain Clash with Protestors," *Associated Press,* January 30, 2009.

102. "Trial starts for Bahrain Shiite Opposition Group," *Kuwait Times,* February 24, 2009, http://www.kuwaittimes.net/read_news.php?newsid = NjYzNDA4MzM.

103. "Bahrain: Freedom in the World 2010," Freedom House, http://www.free domhouse.org/report/freedom-world/2010/bahrain.

104. See "Bahraini Authorities Must Allow Detainees Access to Lawyers" (Amnesty International, October 12, 2010), http://www.amnesty.org/en/news-and-up dates/bahrain-authorities-must-allow-detainees-access-lawyers-2010–10–13; "Bahrain Accuses Shia Activists of 'Terror Campaign,'" *BBC News,* September 4, 2010; "Bahrain: Ali Abdulemam, Blogger and Global Voices Contributor Arrested" (Global Voices Advocacy, September 5, 2010), http://advocacy.globalvoicesonline.org/2010/09/ 05/bahrain-bahraini-blogger-arrested/.

105. Robyn Gedye, "Bahrain's Flying Shaykh Takes a Gamble on Democracy—and Even Women Get the Vote," *Telegraph*, July 22, 2001.

106. Personal interview, chair, National Democratic Action Society, January 21, 2008, Manama, Bahrain.

107. According to a former opposition leader and member of parliament, "The opposition cleverly worked the expatriate vantage point. On the ground in Bahrain, when the envoys would come from the West, such as Human Rights Watch and Amnesty, we met them and sent them around on a tour of the abuses here. We took them to see the impoverished situation but made it clear we were not looking for the end of the al-Khalifa family rule. We won support in the international human rights community by showing we were moderate, neutral, liberals not dreamers. And we were able to neutralize the support for the regime extended by the British and U.S. governments. We were able to meet U.S. Ambassadors many times, and we told them we are liberals, not some sort of Shia revolution or Iranian-conspiracy in waiting." Personal interview, chair, National Democratic Action, Manama, Bahrain, January 21, 2008.

108. Personal interview, senior official, Bahrain Society for Human Rights, Manama, Bahrain, January 23, 2008.

109. Stork, *Routine Abuse, Routine Denial: Civil Rights and the Political Crisis in Bahrain*.

110. Personal interview, chair, National Democratic Action, Manama, Bahrain, January 21, 2008.

111. Human Rights Watch World Report, excerpted and quoted in "Bahrain Brief," *Gulf Centre for Strategic Studies*, no. 1 (January 2001).

112. U.S.-Bahraini cooperation intensified over the course of the 2000s. "Bahrain: Human Rights Developments 1999" (Human Rights Watch), http://www.hrw.org/wr2k/Mena-02.htm.

113. "President Bush arrives in Bahrain," White House, January 2012, 2008, http://georgewbush-whitehouse.archives.gov/news/releases/2008/01/20080112–5.html.

114. While this chapter and book focus on the drivers of political change, many of the economic reform programs introduced in the region during this period followed a similar trajectory and led to a similarly limited outcome. Barkey, *Politics of Economic Reform*; Navtej Dhillon and Tarik Yousef, eds., *Generation in Waiting: The Unfulfilled Promise of Young People in the Middle East* (Washington, DC: Brookings Institution Press, 2009); and Richard Javad Heydarian, "The Economics of the Arab Spring," *Foreign Policy in Focus*, April 21, 2011.

115. Dhillon and Yousef, *Generation in Waiting*; and Heydarian, "Economics of the Arab Spring."

116. Two seminal authors from the authoritarian robustness school acknowledged after the Arab Spring the degree of frustration, anger, and alienation pervasive throughout the region. See Bellin, "Reconsidering the Robustness of Authoritarianism," and Ellen Lust, "Why Now? Micro Transitions and the Arab Uprisings" (paper,

Yale University), http://themonkeycage.org/wp-content/uploads/2011/10/Ellen_Lust_final.pdf.

117. Gamal set up the Future Generation Foundation, which was meant to promote young Egyptians in business and public life, and a private equity firm called MedInvest. Mary Anne Weaver, "Pharaohs-in-Waiting," *Atlantic Monthly*, October 2003.

118. Ibid.

119. Gamal surrounded himself with a group of devoted supporters, whom some called "the shilla" (gang). They endorsed what Egyptian analysts called "managed reform." The group included businessmen, academics, and Egyptians with political pedigrees in their families, in their late thirties or early forties. Many were educated and worked in the West; English was their second language. Williams, "Clearing the Path."

120. Tarek Masoud, "Is Gamal Mubarak the Best Hope for Egyptian Democracy?," *Foreign Policy Magazine*, September 20, 2010.

Chapter 4

1. See Ajami, "Lost Bequest of Hafez Assad."

2. See the discussion of the new post–Arab Spring research agenda for political scientists in Project on Middle East Political Science, "Arab Uprisings: New Opportunities for Political Science."

3. Gause, "Why Middle East Studies Missed the Arab Spring."

4. President George W. Bush quoted the 2003 Arab Human Development Report when he used the term "freedom deficit" in a speech to the National Endowment for Democracy on November 6, 2003, http://georgewbush-whitehouse.archives.gov/news/releases/2003/11/20031106-2.html. See also United Nations Development Programme, "Arab Human Development Report 2004: Towards Freedom in the Arab World" and "Arab Human Development Report 2003: Building a Knowledge Society," http://arabstates.undp.org/subpage.php?spid = 14.

5. For a discussion of this point with extensive historical comparisons, see Bruce W. Jentleson, "Beware the Duck Test," *Washington* Quarterly 34, no. 3 (Summer 2011): 137–149.

6. Charles Tilly, "Processes and Mechanisms of Democratization," *Sociological Theory* 18, no. 1 (March 2000): 1–16; and Anne Sa'adah, "Regime Change: Lessons from Germany on Justice, Institution Building, and Democracy," *Journal of Conflict Resolution* 50, no. 3 (June 2006): 303–323.

7. Thomas Carothers and Marina Ottaway, *Uncharted Journey: Promoting Democracy in the Middle East* (Washington, DC: Carnegie Endowment for International Peace, 2005); Rashid Khalidi, *Resurrecting Empire: Western Footprints and America's Perilous Path in the Middle East* (Boston: Beacon, 2005); Michele Dunne, "The Baby, the Bathwater, and the Freedom Agenda," *Washington Quarterly* 32, no. 1 (January 2009): 129–141; and Wittes, *Freedom's Unsteady March*.

8. Quan Li, "Does Democracy Promote or Reduce Transnational Terrorist Incidents?," *Journal of Conflict Resolution* 49, no. 2 (April 2005): 278–297; and Shadi Hamid and Steven Brooke, "Promoting Democracy to Stop Terror, Revisited," *Policy Review*, no. 159 (February–March 2010), http://www.hoover.org/publications/policy-review/article/5285.

9. Oz Hassan, "American Democracy Promotion and the 'Arab Spring'" (LSE working paper), http://www2.lse.ac.uk/IDEAS/publications/reports/pdf/SR009/hassan.pdf.

10. "Arabs found the idea that Iraq's liberation had inspired their democracy struggle laughable." See Lynch, "Big Think behind the Arab Spring," and Laurence Whitehead, "Losing 'the Force'? The 'Dark Side' of Democratization after Iraq," *Democratization* 16, no. 2 (2009): 215–242.

11. Thomas Carothers, "The Rule of Law Revival," *Foreign Affairs* 77, no. 2 (March–April 1998): 95–106.

12. For instance, in the early 1990s, both the French and U.S. governments publicly criticized the regime of King Hassan for his gross violations of human rights. In addition, the U.S. Senate and the European Parliament began discussing withholding aid to Morocco due to its human rights record, though neither ultimately decided to do so. Personal interview, national commissioner on human rights, Casablanca, June 2007; "Human Rights Development: Morocco and Western Sahara" (Human Rights Watch, 1991); and "Morocco: Country Reports on Human Rights Practices 2000" (Bureau of Democracy, Human Rights, and Labor, U.S. Department of State, February 23, 2001).

13. Anoushiravan Ehteshami, "Is the Middle East Democratizing?," *British Journal of Middle Eastern Studies* 26, no. 2 (November 1999): 199–217.

14. See George W. Bush's speech at the National Endowment for Democracy, November 6, 2003, www.ned.org.

15. "Rice Drops Plan for Visit to Egypt," *Washington Post*, February 26, 2005.

16. Dunne, "The Baby, the Bathwater and the Freedom Agenda."

17. Ibid.

18. Jack Snyder and Edward Mansfield, *Electing to Fight: Why Emerging Democracies Go to War* (Cambridge, MA: MIT Press, 2005); David L. Epstein, Robert Bates, Jack Goldstone, Ida Kristensen, and Sharyn O'Halloran, "Democratic Transitions," *American Journal of Political Science* 50, no. 3 (July 2006): 551–569.

19. Personal interview, professor of women's studies, Kuwait University, Kuwait City, January 31, 2008.

20. Personal interview, member of National Democratic Action Society, Manama, Bahrain, January 21, 2008.

21. Abderrahman al-Nu'aimi, "The Reforms That Never Happened," *Asharq Alawsat*, December 14, 2004, http://www.asharqalawsat.com/.

22. While most democratization experts acknowledge that the international system exerts influence on local democratization, there is less of a consensus regarding

the most common causal pathways linking international pressure to domestic-level processes. The third and fourth waves of democratization, combined with Reagan's neo-Wilsonian policies to democratize the former Soviet states, led to academic hypotheses that democracy could be imported through a "contagion" effect, by inducements or conditions, by coercion and control, or by invasion. See Laurence Whitehead, *The International Dimensions to Democratization* (Oxford: Oxford University Press, 1996). More recently, scholars have expressed skepticism about the efficacy of international tools and levers used in nondemocracies to encourage democratic transitions. See Thomas Carothers, *Confronting the Weakest Link: Aiding Political Parties in New Democracies* (Washington, DC: Carnegie Endowment for International Peace, 2006), and Vickie Langohr, "Too Much Civil Society, Too Little Politics," *Comparative Politics* 36, no. 2 (2004): 198–201.

23. See Lynch, "Big Think behind the Arab Spring."

24. Compare the "Protest Letters, 2009" (Committee to Protect Journalists), http://cpj.org/letters/2009/, with the content of the daily press briefings given at the U.S. Department of State throughout 2008 and early 2009, http://www.state.gov/r/pa/prs/dpb/index.htm.

25. During the Ben Ali era, local activists lamented that the local U.S. embassy personnel did not publicly discuss the widespread civil liberties abuses and the de-democratization measures discussed in Chapter 2. Personal interview, political opposition figure, Tunis, Tunisia, June 2007.

26. By the mid-2000s, to some opposition leaders and human rights activists in the Middle East and North Africa, the U.S. State Department's annual Human Rights Report had become an increasingly effective tool that could help shine a light on the regime internationally. At times, according to opposition leaders, some governments tried to respond to these reports. In Kuwait, for example, partially in response to the outcry created by the 2007 U.S. Human Rights Report criticizing the treatment of the Bidun, residents without citizenship, the Kuwaiti government began building shelters for them as well as for domestic laborers. Personal interview, U.S. embassy Kuwait, Kuwait City, Kuwait, January 4, 2008. In addition, in writing the report, U.S. diplomats asked local civil society organizations to contribute, thus increasing their access to U.S. officials.

27. Susan B. Epstein, Nina M. Serafino, and Francis T. Miko, "Democracy Promotion: Cornerstone of U.S. Foreign Policy?" (Congressional Research Service report to Congress, December 26, 2007).

28. Ibid., 16.

29. The Leahy Amendment to the 2001 Foreign Operations Appropriations Act (Sec. 563 of Pub. L. No. 106-429) states, "None of the funds made available by this Act may be provided to any unit of the security forces of a foreign country if the Secretary of State has credible evidence that such unit has committed gross violations of human rights, unless the Secretary determines and reports to the Committees on

Appropriations that the government of such country is taking effective measures to bring the responsible members of the security forces unit to justice."

30. See House Resolution 343 (commending the state of Kuwait for granting women certain important political rights), which passed the House on July 12, 2005. Congress has used resolutions to commend democratic advancements in transitioning countries outside of the region. See, for example, Senate Resolution 111-56 (U.S. Senate Resolution on Moldova's April 6, 2009 elections) and Senate Concurrent Resolution 5, introduced January 2005 (a concurrent resolution congratulating the people of Ukraine for conducting a democratic, transparent, and fair runoff presidential election on December 26, 2004, and congratulating Viktor Yushchenko on his election as president of Ukraine and his commitment to democracy and reform).

31. Jeremy Sharpe, "Egypt in Transition" (Congressional Research Service report to Congress, March 29, 2011), http://www.fas.org/sgp/crs/mideast/RL33003.pdf.

32. "Egypt: Proposed Constitutional Amendments Greatest Erosion of Human Rights in 26 Years" (press release, Amnesty International, March 18, 2007), http://www.amnestyusa.org/document.php?lang=e&id=ENGMDE120082007.

33. Sean McCormack, quoted in Andrew Exum and Zach Snyder, "Democracy Demotion in Egypt? Is the United States a Willing Accomplice?" (Policy Watch no. 1212, Washington Institute for Near East Policy, March 23, 2007).

34. State Deputy Spokesman Tom Casey, State Department daily press briefing, March 27, 2007.

35. After the October 2009 elections that gave Ben Ali his fifth term, a U.S. State Department spokesperson said that the U.S. government was "concerned": "We are not aware that permission was granted to any credible independent observer . . . We'll continue to pursue bilateral cooperation in areas of mutual interest, and we'll continue to press for political reform and respect for human rights." "Country Summary on Tunisia" (Human Rights Watch, 2010), http://www.hrw.org/sites/default/files/related_material/tunisia_0.pdf.

36. See Hassan, "American Democracy Promotion and the 'Arab Spring.'" See also the list of MEPI projects and grantees at www.mepi.state.gov and a discussion about the efficacy of these grants in Amy Hawthorne, "The Middle East Partnership Initiative: Questions Abound," *Arab Reform Bulletin North Africa* (Carnegie Endowment for International Peace, September 2003).

37. Personal interview, professor of political science, Rabat, Morocco, August 16, 2005.

38. In 2003 and 2004, Morocco received over $20 million of the new funding. See "Morocco and MEPI" (U.S. Embassy Rabat), http://rabat.usembassy.gov/mepi.html.

39. Personal interview, USAID democracy and governance expert; personal interview, head of MEPI's regional director, Tunis, Tunisia, May 2007.

40. Raymond J. Ahearn, "The Morocco-U.S. Free Trade Agreement" (Congressional Research Service report to Congress, May 26, 2005), 2–3.

41. Speaking in Rabat in 2003 at the Forum for the Future, Secretary of State Powell applauded Morocco for "moving forward on political, educational, and economic reform initiatives." Secretary Colin L. Powell, "Remarks at the Conclusion of the Forum for the Future" (Rabat, Morocco, December 11, 2004), www.state.gov/rls/remarks.

42. Noting the "remarkable developments" spreading from Cairo to Kabul, President Bush announced in his weekly radio address on March 5, 2005, that "the trend is clear: In the Middle East and throughout the world, freedom is on the march." See "Freedom Is on the March," CNN, March 5, 2005.

43. Ahearn, "Morocco-U.S. Free Trade Agreement," 4.

44. Dunne, "The Baby, the Bathwater and the Freedom Agenda."

45. Personal interview, U.S. Agency for International Development (USAID) democracy and governance expert, Rabat, Morocco, August 8, 2005; personal interview, human rights lawyer and civil society leader, Casablanca, Morocco, August 2007; Amy Hawthorne, "The New Reform Ferment," in Carothers and Ottaway, *Uncharted Journey*, 72.

46. Larbi Sadiki, "Bin Ali Baba: Tunisia's Last Bey?," Al Jazeera English, September 27, 2010, http://www.aljazeera.com/indepth/opinion/2010/09/20109238338660692.html.

47. Carothers, "How Democracies Emerge," 15.

48. Gorbachev represents the paradigmatic example where the unintended consequences of reform precipitated the regime's demise. He, along with many among the Soviet elite, believed the communist economic system had become untenable, but that the perestroika policies could be protected only through political liberalization. Because the opponents of perestroika were concentrated in the party apparatus, Gorbachev called for a transfer of political and administrative power from the party to the state. Gorbachev expected his strategy of political liberalization to undermine the opponents of economic reform within his party, creating a new pro-perestroika base. Christopher Young, "The Strategy of Political Liberalization: A Comparative View of Gorbachev's Reforms," *World Politics* 45, no. 1 (1992): 47–65.

49. See Barbara Geddes, "Authoritarian Breakdown: Empirical Test of a Game Theoretic Argument" (paper, American Political Science Association meeting, Atlanta, GA, 1999); and Geddes, "What Do We Know about Democratization?"

Index

Abdallah (king of Saudi Arabia), reforms of, 75, 148n16

Abdel Fattah, Esraa, 43

Abdullah (king of Jordan), economic reforms of, 78

activism, Middle Eastern: Egyptian, 39; Islamic, 101–2, 119n6; Moroccan, vii–viii; online, 41; preceding Arab Spring, 6; public participation in, xi; Western influence on, 14. *See also* Arab Spring; protest movements

al-Ahram (Egyptian newspaper), 144n102

Algeria: imprisonments in, 129n17; rule-of-law reforms in, 50

Al Jazeera, 7, 8; Rabat bureau of, 133n64; role in political change, 20

Almassae, defamation case against, 36

Amnesty International, 13; on Bahrain, 86, 155n107; on Mubarak, 107

Anderson, Lisa, 120n12, 138n27, 146n5

anticolonialism, in Middle East, 18

Arab Observatory for the Freedom of the Press and Media, 44

Arab Spring: activism preceding, 6; authoritarian regimes following, 12, 108, 115; catalytic explanations for, 10; challenges following, 103–14; civil society following, 99, 116; conditions leading to, 6–7, 98; consequences of, 116–17; contagion effects in, 10, 38, 125n27; demographic factors in, 12; drivers of change for, 2–10, 98; effect of U.S. policy on, 100; food insecurity in, 11, 125n32; free expression following, 103–4; geographic factors in, 12; indigenous nature of, 103; instability in, 12; Islamists following, 101–2; levels of protest in, 126n37; media innovations in, 39; origins of, 2; patterns in, 120n8; personal desperation in, 11, 125n30; political change following, 116–17; public sphere following, 116; reforms following, 2, 103–4, 114–15; regime types following, 116; regional mobilization during, 44; role of emotions in, 7, 122n4, 123n15, 124n24,

155n116; role of media technologies in, 128n4; role of unemployment in, 11; rule of law following, 99, 156n5; scholarship on, 10, 156n2; spread of, 1–2; terminology of, 122n2; transitions to democracy following, 12; Tunisia in, 45; varied outcomes of, 2, 12, 16

Asharq Alawsat (pan-Arab daily), 31; Bahraini elections in, 89; on Freedom Agenda, 102; Saudi reforms in, 75

al-Assad, Bashar: reforms of, 73, 81–82, 151n56; "Statement of 1,000," 82; succession of, 94

al-Assad, Hafez, 81, 151n50

authoritarianism, and rule of law, 145n112

authoritarianism, Middle Eastern and North African: effect of media technologies on, 128n4; endurance of, vii, ix, xi; factors sustaining, ix; following reforms, 79, 80; liberalized, 146n4; micro foundations of, ix; Tunisian, viii

authoritarian regimes: international treaties of, 145n111; self-justification by, 13

authoritarian regimes, Middle Eastern and North African: appearance of democracy in, 50–51; coercive apparatuses of, 3, 5, 71, 120n8; dissolution of, 2; drivers of change under, 117; elites in, 144n106; flawed assumptions concerning, 4–5, 123n10; following Arab Spring, 12, 108, 115; hereditary succession in, 9–10, 14, 71–75, 94, 146n6, 147nn8,12; hybrid, vii, 76, 119n2; international expectations for, 51, 67–68, 69, 76–77; liberalized, 76; non-hereditary transitions in, 112–14; persistence of, 18; responses to free expression, 25–26; robustness of, viii–ix, 5, 6, 17, 98, 121n15, 123n12, 155n116; survival of, 120n8; toleration for dissent, 20; U.S. responses to, 108, 109–10, 112–13; vulnerability of, 2, 4–5, 6, 17, 116. *See also* resilience, authoritarian

autocrats, Middle Eastern and North African: benefits of reforms for, 115; censorship

Carothers, Thomas, 145n112, 148n24

Casablanca: protests in, 40; terrorist attacks in, 132n62

censorship, Middle Eastern, 23, 44, 130n19; easing of, 7; of Internet, 137n3; media circumvention of, 21; of 1980s, 43; relaxation of, 20; self-, 25, 26, 32, 36; U.S. policy on, 104

Charfi, Mohammed, 138n28

Chebbi, Ahmed Nejib, 142n87

civil liberties: Congressional support for, 106; in Soviet Union, 106

civil liberties, Middle Eastern, 4; following Arab Spring, 99; Moroccan, 29, 30, 35; organizations of, 54, 57; in Tunisia, 158n25; U.S. expectations for, 105

civil society, Middle Eastern: Bahraini, 86; following Arab Spring, 116; Moroccan, 28; Tunisian, 54, 57, 60–62, 69; U.S. policy on, x–xi; Western influence on, 14

Committee to Protect Journalists, 68, 105; on Morocco, 34, 36

Congrès pour la République (Tunisia), 61

Conseil Consultatif des Droits de l'Homme (CCDH, Morocco), 27

constitutional change, Middle Eastern, 3, 48, 72, 107; in Bahrain, 16, 59, 67, 87–88, 90, 153n87; in Egypt, 64–65, 67; in Morocco, 48, 59, 128n7; nineteenth-century, 18; strategic effectiveness of, 64; in Tunisia, 14, 46, 48, 58–63, 65, 141n75, 142n81; Western recognition of, 67–68; in Yemen, 47. See also reforms, Middle Eastern

Constitutional Democratic Rally (RCD, Tunisia), 1, 11, 45, 141n72; under Bourguiba, 52; on constitutional change, 59; dissolution of, 46; dominance of, 58, 60, 63; economic policies of, 60; in elections of 1989, 53; elites in, 144n106; En-Nahda challenges to, 53, 60–61, 139n32; expanded powers of, 55; and Human Rights League, 56, 57, 140n51; under law of association, 56; membership of, 60

Dahl, Robert, 123n8

de-democratization, 8, 97; autocrats' experience of, 66, 144n105; by Ben Ali, 46, 134n7; Egyptian, 64–66; international critiques of, 50, 108–9; legal codification of, 71; private/public critiques of, 109; short-term benefits of, 70; through rule-of-law, 13, 15, 17, 47–70; top-down, xi; unintended consequences of, 68–70, 98, 114–15; U.S. responses to, 107–9. See also reforms, Middle Eastern: rule-of-law

deliberalization, through rule-of-law reforms, 8–9, 15

Demain (satirical newspaper, Morocco), 33

democracy: contagion effect for, 158n22; international norms of, 13; role of elections in, 4. See also transitions to democracy

democracy, Middle Eastern: following Arab Spring, 99; U.S. policy on, x, 100

Democratic Action Society (Bahrain), 153n90

Democratic Forum for Labor and Liberties (FDTL, Tunisia), 61

Democratic Progressive Party (PDP, Tunisia), 61

democratization: fourth wave of, 158n22; and liberalization, 4, 145n1; third wave of, 5, 23, 73, 158n22

democratization, Middle Eastern: academic literature on, 5; contagion effects in, 127n45; effect of Iraq War on, 149n26; effect of liberalizing reforms on, 80; external promotion of, 100–103; following Arab Spring, 98, 99–103; international pressures on, 100, 102–3, 157n22; long-term, 103; negative consequences of, 102; neighborhood pressures on, 125n28; sources of, 6; U.S. support for, 77

al-Din, Khair, Tunisian reforms of, 18

Doumain (satirical newspaper, Morocco), 33

Driss, Rachid, 55

drivers of change, Middle Eastern, xi, 1–20; for Arab-majority states, 122n2; under authoritarian regimes, 117; in Bahrain, 97; de-democratizing, 68–69; domestic, 103; in Egypt, 97, 129n7; implications for U.S., 17, 97–117; indigenous, 102; international influences on, 12–15, 18; macroeconomic, 11, 98, 125n29; microeconomic, 11; in Morocco, 129n7; role in Arab Spring, 2–10, 98; socioeconomic, 11. See also political change, Middle Eastern

Al-Dustur (Egyptian daily), 42

Eastern European Democracy (SEED) Act, 106

Egypt: April 6 political movement, 39; constitutional revisions in, 64–65, 67, 107–8; drivers of change in, 97, 129n7; economic reform in, 94; electoral laws of, 65; following Arab Spring, 124n25; free expression in, 22, 38, 41; human rights in, 106; Internet use in, 39; Muslim Brotherhood in, 64–65, 102, 143n100; National Democratic Party, 42, 64, 65; opposition groups in, 65; press law (2006), 42;

Acknowledgments

This book began with field research conducted in Tunisia, Morocco, Bahrain, and Kuwait, from 2005 through early 2008, supported by the Smith Richardson Foundation, the American Institute for Maghrib Studies, the David E. Boren Fellowship Program, the Columbia Center for International Business Education, and the Saltzman Institute of War and Peace Studies. During my time in North Africa, I was particularly lucky to be affiliated with the Centre d'Etudes Maghrebine à Tunis (CEMAT), and I appreciate that institution's willingness to support an ambitious set of research questions that were largely taboo at the time. The ideas, research, and analysis in this book are entirely my own and do not reflect the views of the Department of State, National Security Staff, or the United States government.

In each of these countries, I interviewed dozens of academics, politicians, opposition activists, and leading civil society members. Some of these individuals are now serving in new capacities in new governments; some remain activists and opposition leaders. For the sake of their privacy, in this book I cite these individuals' positions without offering names in order to protect the points of view they expressed with great candor in their interviews. Many of these interviewees also opened doors, allowing me to visit parliamentary offices, national libraries, and other institutions that were necessary to obtain the full pictures of the cases described in this book. I am grateful for the hospitality and warmth with which I was welcomed, especially given the often sensitive nature of my research questions.

I am deeply appreciative of the many faculty, friends, and graduate students at Columbia University, Yale University, and elsewhere who provided invaluable feedback at different stages of the early research for this book, particularly Aziz Rana, Mona El-Ghobashy, Jesse Sage, Alfred Stepan, Ken

Pollack, Rashid Khalidi, Alex Scacco, Sheri Berman, Eva Bellin, Guy Grossman, Sean Yom, Nate Barksdale, Maria Victoria Murillo, and the late Charles Tilly. Dick Betts, Lisa Anderson, and Jack Snyder were my champions at Columbia, encouraging the development of my converging interests in foreign policy and social science research. I thank Jack for his enthusiasm for the questions motivating this project, as well as for his mentorship.

By 2008, I had already begun to question the theoretical framework offered by Middle East experts at the time regarding autocratic cleverness and strategic success. In early 2009, when David Sorenson asked me to publish a chapter on political change in a Westview Press anthology that he was editing, I was grateful for the opportunity to switch my perspective. Rather than talking about how, somehow, someday, even the most clever leader's best plans could go awry, I realized that the change was already upon us, as I had instinctively felt during my time in the Middle East and North Africa. Writing that chapter set the stage for this book.

I am very grateful to Bill Finan for his sustained interest in helping me to develop the manuscript. In 2009, he understood the extent to which my questions and conclusions broke ranks with the conventional scholarly views. He also saw why, after the Arab Spring, it was important to offer a broader, more accessible argument, as part of the wave of retroactive analyses attempting to explain the dramatic events of 2011. Any mistakes, however, are entirely my own. I am very thankful for the assistance of all the talented professionals at the University of Pennsylvania Press.

At the very end of this project, I relied on a few academic colleagues to check my work and observations, particularly regional experts Frederic Wehrey, Lawrence Rubin, Ahmed Benchemsi, and Samy Ghorbal. The talented Rebecca Goldstein offered invaluable research assistance and intellectual insights. Throughout the time spent writing and rewriting, I was blessed, as I have always been, by the encouragement and love offered by my parents, Esther and Richard, and my sisters, Dalia and Aliza, and their families, as well as the support offered by my aunt and uncle, in-laws, and numerous friends. This small circle cheered me on, forgiving of my utter distraction.

My greatest debt is to my husband and best friend, Douglas Rand. Doug convinced me to carry on with this project, late into the night and before dawn. It is Doug who convinced me that new parenthood could be entirely compatible with continued hard work, when, at the end of this project, the arrival of our delightful daughter, Maya Rose, added a tremendous source of joy. I hope Maya will inherit Douog's industrious approach to all matters, and his daily pursuit of truth and justice.

In tribute to Doug's generosity, this book is dedicated to him.